Dividend Policy

Dividend Policy: A Business Perspective

BY

QUOC TRUNG TRAN

Foreign Trade University, Vietnam

United Kingdom – North America – Japan – India – Malaysia – China

Emerald Publishing Limited
Emerald Publishing, Floor 5, Northspring, 21-23 Wellington Street, Leeds LS1 4DL

First edition 2024

British Library Cataloguing in Publication Data
A catalogue record for this book is available from the British Library

ISBN: 978-1-83797-988-2 (Print)
ISBN: 978-1-83797-987-5 (Online)
ISBN: 978-1-83797-989-9 (Epub)

Printed and bound by CPI Group (UK) Ltd, Croydon, CR0 4YY

INVESTOR IN PEOPLE

Contents

Contents

List of Figures and Tables

About the Author

Quoc Trung Tran is an Associate Professor at Foreign Trade University (Vietnam). He is also the Vice Director of Ho Chi Minh City Campus of Foreign Trade University. He holds a PhD in Management Science from University of Lille (France). He started his academic career in 2008. His research focus is on corporate finance, corporate governance, and international business. He has published many papers in *Economic Modelling, Research in International Business and Finance, The North American Journal of Economics and Finance, Economic Analysis and Policy, The Quarterly Review of Economics and Finance, Journal of Multinational Financial Management, International Journal of Emerging Markets, Australian Journal of Management, Multinational Business Review, Finance Research Letters,* etc. Most of his works are about the effect of business environment on corporate finance and corporate finance in emerging markets. He has many research projects granted by the Vietnam National Foundation for Science and Technology Development (NAFOSTED), the Ministry of Science and Technology of Vietnam (MOST), and Foreign Trade University. He has served as reviewer of many high-quality journals in finance, economics, and business. His most recent book is "Political Corruption and Corporate Finance."

Preface

"Our goal is to increase enterprise value. Which would you rather have us be? A company with our stock price, and $40 billion in the bank? Or a company with our stock price and no cash in the bank?" – Steve Jobs replied when he was asked about Apple's dividend policy. Under this philosophy, the world's largest technology company did not pay dividends from 1996 to 2011. After Tim Cook succeeded Jobs to be the CEO, Apple started to pay dividends in 2012. Although Cook stated: "We can still maintain a war chest for strategic opportunities and have plenty of cash to run our business" (dividends are also considered as residuals), to some extent this dividend payment was interpreted that Cook "actually meets with and listens to investors and shareholders" (Paczkowski, 2012). In fact, dividend decisions are much more complicated in corporations. For example, Boeing Corporation's dividend per share tends to increase steadily while earning per share and stock price experience many fluctuations over the period from 2000 to 2013. Remarkably, dividend per share exceeds earnings per share in the year of 2002. Therefore, dividends are not only residuals and not only completely determined by investment opportunities to some extent. In fact, dividend policy has many determinants from different levels of business environment.

A proper understanding of dividend paying policy is essential for other fields of financial economics including capital structure, mergers and acquisitions, and capital asset pricing (Allen & Michaely, 1995). Firstly, firms paying more dividends tend to use external funds including new share issues and debt to finance their investment projects. On the other hand, paying dividends is considered as a means to disgorge abundant cash which is available for managers to invest in negative net present value projects. Therefore, dividend policy is relevant to capital structure theories including transaction cost theory, pecking order theory, residual theory, and agency cost theory. Secondly, dividend policy is also related to the probability of takeover. The free cash flow theory suggested by Jensen (1986) posits that managers do not use retained earnings to maximize shareholder wealth optimally. High dividends are considered as a signal to the markets that firm managers act prudently and the likelihood of takeover is reduced. For example, to defend Scottish and Southern Energy against a possible takeover, its leaders announced a new dividend policy with an increase in the payout ratio by 18% in the year 2007 and an annual growth rate of at least 4% over three following years (Shelley, 2007). Thirdly, dividends have employed commonly to estimate the intrinsic value of shares over more than 40 years since Gordon (1962) initially suggested the dividend growth model. Fama and French (2015) also use the dividend growth mode to explain the impact of profitability and investment on average returns and add these two factors to their three-factor model to establish a five-factor model. Therefore, understanding dividend policy is useful to asset pricing.

In a classic work, Black (1976) fails to find a reasonable argument to explain why firms distribute cash dividends to their stockholders and consider dividends as a "puzzle." Since then, dividend policy is studied intensely by financial economists and has become one of the most debatable topics in corporate finance. Most prior books consider dividend policy as financial decisions and investigate both theories and practices in dividend policy from a financial perspective, for example, "Dividends and dividend policy" by Baker (2009), "Dividend policy: Theory and practice" by Frankfurter et al. (2003) and "Dividend Policy and Corporate Governance" by Correia da Silva et al. (2004). However, this book analyzes cash dividend decisions and related issues from a business perspective. Cash dividends are a distribution of cash to shareholders; therefore, dividend decisions affect business activities through reducing corporate cash reserves or investors' behavior. On the other hand, dividend decisions are also affected by firms' business environment – the main source of information for managers' decision-making process. Consequently, this book focuses on how different levels of business environment determine cash dividend policy. Particularly, dividend decisions are made under the impacts of internal environment, industry environment, and macro-environment. Besides, we also present how corporate dividend policy affects shareholders' wealth through stock price.

This book is structured as follows. The first three chapters present fundamentals of dividend policy. Chapter 1 introduces corporate dividend policy from a business perspective. Chapter 2 describes dividend policy around the world. Chapter 3 presents dividend theories – the mechanism through which market frictions determine dividend decisions – and their empirical evidence. The next four chapters analyze how firms make dividend decisions under the three levels of business environment. Chapter 4 analyzes the effect of internal environment (i.e., internal management and internal stakeholders) on dividend policy. Chapter 5 presents the relationship between industry environment and dividend decisions. Industry environment includes participants in both the product market and the financial market. Chapter 6 focuses on how macro-environment including political, economic, social, environmental, and legal factors influence corporate dividend policy. Especially, Chapter 7 examines the effect of business environment on dividend smoothing – a special dividend decision. Finally, Chapter 8 presents the reaction of stock price to dividend payments. It provides readers with comprehensive understandings in dividend policy and related issues under the impact of business environment. In this book, dividend policy is examined as both business-related and financial decisions. Therefore, it is attractive to both academics (e.g., researchers, lecturers, and students) in Finance and Business Administration and practitioners (e.g., investors, managers and policymakers).

Acknowledgments

First and foremost I would like to sincerely thank Professor Pascal Alphonse, one of the greatest teachers in my academic life. He inspired and taught me with patience and kindness.

I also thank Foreign Trade University for supporting me to publish this monograph. I would like to express our sincere gratitude to my colleagues for their valuable comments on my work.

This book is for my little son and daughter, Yoyo and Pony. You made me take this leap. You study hard every day and so do I. I hope you grow up safe, strong, free, and fearless. Thank you for being my children. I love you.

Although I have spared no efforts to write this book and made it as perfect as possible, mistakes and errors may be unavoidable. Therefore, I hope that colleagues and readers sympathize with me for these problems. I look forward to your valuable comments and criticisms so that I can improve it in the future.

Chapter 1

Introduction of Dividend Policy

Abstract

This chapter introduces dividend policy as both financial and business
decisions. First, it presents the history of dividend payment, definition of
dividend, and typical types of dividend. Dividends originate from liquidating
payments of sailing vessels in the early 16th century and become popular
with the development of corporations. In this book, a dividend is defined as a
cash payment to shareholders. By payment time, there are three typical types
of dividend including final dividend, interim dividend, and special dividend.
Second, it presents definition, important dates, measures, and patterns of
dividend policy. Dividend policy includes two decisions: the first is to pay or
not to pay dividends, and the second is the dividend magnitude. Investors
have to follow important dates of dividend payments in order to make their
investment decisions. Important dates include declaration date, record date,
ex-dividend date, and payment date. Dividend payout ratio and dividend
yield are two common measures of dividend policy. Common patterns of
dividend policy are no dividend policy, residual dividend policy, stable
dividend policy, and irregular dividend policy. Finally, dividend policy is
both financial and business-related decisions. Therefore, dividend decisions
are affected by various levels of business environment such as internal, micro
(industry), and macro-environment. Dividend theories are the behind
mechanisms to explain the effect of each factor in the business environment
on corporate dividend policy. Dividend policy, in turn, determines shareholders' wealth through its impact on stock price.

Keywords: Dividend; dividend policy; types of dividends; important dates;
cash holdings; analytical framework; business perspective

1.1 What Is Dividend?

1.1.1 History

The term "dividend" originates from a Latin word "dividendus," which means
"something divided." The history of dividends goes with the development of joint

Dividend Policy, 1–11
Copyright © 2024 Quoc Trung Tran
Published under exclusive licence by Emerald Publishing Limited
doi:10.1108/978-1-83797-987-520241001

stock corporations. According to Williston (1888), the embryonic form of corporation was developed in Greek/Roman times. However, until 14th century, precursors of modern corporations were initially established as federations of traders in Italy and Denmark (Kindleberger, 2000; Scott, 1912). These federations have limited goals, simple principles, and loose organization (Frankfurter & Wood, 1997). In the early 16th century, captains of sailing vessels started calling for investors to finance their voyages. They sell ventures on parts to investors in order to raise funds. Later, these parts were standardized and traded publicly in the open market. A vessel property was divided into fixed denomination shares such as 8, 16, 32, 48, and 56 and sold to investors. Investors could buy shares from different vessels to avoid risk of loss (Masselman, 1963). At the end of each voyage, all of the vessel's assets were liquidated and the profit was distributed to investors in proportion to their shares. If investors were willing to continue their investment, they negotiated with the captain for a new voyage (Lease et al., 1999). This basic mechanism is called liquidating dividend policy. Although investors could avoid the captain's fraudulent behavior by receiving all proceeds, this distribution practice was not economically efficient. Investors had to receive nonfinancial assets that they failed to utilize and manage efficiently. In addition, human capital gained from previous ventures was not exploited (Kindleberger, 2000).

Based on the original cooperation between investors and sea captains, joint stock companies were established since merchants needed more capital for their foreign trade (Kindleberger, 2000). Investors gave their money to corporations where captains use capital with their expertise to create profits. Then, the corporations pay dividend to their investors. According to Frankfurter and Wood (1997), Eastland Trading Company was the first joint stock corporation in Great Britain which received exclusive rights to trade with the Baltic countries. Then, the Muscovy and Levant corporations were granted charters to trade with Russia and Turkey, respectively (Scott, 1912). However, these charters were valid within certain periods. When they were renewed, the government could amend their terms and collect more charges and taxes. According to Van Loon (1913), the first corporation that granted a perpetual charter was the Dutch East India Company whose name is the Verenigde Oostindische Compagnie (VOC) in Dutch. It was founded by Amsterdam merchants in the Netherlands on March 20th, 1602. These wealthy merchants raised about 64 tons of gold to make many vessels for their international trading activities. The Dutch government provided the VOC with the exclusive right to trade with Asia. The VOC's shares were traded publicly in the open market until 1613 when the first stock exchange (in the world) was built in Amsterdam. At the initial public offering (IPO) launched in 1604, its share price was 500 pounds. After about 10 years of development, the company started paying a dividend of 287.50 pounds per share in 1612. This amount was equivalent to 57.5% of the initial share price (Freedman, 2006). Over the first 15 years, the VOC's average dividend yield is 25% (Scott, 1912). In 1799, the VOC was dissolved after 198 years of business.

Along with the development of corporations, law makers recognized and developed legal regulations on dividend payment. In the late 17th century, regulations on profit and impairment were approved by the British Parliament. They are legally fundamental rules to govern corporate dividend policy (Lease et al., 1999). Corporations are free to conduct their dividend policies based on legal regulations, their charter provisions and practices (Scott, 1912). Consequently, modern corporations have not followed liquidating dividend policy. Their dividends are now a symbolic vehicle of liquidation. They pay dividends to maximize shareholders' wealth.

1.1.2 Definition

From a broad view, a dividend is any kind of property distributed to shareholders. Accordingly, a dividend may be in different forms, such as cash, stock, and other assets. While corporations are obliged to pay interest to their debtholders periodically, they are flexible to decide whether to distribute or not to distribute dividends, and which forms of dividends are distributed. If a corporation fails to pay dividends, there shall not be a breach of contract.

Based on the broad definition, stock dividend is a common form of dividend when firms do want to disgorge cash. According to Ross et al. (2010), stock dividend is not a real dividend since the corporation loses no cash. A stock dividend reduces stock price since it raises the number of shares outstanding. A stock dividend is paid as a percentage. For example, a 5% stock dividend means a shareholder obtains five additional stocks for every 100 stocks held. A stock split also leads to a larger number of shares outstanding and a lower level of stock price. However, the effects of a stock split are commonly stronger. When a corporation launches a stock split with the ratio 2:1, a shareholder holding 100 stocks receive 50 additional stocks and the stock price declines from $75 to about $25 per stock.

From a narrow view, a dividend is defined as a cash payment made by a corporation to its shareholders. Corporations may pay dividends from two sources of funds. The first is their current net income or accumulated retained earnings. The second is other funds. Some academics claim that a payment from other funds should be called as a distribution instead of a dividend. However, it is commonly acceptable to define a cash distribution as a dividend regardless of its source of fund (Ross et al., 2010). When a corporation pays a dividend except a liquidating dividend, its retained earnings and cash reserves decrease. A dividend is the return of shareholders' investment. This book follows the narrow definition.

1.1.3 Types of Dividends

Based on the narrow definition, dividends are classified into three groups by payment time. Table 1.1 shows that they are final dividend, interim dividend, and special dividend.

First, a corporation pays its final dividend after its financial reports are audited. Commonly, the final dividend is suggested by the board of directors and approved by the shareholders' annual meeting. The board of directors often

Table 1.1. Different Types of Dividend.

Criteria	Final Dividend	Interim Dividend	Special Dividend
Time of payment	After the release of final financial reports	Before the release of final financial reports	Regardless of the release of final financial reports
Frequency	Annually	Monthly, quarterly, or semiannually	Nonrecurring
Common source of fund	Current earnings	Accumulated retained earnings	Excess cash reserve

suggest a final dividend as a ratio of the current income and pay it on a per share basis.

Second, an interim dividend is distributed to shareholders before the final financial reports are released. The board of directors often announce interim dividends when releasing interim financial reports. However, the final decision to pay interim dividends is made by shareholders. Interim dividends are commonly paid monthly, quarterly, or semiannually from accumulated retained earnings since the current income has not been available.

Third, a special dividend is an exceptional payment to shareholders. It is not a regular dividend like final and interim dividends. A corporation may pay a special dividend in order to reduce the extra-large cash reserve, change its financial structure, or create a signal to investors.

1.2 What Is Dividend Policy?

1.2.1 Definition

When a corporation creates a dollar of profit, it faces many choices to use the dollar. It may hold the whole net income for future investment or distribute the whole net income to its shareholders or use a certain proportion to pay dividend and keep the rest for future investment. It needs to find an optimal approach in order to maximize its shareholders' wealth. Dividend policy is defined as a set of principles to distribute a corporation's profit. With these principles, corporate managers have to make two decisions: (1) whether their corporation should pay or not pay a dividend and (2) if yes, how much their corporation should use their earnings to pay the dividend. In other words, a dividend policy is reflected by the decision to pay and the dividend magnitude.

In practice, corporations may have other ways to distribute cash to shareholders without paying dividends as shown in Table 1.2. For example, a corporation may use its cash to repurchase shares. Share repurchasing is an alternative of dividend payment. When a corporation buys back its shares, the number of

Table 1.2. Comparison of Cash Dividend, Stock Dividend, Stock Split, and Share Repurchase.

Criteria	Cash Dividend	Stock Dividend	Stock Split	Share Repurchase
Par value	Constant	Constant	Lower	Constant
Number of shares outstanding	Constant	Higher	Higher	Lower
Ex-day stock price	Lower	Constant	Lower	Higher
Common stock	Lower	Higher	Constant	Lower
Common source of fund	Earnings	No need	No need	Earnings

shares outstanding is reduced. Therefore, a share purchase increases shareholders' capital gains and stock price. The corporation decides to repurchase its shares when its managers recognize or want to show that its stocks are undervalued. In this book, we only focus on cash payments as the only way to conduct corporate dividend policy.

1.2.2 Important Dates

Dividend payment procedures start when a corporation releases a declaration of dividend distribution. Main contents of this declaration include the amount of payment, the date of record, and the date of payment. There are four important dates that investors have to remember so that they can make right investment decisions:

- *Declaration date:* The date at which the dividend distribution is officially announced.
- *Record date:* The date at which investors are recognized as the corporation's shareholders to receive the declared dividend. Shareholders who are in the corporation's books after the record date shall not be allowed to obtain the dividend.
- *Ex-dividend date:* The date is commonly from 1 to 3 days before the record date. The gap between the record day and the ex-dividend date relies on the settlement cycle (T + n). When a person buys a stock today, he/she will receive the stock and be officially recognized as a stockholder in the corporation's books after n working days. The ex-dividend date is the most important date to investors who intend to sell or buy stocks. If an investor buys stocks on that day or later, he/she will not receive dividends for them. In principles, the corporation's stock price is reduced by a dividend per share as a compensation for investors who fail to obtain the dividend on the ex-dividend day. The

differences between the ex-dividend date and the record date are presented in Table 1.3.

- *Payment date:* The date at which shareholders receive dividends for their stocks in their bank accounts.

For example, XYZ Corporation announces a dividend of $3 per share on February 5th, 2023. Its announcement shows that the record date is March 31st, 2023 and the payment date is June 30th, 2023. After receiving this declaration of dividend, the stock exchange calculates and announces the ex-dividend date is March 29th, 2023 if the settlement cycle is T + 2. Investors who officially hold XYZ stocks on March 29th, 2023 or later shall not receive the dividend of $3 per share. If you want to obtain this dividend, you should buy the stock before March 29th, 2023 or sell it after March 29th, 2023. In principles, the stock price on March 29th, 2023 decreases by $3.

1.2.3 Measures of Dividend Payment

As discussed above, a dividend policy includes the decision to pay or not to pay and the decision to determine the dividend magnitude. The dividend magnitude is commonly represented by dividend payout ratio and dividend yield. First, dividend payout ratio is defined as the proportion of net income paid to shareholders. Accordingly, the payout ratio is computed by the amount of dividend divided by net income. However, corporations may not pay dividends only from their current earnings but also from their accumulated retained earnings. If the current net income is negative, it is difficult to interpret the negative value of payout ratio. Therefore, academics usually replace net income as a deflator by total assets or

Table 1.3. Ex-Dividend Date Versus Record Date.

Criteria	Ex-Dividend Date	Record Date
Importance	Important to investors to buy or sell their stocks	Important to corporations to identify shareholders who are eligible for dividends
Source	Announced by stock exchanges	Announced by corporations
Calculation	Calculated from the record day and the settlement cycle (T + n)	Set by corporations
Eligibility for dividend	Stocks bought on the ex-day or later shall not be eligible for dividends	Stocks bought on the record day or earlier shall be eligible for dividends
Stock price adjustment	Decreased by a dividend per share	No adjustment

sales revenue in order to avoid this problem. In several academic papers, dividend to assets and dividend to sales are used commonly as proxies of dividend payout ratio.

Second, dividend yield is computed by dividend per share divided by stock price. As a result, dividend yield is determined by stock price which is beyond the corporation's control to some extent. According to Fama and French (1988), dividend yield is more effective than dividend payout ratio in forecasting stock returns. This implies that dividend yield is more informative. However, McManus et al. (2004) show that dividend payout ratio is more effective in signaling outside investors, since it reflects internal information only. Chapter 2 presents dividend policy around the world.

1.2.4 Patterns of Dividend Policy

Although dividend policy is determined by many factors including firm characteristics and business environment, there are common patterns of dividend policy as follows:

- *No dividend policy:* This pattern is followed by firms with many attractive investment opportunities. When they need to save much cash for future investment, they are less likely to pay dividends. According to DeAngelo and DeAngelo (2006) and Grullon et al. (2002), young firms have more investment opportunities than older ones, and thus they have high incentives to conduct no dividend policy. However, no dividend policy cannot be implemented without shareholders' support. Shareholders may insist on dividend distribution rather than retained earnings when they are concerned about the future prospect (Gordon, 1959). Therefore, the management has to persuade shareholders so that they are optimistic about their firms' future development. Long-term investors tend to prefer capital gains to dividends. Therefore, they support no dividend policy more than speculators.
- *Residual dividend policy:* This pattern considers a dividend as a residual left-over. If firms still have cash after financing all profitable investment opportunities and business activities, they resort to pay dividends in order to improve their asset management efficiency (Weston & Brigham, 1979). Excess cash creates no added value; therefore, dividend payment is necessary to clear it. In other words, firms following residual dividend policy only distribute dividends when they do not have to raise external funds.
- *Stable dividend policy:* This pattern focuses on maintain a stable payout ratio or dividend per share. Firms may set a specific percentage of their earnings annually to pay dividends or keep their dividend per share constant for many years despite fluctuations of their earnings. Stable dividend policy is a financial burden to firms when their earnings are low. However, it is a good opportunity for many shareholders such as retired people, low-income households, and blue-collar workers. These people need stable investment returns in order to pay for their living expenses.

- *Irregular dividend policy:* This pattern fails to consider dividend payment as an obligation. Firms following this pattern never pay dividends periodically and thus investors cannot predict when they make payment and how much they pay. Unlike stable dividend policy, irregular dividend policy fails to create pressure to firms when their financial performance is limited. Their investors are not shocked when receiving no dividends.

1.3 Why Do Firms Hold Cash?

When firms pay cash dividends, their cash reserves decline. Therefore, motives of cash holdings provide a better understanding of dividend policy. Common cash holding motives include transaction motive, precautionary motive, agency motive, predation motive, and tax motive. First, transaction motive drives firms to save cash when transaction costs are significant. A lack of internal funds may force firms to sell noncash assets, raise external funds, and reduce dividends. Selling noncash assets leads to advertising costs and brokerage fees. Raising external funds results in floatation costs including but not limited to brokerage, underwriting, legal, registration, and audit fees. Therefore, firms are more likely to reduce dividends if they want to avoid these transaction costs. Second, precautionary motive drives firms to hold cash in order to handle unpredictable events and have enough resources for emerging investment opportunities. Firms with insufficient cash reserves face high probability of bankruptcy and miss profitable investment projects, which leads to low profitability (Campello et al., 2010). Consequently, cash holdings play the role of a safety buffer. Firms tend to save more cash from their cash flows when they are financially constrained and their cash flows are more volatile (Almeida et al., 2004; Bates et al., 2009). Third, agency motive makes corporate managers prefer cash. As an agent, corporate managers have high incentives to expropriate shareholders since they control resources that they do not own. Accordingly, managers prefer to hold more cash for overinvestment in order to build their empire and strengthen their positions (Jensen, 1986). Fourth, predation motive drives firms to accumulate cash when they face aggressive competition. Cash reserves can play the role of a deterrent to predation, prevent potential entrants, and create cash flow pressure on weak rivals (Haushalter et al., 2007; Hoberg et al., 2014; Root & Yung, 2022). Finally, tax motive drives multinational corporations to save cash in order to avoid the tax burden. When home countries impose high tax rates on foreign income, multinational corporations are less likely to transfer foreign income to their home countries. Their foreign subsidies hold high levels of cash in host countries which have low income tax rates to avoid repatriation costs. Many US firms have high levels of cash holdings due to tax motive (Fritz Foley et al., 2007).

1.4 What Drives Dividend Policy?

1.4.1 From a Theoretical Perspective

Initially, Miller and Modigliani (1961) propose the irrelevance theory of dividend policy assuming that capital markets are perfect and complete. In fact, dividend policy is affected by market frictions including information asymmetry, agency problems, transaction costs, firm maturity, catering incentives, and taxes. From these market fictions, many theories of dividend policy are developed to explain the dividend puzzle. Signaling theory argues that there is asymmetric information between corporate managers and outside investors, thus managers use dividends as a signal of corporate expected profitability (Bhattacharya, 1979). When firms face more information asymmetry, they are more likely to pay dividends. Agency theory focuses on the conflicts of interest between managers and shareholders and considers dividend payment is a device to mitigate agency problems and reduce agency costs (Easterbrook, 1984; Jensen, 1986; Jensen & Meckling, 1976). Transaction cost theory and pecking order theory argue that firms prefer internal funds to external funds; therefore, firms are less likely to pay dividends in order to save cash for investment opportunities (Higgins, 1972; Myers & Majluf, 1984; Rozeff, 1982; Weston & Brigham, 1979). Life cycle theory states that mature and established firms pay more dividends due to fewer investment projects and abundant resources, while young firms with limited resources tend to pay less dividends to finance their investment opportunities (DeAngelo & DeAngelo, 2006; Grullon et al., 2002). Catering theory argues that firms pay dividends since they follow investors' demand (Baker & Wurgler, 2004b). Tax clientele theory explains dividend policy by the difference between tax rates imposed on capital gains and dividends. The favorable treatment of capital gains to dividends leads to dividend restrictions since firms tend to maximize their shareholders' wealth (Litzenberger & Ramaswamy, 1979). Chapter 3 analyzes these theories from theoretical arguments to empirical evidence.

1.4.2 From a Business Perspective

Firms do business in a dynamic environment. Adaptation to business environment and its changes is vital for firms' survival and development. Therefore, business environment plays an important role in corporate decisions. A typical business environment commonly has three levels, namely internal environment, industry environment (micro-environment), and macro-environment. As one of the three main corporate financial decisions, dividend policy is certainly determined by the three levels of business environment as shown in Fig. 1.1. In principles, there are more factors in each level of business environment but Fig. 1.1 only shows the factors that may have effects on dividend policy based on dividend theories.

First, the internal environment includes all things within a firm and under its control. Dividend policy is not only influenced by corporate operations and resources but also internal stakeholders whose benefits are closely connected with dividend decisions. These internal stakeholders are commonly shareholders (owners), the board of directors, the Chief Executive Officer (CEO), and employees. Each internal stakeholder has their own rights, benefits, and characteristics which lead their behaviors. Chapter 4 clearly presents how the internal environment affects dividend policy.

Second, the industry environment includes all outside individuals and organizations whose benefits are related to a firm's operations. As a business-related decision, dividend policy is affected by participants in the product market like competitors, suppliers, and customers, since the interaction between the firm and these micro-stakeholders determine its profitability and future prospects. In addition, as a financial decision, dividend policy is also affected by participants in the financial market like investors, creditors, and auditors since their behaviors determine shareholders' wealth through stock prices. Chapter 5 analyzes the effect each participant on dividend decisions in details.

Third, the macro-environment includes all external and general conditions for all firms in an economy. Macro-environment factors are beyond firms' control. A macro-environment factor may be an opportunity for a firm but a challenge for another firm, since the two firms have different characteristics and resources. The common model to analyze the macro-environment is PESTEL – the abbreviation of six groups of factors: political, economic, social, technological, environmental, and legal. However, there has not been theoretical mechanism and empirical evidence for the impact of technological factors on dividend policy. Consequently, Fig. 1.1 only presents five factors. The relationship between the macro-environment factors and corporate dividend decisions is presented in Chapter 6.

Moreover, dividend policy is commonly defined as two decisions: The first is to pay or not to pay dividends and the second is the dividend magnitude. Actually, corporate managers also consider dividend smoothing – the third decision since dividend stability is a signal to outside investors and determines firm value (Lintner, 1956; Pruitt & Gitman, 1991). Therefore, Chapter 7 is reserved to analyze how the three levels of business environment influence the dividend smoothing behavior.

Finally, all dividend decisions may affect stock price. Theoretically, a dividend payment leads to a price drop equivalent to the dividend amount. Nevertheless, market frictions create a bias in this change. Furthermore, a dividend announcement may convey information to outside investors who have less information than corporate managers and thus change their valuation of firms. Besides, dividend smoothing may be considered as a signal about firms' quality. Consequently, Chapter 8 analyzes how dividend policy affects stock price.

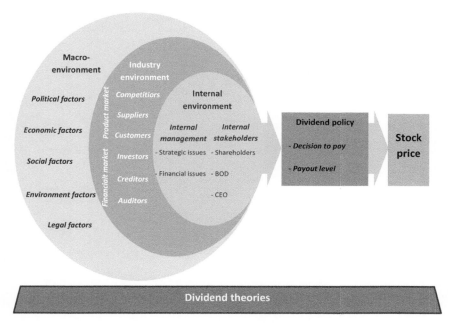

Fig. 1.1.   The Analytical Framework.

In conclusion, this book analyzes dividend policy from a business perspective. As both business-related and financial decisions, dividend decisions are made under the impacts of different business environment levels (internal, micro, and macro). Besides, dividend policy affects stock price from various aspects.

Chapter 2

Dividend Policy Around the World

Abstract

This chapter analyzes how firms conduct their dividend policy around the world. In principles, firms are free to pay or not to pay dividends and choose dividend levels. However, in some countries, the government requires firms to pay dividends annually in order to protect minority shareholders. Brazil, Chile, Colombia, Greece, and Venezuela are five countries of mandatory dividend payments. In addition, using the Compustat database, we investigate how nonfinancial firms pay dividends over the period 2001–2020. The percentage of payers tends to decrease across four time periods including 2001–2005, 2006–2010, 2011–2015, and 2016–2020. Newly listed firms are less likely to distribute dividends than old firms. "Payers," "Always payers," and "Former payers" have positive earnings while "Nonpayers" and "Never payers" experience negative earnings. "Never payers" have the highest level of cash while "Always payers" and "Former payers" have the smallest cash reserves. Moreover, Asia-Pacific has the largest proportion of payers but it tends to decrease. America has the lowest proportion of dividend payers, but it tends to increase. Firms in developing countries are more likely to pay dividends. Both the proportion of payers and the average payout ratio of civil law countries are much higher than those of common law countries. The United States has the lowest percentage of paying firms and dividend payouts. Furthermore, construction and wholesale trade industries have the highest proportions of payers and payout ratios. Mineral and services industries are less likely to pay dividends. Tax rates for dividends and capital gains are diverse across countries.

Keywords: Mandatory dividends; payers; nonpayers; civil law; common law; dividend taxes

2.1 Countries of Mandatory Dividend Policy

In principles, firms are not obliged to pay dividends since dividend payment depends not only on earnings but also on investment plans, capital structure, and

Dividend Policy, 13–28
Copyright © 2024 Quoc Trung Tran
Published under exclusive licence by Emerald Publishing Limited
doi:10.1108/978-1-83797-987-520241002

other factors. Therefore, most countries tend to let firms be flexible in their dividend policy. However, there are five countries in which dividend payment is a legal obligation. Brazil, Chile, Colombia, Greece, and Venezuela require their firms to distribute dividends annually. This obligation is only suspended in special cases.

According to La Porta et al. (2000), mandatory dividend payment is a means to protect minority shareholders. In a corporation, there may be a conflict of interest between controlling shareholders and minority shareholders. When controlling shareholders make all corporate decisions, they have incentives to expropriate minority shareholders. Instead of distributing excess cash to minority shareholders in the form of dividend, controlling shareholders are likely to hold all of the profits and use them to serve controlling shareholders' benefits. Recognizing this mechanism, policymakers develop legal regulations on mandatory dividend policy in order to restrict controlling shareholders' opportunistic behaviors and create a level playground for all shareholders. Moreover, mandatory dividend policy may also be effective in improving stock market liquidity. When minority shareholders are strongly protected, investors are more willing to invest in equity securities (Mahenthiran et al., 2020).

According to the Brazilian corporate law, corporations are required to have stipulations on mandatory dividend payment in their bylaws. When their annual income is positive, they have to distribute at least 25% of their adjusted income to shareholders. This distribution may be conducted in the form of dividend or interest on shareholders' equity, unless otherwise, dividends are paid within 60 days from the declaration date. Although lawmakers impose strict regulations on mandatory dividend policy, they recognize the importance of internal funds in corporate investment. Corporations are allowed to set aside 5% of their earnings at the maximum to finance new investment opportunities. This adjustment is recorded as a legal reserve in financial reports. Then, the remaining income is used to calculate the amount of dividend distributed to shareholders in accordance with the statutory rate. In addition, the law also stipulates some exceptions, allowing firms to set a lower payout ratio. However, most profitable firms in Brazil follow the statutory rate (Martins & Novaes, 2012).

In Chile, the corporate law requires profitable corporations to use at least 30% of their net income in order to pay dividends every fiscal year (Saens & Tigero, 2021). In Colombia, the minimum percentage of net income for dividend payment is 50%. Where all reserves are greater than the total subscribed capital, firms have to distribute at least 70% of their income in the form of dividend (Capaul, 2003). In Greek, there are two approaches to calculate the mandatory dividend level: (a) 6% of common equity and (b) 35% of earnings after tactical reserves. Firms have to choose the approach with the larger amount. Where the amount of (b) is greater than that of (a), firms are allowed to follow (a) with the acceptance of at least 65% of voting rights. Besides, firms are allowed not to distribute dividends if no dividend policy is accepted by at least 80% of voting rights (Asimakopoulos et al., 2007; Dasilas & Leventis, 2011).

2.2 Trends in Dividend Policy Over Time

We use the Compustat database to collect information on dividend policy and other financial ratios of nonfinancial firms over the period 2001–2020 for our analysis. Financial and utility firms are excluded from our data since they are highly regulated. After removing observations and firms with missing information, we obtain 39,154 firms with 365,320 observations. These firms are incorporated and listed in 46 countries.[1] Following Fama and French (2001), we define a firm as a "Payer" if it pays a dividend in the current year. A firm is labeled as "Never payer" or "Always payer" if it has no dividend payments or continuous dividend payments during the period 2001–2020, respectively. A firm is a "Former payer" if it fails to pay a dividend in the current year but paid dividends in previous years. Moreover, a firm is defined as "Newly listed" if it is present in the Compustat database for the first time.

Table 2.1 presents how firms decide to pay dividends across four time periods including 2001–2005, 2006–2010, 2011–2015, and 2016–2020. Panel A shows that the majority of firms are "Payers" and firms are more likely to pay dividends over time. "Payers" constitute 50.07% in the first period and then their proportion increases significantly in the following periods. Paying firms account for 58.12% in the period 2016–2020. Consistently, firms with continuous dividends constitute about 30% over the period 2001–2005 and have larger percentages in the next two periods to reach a peak at 39.69%. Over the period 2016–2020, their proportion slightly drops to 38.92%. By contrast, "Never payers" and "Former payers" become less popular over time. Firms without dividends constitute 39.26% in the first period, but their percentage considerably declines to 32.84% in the last

Table 2.1. Trends in Dividend Policy Over Time.

	2001–2005	2006–2010	2011–2015	2016–2020
Panel A. All firms				
Number of observations	75,429	87,298	98,053	104,560
Number of firms	9,257	7,826	8,885	13,008
Payers (%)	50.07	54.78	57.67	58.12
Always payers (%)	29.76	33.40	39.69	38.92
Never payers (%)	39.26	35.70	33.04	32.84
Former payers (%)	10.67	9.51	9.28	9.04
Panel B. Newly listed firms				
Number of firms	19,634	8,030	7,015	5,741
Payers (%)	11.54	3.93	2.68	2.08

---

[1]Countries with mandatory dividend policy are excluded.

period. The proportion of "Former payers" also has a slight decrease from 10.67% to 9.04% over the four periods.

Panel B shows the number of newly listed firms and the percentage of newly listed payers. Unlike old firms, newly listed firms are less likely to pay dividends over time. Paying firms occupy 11.54% of newly listed firms over the period 2001–2005; however, their proportion drops significantly in the next period and reaches 2.08% in the last period. This trend is consistent with the life cycle theory. Young firms have more investment opportunities, and thus they tend to retain earnings to finance emerging projects instead of paying dividends.

2.3 Characteristics of Different Payer Groups

In order to investigate the characteristics of different dividend policy groups, we calculate main financial ratios of each group over time. "Nonpayers" are firms that fail to pay dividends in the current year. These main financial ratios include firm profitability, cash holdings, financial leverage, firm size, and firm value. Firm profitability is measured by earnings before interest, taxes, depreciation, and amortization deflated by total assets. Cash holdings are computed by total cash and short-term investments deflated by total assets. Financial leverage is calculated by total liabilities deflated by total assets. Firm size is the natural logarithm of total assets in USD. Firm value is measured by total market value of equity and liabilities deflated by total assets.

Table 2.2 shows that all paying groups including "Payers," "Always payers," and "Former payers" have positive profitability ratios, while "Nonpayers" and "Never payers" have negative earnings across the four periods. "Always payers" are slightly more profitable than "Payers," while "Former payers" have much lower levels of profitability. "Never payers" face the largest losses among the five groups. These findings imply that firm profitability is important in corporate dividend policy. However, it is not the only determinant. Although Table 2.2 reports that "Payers" and "Always payers" face steady declines in their profitability levels, Table 2.1 shows that their propensity to pay dividends are higher over time.

Moreover, we find that "Never payers" have the highest levels of cash holdings in all time periods, followed by "Nonpayers." "Always payers" and "Former payers" hold the smallest cash reserves in the first two periods and the last two periods, respectively. Cash holdings of "Payers," "Always payers," and "Former payers" tend to increase over time, while "Nonpayers" and "Never payers" witness declining cash reserves. These can be explained that dividend payment reduces corporate cash holdings.

Besides, financial leverage tends to decrease in the two lowest financial leverage groups including "Payers" and "Always payers." "Nonpayers" and "Never payers" have a similar pattern of financial leverage. Their debt ratios drop sharply in the second period and then recover in the next two periods. Firms with low financial leverage face lower risk of default; therefore, they can raise external funds with lower costs. This makes them less likely to retain earnings.

Table 2.2. Characteristics of Different Payer Groups.

	2001–2005	2006–2010	2011–2015	2016–2020
Profitability (%)				
Payers	10.42	11.12	10.24	9.77
Always payers	10.48	11.72	10.64	10.02
Nonpayers	−5.52	−4.94	−5.55	−5.45
Never payers	−8.71	−7.93	−8.65	−8.52
Former payers	6.24	6.29	5.50	5.69
Cash holdings (%)				
Payers	13.64	14.78	16.20	17.59
Always payers	13.31	14.25	16.07	17.50
Nonpayers	20.67	20.77	18.23	19.59
Never payers	22.53	22.38	19.40	20.78
Former payers	13.85	14.74	14.07	15.29
Financial leverage (%)				
Payers	51.30	50.07	47.27	46.01
Always payers	50.86	49.83	46.95	45.76
Nonpayers	55.97	52.51	55.29	55.77
Never payers	55.49	51.95	55.82	56.84
Former payers	57.73	54.60	53.39	51.89
Firm size				
Payers	12.65	12.81	12.90	13.03
Always payers	13.02	13.26	13.18	13.37
Nonpayers	11.01	11.14	11.03	11.04
Never payers	10.77	10.96	10.81	10.83
Former payers	11.91	11.84	11.83	11.82
Firm value				
Payers	1.50	1.59	1.71	1.87
Always payers	1.44	1.57	1.67	1.81
Nonpayers	2.26	2.12	2.15	2.39
Never payers	2.44	2.28	2.31	2.54
Former payers	1.60	1.50	1.60	1.82

Furthermore, Table 2.2 shows that "Always payers" are the largest firms. The second largest is "Payers" and the third largest is "Former payers." Larger firms have better reputation; therefore, they have better access to external funds. They are also well-organized to reduce possible risks. Consequently, they have higher incentives to pay dividends.

Remarkably, "Never payers" are the most valuable firms, followed by "Nonpayers." Other groups have much lower value. These findings imply that firms are less likely to pay dividends in order to signal outside investors when their market value is high.

2.4 Dividend Policy Across Groups of Countries

Fig. 2.1 presents the percentage of dividend payers across six geographic regions namely America, Asia-Pacific, Europe and Central Asia, Middle East and North Africa, Sub-Saharan Africa, and Western Europe/EU during the period 2001–2020. Asia-Pacific has the highest proportion of payers ranging from 66% to 75%, while America has the lowest proportion of dividend payers varying from 21% to 33%. However, Asia-Pacific firms are less likely to pay dividends, while American firms have higher propensity to pay dividends over time. Sub-Saharan Africa experiences a sharp increase in the percentage of payers from 28% to 70% over the period 2001–2005, then a stable level during the next 10 years and a decline from 2016 to 2020. Furthermore, the percentage of paying firms in Europe & Central Asia, Middle East & North Africa, and Western Europe/EU strongly fluctuates from 40% to 60% over the period 2001–2020.

Table 2.3 shows the percentage of payers and dividend payout ratio of different groups of countries in four periods including 2001–2005, 2006–2010, 2011–2015, and 2016–2020. Dividend payout ratio is measured by total cash dividends deflated by earnings before interest, taxes, depreciation, and amortization. Although

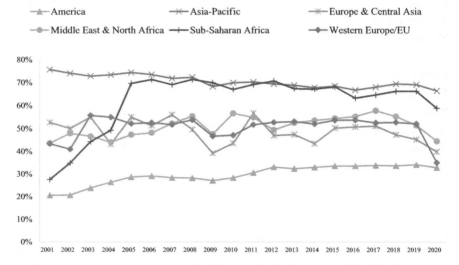

Fig. 2.1.   Dividend Payers Across Geographic Regions.

Table 2.3. Dividend Policy Across Different Groups of Countries.

Group of Countries	2001–2005			2006–2010			2011–2015			2016–2020		
	No. of Obs	Payers (%)	Dividend to Earnings (%)	No. of Obs	Payers (%)	Dividend to Earnings (%)	No. of Obs	Payers (%)	Dividend to Earnings (%)	No. of Obs	Payers (%)	Dividend to Earnings (%)
Geographic regions												
America	28,149	23.89	3.92	24,192	28.25	5.86	21,149	32.51	6.80	18,615	33.61	6.97
Asia-Pacific	31,406	73.97	14.36	43,790	71.00	14.31	56,058	68.86	15.39	64,555	67.87	15.30
Europe and Central Asia	309	51.78	12.57	696	47.27	14.11	1,476	48.44	12.49	1,591	46.51	12.46
Middle East and North Africa	450	46.00	15.12	1,156	52.34	19.14	2,297	52.85	20.59	2,290	52.79	17.94
Sub-Saharan Africa	662	46.07	10.87	903	69.66	17.04	1,049	68.45	16.58	1,011	63.80	15.56
Western Europe/EU	14,453	49.36	9.31	16,561	50.34	11.37	16,024	52.58	13.11	16,498	49.15	12.54
Economic development												
Developed economies	57,285	43.23	6.69	57,410	46.52	8.90	53,002	50.02	9.86	50,856	50.87	10.53
Developing economies	18,121	71.65	18.22	29,710	70.86	16.56	44,524	66.78	17.34	53,188	65.05	16.13

Table 2.3. *(Continued)*

Group of Countries	2001–2005			2006–2010			2011–2015			2016–2020		
	No. of Obs	Payers (%)	Dividend to Earnings (%)	No. of Obs	Payers (%)	Dividend to Earnings (%)	No. of Obs	Payers (%)	Dividend to Earnings (%)	No. of Obs	Payers (%)	Dividend to Earnings (%)
Transition economies	23	60.87	4.71	178	35.96	3.90	527	57.87	9.39	516	58.72	14.71
Legal systems												
Civil law	30,666	74.33	13.53	37,331	72.19	15.01	46,369	72.39	17.01	54,614	71.91	16.63
Common law	44,763	33.45	6.68	49,967	41.78	8.88	51,684	44.47	9.89	49,946	43.04	9.85

Asia-Pacific has the highest proportion of dividend payers, its dividend payout levels are the second highest across the four periods. Middle East & North Africa is the highest payout region. Its payout ratios range from 15% to 20%. America has the lowest payout ratios which vary from 4% to 7%.

In addition, we also investigate dividend policy in developed, developing, and transition economies. Firms in developing countries are more likely to pay dividends than those in developed countries. The average payout ratios in developing countries are from one half to three times than in developed countries across the four periods. Besides, the number of observations from transition economies in our data is small; therefore, there are many fluctuations in their percentages of payers and payout ratios over time. Moreover, Table 2.3 points out that both the proportion of payers and the average payout ratio of civil law countries are much higher than those of common law countries. According to La Porta et al. (2000), the former are less effective than the latter in investor protection; therefore, firms in civil law countries tend to pay more dividends as a compensation for this weakness.

2.5 Dividend Policy Across Industries

Table 2.4 presents dividend policy across different industries defined by the Standard Industrial Classification (SIC). Firms in Construction and Wholesale trade industries are most likely to pay dividends and have the highest dividend payout ratios over time. The proportion of "Payers" in the two industries range from 65% to 70% and their "Always payers" also constitute from 40% to 50% of firms. Mineral has the lowest proportion of "Payers." Paying firms constitute less than 10% of firms in the industry in each period. Moreover, most mineral firms follow no dividend policy. Over 60% of firms in the industry never pay dividends. Besides, many service firms also prefer no dividend pattern. The proportion of "Never payers" account for at least 40% of firms in this industry across the four periods.

2.6 Dividend Policy Across Countries

Table 2.5 shows the distribution of all firms, observations, newly listed firms by country, the proportion of payers, and the dividend magnitude in each country during the period 2001–2020. The United States has the lowest percentage of paying firms and dividend payout ratios among 46 countries. Payers account for only 27.55% of the US firms between 2001 and 2020. The country' average dividend to earnings and dividend to assets are only 4.82% and 0.67%, respectively. They are about half of those in Australia – the second lowest. The third lowest country is Canada, where dividend payers constitute 30.55% and dividend to earnings is 8.57%. In addition, the highest propensity to pay dividends is China. Although the country has 10.7% of newly listed firms, 93.86% of all firms pay dividends from 2001 to 2020. On average, Chinese firms use 29.81% of their net income to pay cash dividends. Moreover, Japanese firms are also highly willing to

Table 2.4. Dividend Policy Across Industries.

Industry	2001–2005						2006–2010					
	No. of Obs	Payers (%)	Never Payers (%)	Always Payers (%)	Former Payers (%)	Dividend to Earnings (%)	No. of Obs	Payers (%)	Never Payers (%)	Always Payers (%)	Former Payers (%)	Dividend to Earnings (%)
Mineral industries	5,012	30.23	60.63	15.36	9.14	6.94	7,415	28.16	65.54	16.25	6.30	6.30
Construction industries	2,379	65.95	20.64	40.56	13.41	11.52	2,892	69.26	17.95	41.49	12.79	12.54
Manufacturing	39,395	56.43	33.60	35.17	9.97	10.66	46,839	59.39	31.28	36.71	9.33	11.92
Transportation, communications	4,940	53.48	33.56	31.88	12.96	9.98	5,582	61.27	29.65	39.50	9.08	14.18
Wholesale trade	3,735	63.13	25.60	38.55	11.27	11.74	3,985	68.26	21.36	43.66	10.39	16.00
Retail trade	4,134	54.72	34.25	32.90	11.03	9.41	4,097	62.19	29.00	40.64	8.81	13.16
Service industries	15,834	32.76	55.70	15.69	11.53	6.29	16,488	43.84	45.15	23.93	11.01	10.06
	2011–2015						*2016–2020*					
Mineral industries	7,975	30.73	61.83	19.24	7.44	7.33	6,459	31.32	59.62	18.83	9.06	7.08
Construction industries	3,205	66.12	21.93	45.55	11.95	13.34	3,335	65.46	22.94	42.91	11.60	14.91

Manufacturing	55,038	61.61	29.31	43.56	9.08	13.90	60,350	61.60	29.78	42.04	8.61	13.87
Transportation, communications	5,817	64.21	25.65	45.38	10.14	14.66	5,903	64.41	25.85	44.16	9.74	14.52
Wholesale trade	4,457	66.91	23.06	48.24	10.03	16.18	4,665	64.48	26.95	47.93	8.57	16.48
Retail trade	4,198	65.41	25.01	41.64	9.58	15.03	4,640	63.47	28.23	42.67	8.30	14.85
Service industries	17,363	49.58	40.68	31.19	9.74	12.27	19,208	50.14	39.83	30.45	10.03	12.31

Table 2.5. Dividend Policy Across Countries.

Country	Number of Firms	Number of Observations	Newly Listed Firms (%)	Payers (%)	Dividend to Earnings (%)	Dividend to Assets (%)
The United States	9,086	73,321	11.29	27.55	4.82	0.67
Australia	2,217	18,236	14.89	29.51	8.86	1.26
Canada	2,109	15,876	13.01	30.55	8.57	1.08
Poland	720	5,529	11.54	35.21	9.37	1.16
Ireland	79	599	13.86	36.56	7.13	0.87
Croatia	84	784	11.10	37.88	8.87	0.87
Norway	337	2,475	14.67	41.13	12.28	1.47
Turkey	315	2,828	5.48	44.48	13.65	1.63
Sweden	811	6,044	12.54	45.04	14.01	1.82
Israel	425	3,718	11.75	45.29	14.99	1.76
The United Kingdom	1,737	13,874	14.23	45.65	10.70	1.42
Indonesia	551	5,327	14.10	45.95	9.01	1.30
Denmark	157	1,486	12.31	47.04	10.62	1.43
Jordan	112	931	10.42	47.37	22.36	2.35
Argentina	52	604	10.43	49.34	9.59	1.46
Germany	829	8,272	9.93	50.16	10.43	1.27
Hungary	34	271	12.18	50.92	12.25	1.93
The Philippines	173	1,858	14.75	53.88	13.45	1.56
India	3,487	30,772	11.71	54.57	6.84	0.87
Italy	417	3,550	11.41	54.65	11.06	1.20
Lithuania	35	362	12.43	54.70	12.91	1.93
Mexico	118	1,385	10.40	54.95	10.61	1.51
Russia	186	1,244	9.08	55.14	10.73	1.68
France	851	8,613	10.47	55.60	9.89	1.09
Singapore	714	7,950	11.91	55.97	16.77	1.63
Portugal	59	712	8.15	56.46	12.02	1.24
Malaysia	959	11,667	10.54	56.53	14.35	1.51
Spain	163	1,653	7.74	57.65	12.08	1.37
New Zealand	163	1,417	13.13	57.73	19.21	2.49

Table 2.5. *(Continued)*

Country	Number of Firms	Number of Observations	Newly Listed Firms (%)	Payers (%)	Dividend to Earnings (%)	Dividend to Assets (%)
South Korea	2,035	18,452	11.33	59.13	7.59	0.60
The Netherlands	221	2,101	10.90	59.92	13.00	1.63
South Africa	226	2,343	11.10	61.03	14.36	2.18
Belgium	127	1,362	9.25	62.41	12.55	1.61
Nigeria	100	977	11.87	63.36	15.80	2.37
Peru	82	919	11.97	63.66	16.93	2.33
Switzerland	243	2,873	8.91	65.99	15.34	2.02
Sri Lanka	204	2,493	8.58	67.27	14.65	1.55
Egypt	149	1,205	9.21	68.96	25.23	3.10
Austria	90	848	10.85	71.11	13.22	1.53
Pakistan	302	3,290	12.07	71.61	13.94	2.15
Thailand	643	7,556	10.01	73.21	24.71	2.99
Finland	194	2,128	9.02	74.81	23.84	2.91
Kenya	29	305	11.80	81.31	21.73	3.39
Morocco	52	339	3.54	82.30	30.52	4.29
Japan	3,448	46,167	7.66	87.96	11.58	0.90
China	4,029	40,624	10.70	93.96	29.81	2.18

pay dividends. Payers constitute 87.96% of Japanese firms. Despite its high percentage of dividend payers, Japan has extremely low payout ratios. Its average dividend to earnings and dividend to assets are 11.58% and 0.9%, respectively. The maximum average dividend to earnings ratio is approximately 30% in Morocco. About two thirds of countries have over 50% of firms to pay dividends during the period 2001–2020.

Fig. 2.2 presents the percentage of dividend paying firms in 10 countries which have the largest number of observations in our data. While Fama and French (2001) show that dividends tend to disappear in the US firms over the period 1927–1999, we find an opposite trend in the next 20 years. Firms in the United States, Canada, and Japan are more likely to pay dividends over the period 2001–2020. China has a steady percentage of payers annually from 2001 to 2013;

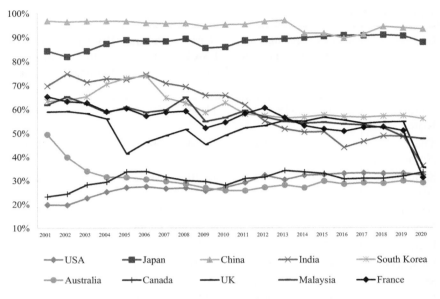

Fig. 2.2.   Dividend Payers in the Ten Largest Countries.

however, Chinese firms become less likely to pay in the following years. Australia experiences a sharp decline in the proportion of dividend payers from 2001 to 2005, then it is steady in the next 15 years. Firms incorporated in other countries are less likely to pay dividends over time.

2.7 Dividend Tax Across Countries

In principles, dividends are considered as shareholders' income; therefore, dividends are taxable. If firms fail to pay dividends, stock price reflects the value of retained earnings. Therefore, investors have to pay taxes on capital gains when they sell their stocks. Investors tend to compare the after tax value of dividends and capital gains in order to value stocks and make their investment decisions. Firms also conduct investment policy based on tax policy. Fig. 2.3 presents top marginal tax rates for dividends and capital gains across 46 countries. There are 16 countries with equal tax rates for dividends and capital gains, 16 countries with higher tax rates for dividends, and 14 countries with lower tax rates for dividends. In addition, Ireland has the highest dividend tax rate at 51%, followed by South Korea (44%), and Denmark (42%). Singapore is the only country that has no tax for dividend payment. Peru and Kenya have the second lowest dividend tax rate with only 5%.

Moreover, the country that supports dividend payment most with its tax policy is Singapore. Its tax rate for capital gains is 18% higher than that for dividends (0%). The next supporters for dividend distribution are China and Malaysia.

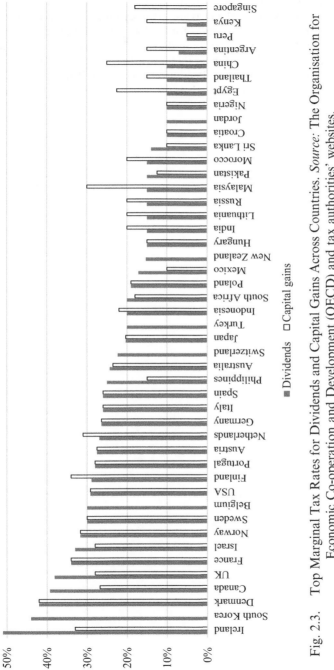

Fig. 2.3. Top Marginal Tax Rates for Dividends and Capital Gains Across Countries. *Source:* The Organisation for Economic Co-operation and Development (OECD) and tax authorities' websites.

Their tax rates for dividends are 15% lower than those for capital gains. On the other hand, South Korea has the heaviest tax discrimination against dividends. It has the largest gap between tax rates for capital gains and dividends with 44%. Belgium and Turkey are the next "anti-dividend" countries. Their tax rates for capital gains are 30% and 20% higher than those for dividends, respectively. In six countries including South Korea, Belgium, Switzerland, Turkey, New Zealand, and Jordan, the tax rate for dividends is 0%.

Chapter 3

Dividend Policy Theories and Empirical Evidence

Abstract

This chapter presents both main arguments of dividend policy theories and their empirical evidence. According to Miller and Modigliani (1961), dividend decisions are not relevant to firm value in a perfect capital market. Nevertheless, there are several market frictions in the real world (e.g., information asymmetry, agency problems, transaction costs, firm maturity, catering incentives and taxes). Therefore, academics use them to develop theories which help them explain corporate dividend decisions. Particularly, signaling theory considers dividend payments as a signal about firms' future prospects since outside investors face information disadvantage. "Bird-in-hand" theory argues that investors prefer dividends to capital gains since the former have lower risk than the latter. Agency theory is developed from the conflict of interest between corporate managers and shareholders. Corporate managers have high incentives to restrict dividend payments. Furthermore, transaction cost theory and pecking order theory posit that firms prefer internal to external funds. This drives firms to hold more cash and pay less dividends. Life cycle theory explains dividend policy by firm maturity. Mature firms have fewer investment opportunities, and thus, they tend to pay more dividends. Catering theory states that dividend decisions are based on investors' demand. Firms pay more dividends since investors prefer dividends and assign higher value to dividend payers. Tax clientele theory argues that firms that have corporate dividend policy rely on the comparative income tax rates for dividends and capital gains. Under the tax discriminations against dividends, firms tend to restrict their dividends in order to increase their stock prices.

Keywords: Signaling theory; "bird-in-hand" theory; agency theory; transaction cost theory; pecking order theory; life cycle theory; catering theory; tax clientele theory

Dividend Policy, 29–41
Copyright © 2024 Quoc Trung Tran
Published under exclusive licence by Emerald Publishing Limited
doi:10.1108/978-1-83797-987-520241005

3.1 Dividend Irrelevance Theory

3.1.1 Main Arguments

Dividend irrelevance theory is developed by Miller and Modigliani (1961). When many academics and practitioners consistently believed that dividends have a positive effect on stock price, Miller and Modigliani (1961) argue that dividend policy is irrelevant to firm value in a perfect business environment. In other words, firms' value remains unchanged no matter whether they decide to pay or not to pay dividends and how much cash they distribute as dividends.

This theory is based on three assumptions: perfect capital market, rational behavior, and perfect certainty. First, in a perfect capital market, no buyers or sellers are price takers who cannot affect the market price of securities. They have equal access to information without costs. Besides, transaction costs and taxes do not exist in the market. Second, all market participants are perfectly rational. They prefer an increase to a decrease in their wealth. They are indifferent to the source of an increase in their benefits. Particularly, they fail to prefer a dividend to a capital gain if the dividend and the capital gain provide them with the same additional interest. Finally, perfect certainty implies that all market participants have equal information and recognize future return of each security. Consequently, there is no difference between equity and debt securities as a source of finance. According to Miller and Modigliani (1961), equity and debt securities are the same, and they can be called as stocks.

Miller and Modigliani (1961) posit that in a perfect business environment, firm value is solely determined by real factors including the earning power of assets and investment decisions. Financial illusions cannot appear when the capital market is perfect and investors are rational. Dividends are just fruits of firm profitability; therefore, they are not "real." When a firm pays a dividend, its retained earnings are lower. Therefore, it has to issue new stocks as a compensation for the distributed cash. New security issuance leads to a decline in stock price which is equivalent to the distributed dividend. In other words, investors' wealth is unchanged since their marginal benefit (the dividend) and marginal cost (the stock price drop) are equal. Rational investors never value dividend payers higher than nonpayers. Consequently, investors are indifferent to corporate dividend policy. Although firms follow no dividend policy or stable dividend policy, their value is not affected by their dividend policy patterns.

3.1.2 Empirical Evidence

Black and Scholes (1974) initially investigate the effect of corporate dividend policy on firm value by testing the relationship between dividend yield and stock return. Using data from firms listed in the New York Stock Exchange, they show that firms with high (low) dividend yields have high (low) dividend payout ratios; however, high (low) dividend yields fail to result in low (high) stock returns. Therefore, the magnitude of payout ratios is not related to stock prices. This finding implies that corporate dividend policy has no significant effect on firm value. Miller and Scholes (1978) extend this line of research by examining whether dividends determine firm value under the US tax system. Although the tax burden on dividends is heavier than that on capital gains, their findings show that dividends are not associated with stock prices. In other words, investors fail to consider dividends as a determinant of firm value despite a tax discrimination against dividends. With a sample of 362 firms in the Compustat database from 1963 to 1980, Jose and Stevens (1989) find that firms with stable and steady growing dividends per share attract market value premiums. However, there is no significant evidence for the association between payout ratios and market value premiums. These findings indicate that firm value is not determined by payout ratios.

In addition, Habib (2004) tests the dividend irrelevance theory in Japan where information asymmetry is extremely low due to the predominance of intercorporate and interlocking ownership. Using the accounting-based valuation approach developed by Ohlson (1995), Habib (2004) finds that dividends are less effective in reducing information asymmetry between insiders and outsiders in Japan. This result supports the theory. Recently, Ofori-Sasu et al. (2022) investigate the effect of dividend policy on investors' wealth in 528 banks from 29 African countries over the period 2006–2018. In line with the dividend irrelevance theory, they find that payout policy has a negative effect on investors' wealth creation in the market.

Although many prior studies show supporting evidence for the dividend irrelevance theory, its assumptions fail to exist completely in the real world. Market frictions make both corporate managers and investors have different preferences toward dividends. Common market frictions are information asymmetry, agency costs, financing costs, corporate life-cycle, catering incentives, and tax clientele. Consequently, other theories are developed to reflect the role of market frictions in corporate dividend decisions.

3.2 Signaling Theory

3.2.1 Main Arguments

Signaling theory is originally an economic theory. According to Akerlof (1970), information asymmetry is an obstacle for economic efficiency. He uses the lemon market to illustrate how information asymmetry makes exchanges impossible. He claims that sellers have more information than buyers about secondhand cars; therefore, buyers cannot distinguish high-quality cars from lemons. Buyers tend to assume that all cars for sale are lemons and never pay high prices for high-quality cars. Consequently, sellers of good cars cannot sell their products. In order to sell their good cars successfully, sellers need to discriminate their cars from low-quality ones by signaling. Signals such as warranties and quality certificates provide buyers with enough information to recognize the quality of different cars and pay them what they are worth. Riley (1975) and Spence (1973) developed signaling equilibrium models which show conditions for buyers to have enough information and distinguish different cars.

In a financial market, information asymmetry is also present. Insiders have more information on business performance of a firm than outside investors. If there is no signal, its stock price is always lower valued. Therefore, firms need to pay dividends in order to send a signal of its positive future performance to outside investors. In other words, as a signal, a dividend is paid to increase the firm's market value. Heinkel (1978) develops an initial model to illustrate how dividend payment determines stock price. Dividends provide information on firms' expected cash flows. When firms with good expected performance are rare, investors perceive implications of firm performance from dividends to make their investment decisions. Later theoretical studies continue to develop and improve models in order to describe the role signaling role of dividends effectively (Ambarish et al., 1987; John & Williams, 1985; Kale & Noe, 1990; Rozeff, 1982).

3.2.2 Empirical Evidence

Several empirical studies with various methods find supporting evidence for the dividend signaling theory in different countries. Baker et al. (1985) use mail questionnaires to survey chief financial officers of 562 corporations listed in the New York Stock Exchange (NYSE) from February to April 1983 in order to examine how chief financial officers think about the effect of dividend policy on firm value. They find that about 90% of participants agree on significant impacts of dividend decisions on both firm value and stock price volatility. Remarkably, among four explanations of this relationship, the signaling mechanism has the highest level of agreement. Baker and Powell (1999, 2000) survey listed firms in NYSE in 1997 with various dividend hypotheses and compare the results with those of the survey conducted in 1983. They find that current and forecasted earnings are important determinants of corporate dividend policy. These earnings have highly similar explanatory power in both studies conducted in 1983 and 1997. In addition, Baker et al. (2001) conduct a survey of 188 managers of firms listed in NASDAQ and find consistent results. Similar findings from surveys are released in Australia (Partington, 1989), Norway (Baker et al., 2006), France (Albouy et al., 2012), Canada (Baker et al., 2007), and 16 European countries (Bancel et al., 2009).

Moreover, the dividend signaling mechanism is also supported by many empirical studies with secondary data. Asquith and Mullins (1983) argue that dividends are more attractive than other accounting data in transmitting information due to two main reasons. Firstly, dividends are a simple and comprehensive signal for managers to convey firms' current and expected performance. Secondly, dividend announcements are supported by cash; therefore, they are clearly more visible than other announcements. With a sample of 168 firms paying dividends for the first time or after a hiatus of at least 10 years in the United States, they find that dividend initiation announcements have a positive effect on excess returns. This finding implies that dividends provide investors information on firms' future performance, and this information is more valuable than any costs arising from dividend distribution. Healy and Palepu (1988) remove 37 firms with missing information from the Asquith and Mullins' sample to test the information content of dividend changes. Their findings are consistent with the signaling theory. Consistently, Nie and Yin (2022) investigate whether dividend payment conveys information about the volatility of future cash flows in China. They find that cash flow volatility changes in the opposite way after dividends changes are announced. Adjaoud (1984), Ahmed and Javid (2009), Mulchandani et al. (2020) and Raaballe and Hedensted (2008) also find supporting consistent results in Canada, Denmark, India, and Pakistan.

However, other empirical studies show that managers fail to communicate with the market through distributing dividends. Watts (1973) investigates whether current and past cash dividends are stronger estimates of future earnings than current and past earnings. With a sample of 310 firms, he finds that the information conveyed by dividends is insignificant. Gonedes (1978) argues that dividend signals do not represent any special information about forecasted distributions of earnings. Moreover, DeAngelo et al. (1996) also document no supporting evidence for the dividend signaling hypothesis with two explanations. Firstly, managers tend to overestimate future earnings because they are over-optimistic. Secondly, managers tend to make limited cash commitments when they raise dividends.

Furthermore, Benartzi et al. (1997) find that a dividend increase (decrease) leads to a positive (negative) abnormal return at the time of dividend announcement. However, they document that there are insignificant abnormal returns for firms cutting dividends, while firms with dividend increases have significant positive excess abnormal returns. These results indicate that even if firms convey signals to the market, these signals are not about firms' expected performance, and the market fails to perceive them. Besides, Grullon et al. (2002) show that an increase in dividends leads to a decrease in the future profit. Brav et al. (2005) conduct a survey and find that the information content of dividends is not significant. In addition, analyzing determinants of dividend policies with a sample of 76 firms listed in the New Zealand Stock Exchange between 1991 and 1999, Chen and Dhiensiri (2009) show no evidence to support the signaling theory.

3.3 "Bird-in-hand" Theory

3.3.1 Main Arguments

In a pioneer paper, Gordon and Lintner (1956) suggest that investors are risk-averse; therefore, they prefer dividends to capital gains. The name of this theory derives from the expression "a bird in the hand is worth more than two in the bush." From a financial perspective, investors have high incentives to buy a stock that distribute a current dividend instead of a stock that fails to pay a current dividend and promises to pay dividends in the future. Stock prices mainly rely on market forces and are beyond shareholders' control; consequently, capital gains are less predictable and controllable than dividends (Gordon, 1959).

Even if the return from capital gains in the future is higher than that from the current dividend, investors are still afraid of uncertainty. They cannot assure that they accumulate a higher return in the future. Investors understand that time horizon and risk are strongly correlated; therefore, they decide to hold dividends – a bird in their hand – rather than wait for two birds in the bush. This behavioral pattern implies a positive relationship between dividends and stock prices. Investors are willing to pay higher prices for firms with high dividends and use a high discount rate for nonpayers or low-dividend firms.

3.3.2 Empirical Evidence

Gordon (1959) investigates dividend policy across four manufacturing industries including chemicals, steels, machine tools, and foods. He finds that dividends have a stronger positive effect on stock price than capital gains. This finding is consistent with the bird-in-hand theory. Fisher (1961) also documents a positive relationship between dividends and share prices. Moreover, La Porta et al. (2000) investigate corporate dividend policy of 4,000 companies across 33 countries and find that firms in countries of poor shareholder protection tend to pay more dividends despite several investment opportunities. This finding can be explained by the bird-in-hand mechanism. When legal regulations fail to provide share-holder rights effectively, shareholders are more likely to force firms to pay dividends in order to avoid uncertainty. They cannot wait to collect future returns from capital gains when corporate managers have many opportunities to exploit retained earnings. With a sample of 154,090 observations from the US firms over the period 1972–2016, Karpavičius and Yu (2018) show that economic uncertainty increases dividend premium. Under high economic uncertainty, investment in equity securities become riskier, and thus, investors tend to value dividend payers higher. Recently, Tran et al. (2022) investigate dividend policy under the impact of the global financial crisis in Vietnam – a country of weak corporate governance. Consistent with La Porta et al. (2000), they find that firms are more likely to pay dividends, and their payout ratios are higher in the crisis period. These findings imply that the financial crisis leads to higher uncertainty, and thus, investors have higher incentives to hold "a bird in hand."

However, Sahu (2000) investigates the effect of dividend policy on abnormal returns of 533 Indian firms from 1993 to 1998 and find no supporting evidence for the bird-in-hand theory. Baker et al. (2007) conduct a survey of Canadian firms with at least one dividend payment from June 2001 to June 2004 in order to examine how top financial officers explain corporate dividend policy. Their findings show that there is little support for the bird-in-hand theory.

3.4 Agency Theory

3.4.1 Main Arguments

Agency theory is initially developed by Berle and Means (1932) to describe the impact of the gap between ownership and control on modern companies. Agency relationship is defined as an agreement under which agents perform some service on behalf of principals who delegate decision-making authority agents (Jensen &

Meckling, 1976). Agency problems arise from the information asymmetry between agents and principals. Although agents are not owners of resources, they can manage and control resources. Therefore, agents tend to make decisions on their own interest instead of maximizing principals' wealth. From a financial perspective, there are two common agency problems including shareholders–managers and bondholders–shareholders (Jensen & Meckling, 1976).

First, corporate managers tend to take advantage of financial decisions in order to expropriate shareholders. This problem results in agency costs of equity. Shareholders have to pay monitoring costs in order to control corporate managers. However, shareholders cannot restrict managers' expropriation completely and still incur residual loss. Managers have to pay bonding costs to show that their behaviors are aligned with shareholders' benefits. Among corporate financial decisions, dividend payment is a device to mitigate the agency problem and reduce agency costs of equity. According to Easterbrook (1984), both monitoring costs and costs arising from managers' risk aversion become less serious with firms paying cash dividend to shareholders. When firms issue new shares or debt securities to finance business opportunities, their affairs are monitored by investment banks, outside investors, and other monitoring institutions in the market. In addition, issuing firms can adjust leverage level so that shareholders cannot exploit bondholders' welfare. Jensen (1986) and Rozeff (1982) propose free cash flow hypothesis which states that firms should reduce their free cash flows to mitigate the agency problem. Corporate managers tend to divert corporate resources into unprofitable projects in order to serve their interest. Free cash flows are opportunities for their overinvestment; therefore, paying dividends to reduce free cash flows is a means to decrease agency costs of equity.

Second, firms tend to expropriate their bondholders by making riskier financial decisions. This behavior is a moral hazard. Myers (1977) posits that in some cases, shareholders try to expropriate bondholders by paying excessive dividends. Firms pay dividends to their shareholders and raise external funds to finance their investment and dividend payment. These actions transfer wealth from bondholders to shareholders. Therefore, bondholders also have to pay monitoring costs and incur residual loss. Firms have to restrict their risky decisions and limit their dividends through debt covenants.

3.4.2 Empirical Evidence

Ang et al. (2000) use a zero agency-cost firm as a base case to measure both absolute and relative agency costs of equity under various ownership and management structures. With a sample of 1,708 small firms from the 1997 National Survey of Small Business Finances data, they find that agency costs of equity are higher with outsider managers than insider managers, negatively related to the managers' ownership, positively related to the number of nonmanager shareholders and lower with greater bank monitoring.

Empirical studies yield mixed results in the impact of free cash flow on dividend policy. Holder et al. (1998) initially use free cash flow to investigate the impact of agency problems on dividend decisions. With the sample of 477 US listed firms during the period 1983–1990, they find strong supporting evidence for the free cash flow hypothesis. Adjaoud and Ben-Amar (2010) also find that free cash flow is positively correlated with dividend payment in Canadian stock market. This positive relationship is present in Ghana (Amidu & Abor, 2006) and Thailand (Thanatawee, 2011). However, with a sample of 26 firms listed in Indonesia from 1994 to 2007, Utami and Inanga (2011) find no significant evidence to support the free cash flow hypothesis. Basil Al-Najjar and Hussainey (2009) show that levels of free cash flows are negatively related to dividend distribution, but this relationship is not significant in the UK stock market.

Moreover, many empirical studies show that strong corporate governance has a positive effect on corporate dividend policy. Using governance data of the Institutional Shareholder Services with 4,771 firm-year observations of dividend-paying firms in US stock markets from 2001 to 2004, Pornsit Jiraporn (2006) finds that strength of corporate governance is positively related to dividend policy. In addition, Bebczuk (2005) and Kowalewski et al. (2007) find that there is a positive association between Transparency and Disclosure Index and dividend policy in Argentina and Poland, respectively. These findings imply that firms with stronger corporate governance pay more dividends. Moreover, with a sample of 714 firm-years from Canadian firms from 2002 to 2012, Adjaoud and Ben-Amar (2010) find that Corporate Governance Score is positively related to dividend payout ratio.

Furthermore, Handjinicolaou and Kalay (1984) investigate the impact of dividend change information on both bond prices and equity prices. Using a research sample with 255 straight bonds randomly selected from the NYSE and 1,967 dividend announcements over the period 1975–1976, they find that bond prices fall significantly with dividend decrease announcements and remain significantly constant with dividend increase announcements. These findings are not consistent with the shareholders–bondholders agency hypothesis, but they support the information content of dividends. In addition, Kalay (1982) uses the data of debt indentures of 150 firms randomly selected from Moody's Industrial Mutual to examine dividend policy under the impact of bond covenant. They document that firms hold considerably more cash than the lowest cash level stipulated in the bond covenants. This finding implies that firms do not intend to expropriate their creditors or they need more cash than the stipulated level. Nash et al. (2003) use bonds issued in 1989 and 1996 to investigate bond covenants' costs and benefits. They find that firms with high firm growth tend to preserve flexibility in their future financing options by ignoring dividend or debt issuance constraints in their bond contracts. These also imply that contractual relations between shareholders and bondholders represent the specific needs of the both parties.

3.5 Transaction Cost Theory and Pecking Order Theory

3.5.1 Main Arguments

According to transaction cost theory, firms need to accumulate enough cash in order to finance their business activities since transaction costs of selling noncash assets are significant (Manos, 2001). When firms pay dividends, they may fail to have enough cash and resort to sell their noncash assets. Consequently, dividend payment is more expensive than retained earnings due to transaction costs. Firms only pay dividends from their excessive cash (Higgins, 1972).

Pecking order theory is originally a capital structure theory developed by Myers and Majluf (1984). This theory states that firms choose sources of financing by priority. Since corporate managers have more information on firm performance, risk, and future prospects than outsiders such as investors and creditors, outsiders tend to pay lower prices for newly issued securities. In order to make newly issued securities obtain their actual value, issuers have to incur signaling costs. Consequently, external funds are more expensive than internal funds. Moreover, debt and equity securities are two sources of external finance, but the former is cheaper than the latter. When firms issue debt securities, outsiders perceive a signal of good future performance, and thus, they use low discount rates. However, issuing equity securities is considered as a signal of overpriced stocks, and outsiders set high discount rates. Based on this pecking order, firms have low incentives to pay dividends to avoid external financing. Retained earnings are transferred internally; consequently, firms do not face obstacles caused by information asymmetry. On the other hand, firms fail to take advantage of tax shield when using retained earnings to finance their investment. Therefore, corporate managers consider marginal costs and benefits when making dividend decisions.

3.5.2 Empirical Evidence

There are several studies supporting transaction cost theory and pecking order theory. Since firms prefer internal to external funds; they tend to restrict dividends in order to save cash for future investment. Higgins (1972) finds that investment opportunities have a negative impact on corporate dividend policy. Firms with high investment opportunities pay less dividends. With a sample of 1,000 US firms listed between 1974 and 1981, Rozeff (1982) shows that firm growth is negatively associated with dividend decisions. In addition, when investigating why dividends disappear in the US market from 1978 to 1999, Fama and French (2001) find that this phenomenon is partly due to firm characteristics. Firms which have never paid dividends experience the highest investment opportunities. Their asset growth and market-to-book ratio are much higher than other groups of firms. With a sample of firms listed in the United States, Canada, the United Kingdom, Germany, France, and Japan over the period 1994–2002, Denis and Osobov (2008) also find supporting evidence for the negative effect of investment opportunities on dividend payment. Moreover, Thanatawee (2011) uses a data including 416 nonfinancial firms to examine determinants of dividend policy in Thailand. Their results show that market-to-book value is negatively associated with dividend policy, while asset growth has insignificant correlation with dividend policy. Nevertheless, some empirical studies show no supporting evidence for the two theories. Al Shabibi and Ramesh (2011) and Basil Al-Najjar and

Hussainey (2009) show no significant relationship between investment opportunities and dividend decisions in the UK stock markets. Similar findings are found in Canada (Adjaoud & Ben-Amar, 2010), Indonesia (Utami & Inanga, 2011), and Jordan (Al-Malkawi, 2007).

3.6 Life Cycle Theory

3.6.1 Main Arguments

Life cycle theory is originally developed by Grullon et al. (2002) to explain why firms with low profitability and high growth have lower propensity to pay dividends in the US market. They argue that young firms have low levels of profitability, but they have many investment opportunities and thus retain more earnings instead of paying dividends. However, mature and established firms have difficulties in finding profitable projects, and thus, their resources are more abundant. They tend to accumulate more retained earnings, and this pile of cash erodes their financial performance. Consequently, they are more likely to distribute cash to improve their economic efficiency (DeAngelo & DeAngelo, 2006; Grullon et al., 2002).

3.6.2 Empirical Evidence

DeAngelo et al. (2006) use the earned/contributed capital mix as a proxy for firm maturity to test life cycle hypothesis in the US market from 1973 to 2002. Their findings show that firms with higher earned/contributed capital mix have higher probability to pay dividends. The positive relationship between maturity of firm and the probability of dividend payment is a supporting evidence for life cycle hypothesis. Furthermore, Denis and Osobov (2008) investigate the predictability of firm maturity on the propensity to pay dividend in six developed countries, namely the United States, Canada, the United Kingdom, Germany, France, and Japan over the period from 1989 to 2002. Their results illustrate that firms with greater proportion of retained earnings to total equity are more likely to pay dividends. Brockman and Unlu (2009) also find that retained earnings scaled by the book value of assets ratio is positively related to both the likelihood of paying dividends and dividend payout ratio across 52 countries with 120,507 firm-year observations. Besides, the survey of top financial officers conducted by Baker et al. (2007) shows that respondents strongly support explaining corporate dividend decisions by firm maturity.

3.7 Catering Theory

3.7.1 Main Arguments

Baker and Wurgler (2004b) propose catering theory to explain corporate dividend policy on the basis of investor demand. While the irrelevance dividend theory assumes that capital market is efficient, Baker and Wurgler (2004b) assume that capital market is inefficient and firms have to satisfy investor demand. This theory states that the relative stock price of dividend payers with respect to nonpayers changes since investors' demand for dividends changes over time. When investors' demand for payers (nonpayers) increases, payers (nonpayers) are value higher. As a result, the decision to initiate or omit dividends relies on the relative stock price of payers with respect to nonpayers.

Li and Lie (2006) argue that corporate dividend policy is not limited to the decision to initiate or omit dividends but include the decision to specify dividend levels. They criticize Baker and Wurgler's model for explaining initiations or omissions rather than the whole dividend policy. Accordingly, they suggest a modified catering theory to explain both dividend decisions. Firms cater to investors' demand through their dividend policy.

3.7.2 Empirical Evidence

Baker and Wurgler (2004b) initially investigate the effect of the current dividend premium on the rates of firms initiating and omitting dividends in the United States during the period 1963–2000. Dividend premium is defined as the difference between the current share prices of paying firms and nonpaying firms. Using four different stock price-based measures to calculate the dividend premium, they find that the total initiation (omission) rate has a significantly positive (negative) relationship with dividend premium. In addition, Baker and Wurgler (2004a) examine the relationship between the propensity to pay dividends and catering incentives. Firstly, they use Fama and French's methodology (2001) to recognize four distinct trends in the propensity of paying dividends from 1963 to 2000 and find that there are two appearances and two disappearances over the period. Secondly, they report that each of these trends is related to a corresponding change in catering incentives when dividend premium variable is measured in line with Baker and Wurgler (2004b).

Li and Lie (2006) argue that the empirical study conducted by Baker and Wurgler (2004b) contains two drawbacks. First, their discrete model cannot explain the catering effects on dividend levels. Second, their empirical findings show no supporting evidence for the catering theory with a statistically insignificant relationship between dividend announcement returns and dividend premium. Therefore, they extend the dividend catering model with continuous dividend levels. Using a research sample of 20,779 dividend announcements (1,815 decreases and 18,964 increases) over the period from 1963 to 2000, they find that both the likelihood of decreases and increases in dividends and the amount of the dividend changes are associated with dividend premium. Particularly, the likelihood of dividend decreases is higher for the group of low dividend premium, and the probability of dividend increases is higher for the group of high dividend premium. In addition, dividends decrease with higher rates if the dividend premium is low and increase with higher rates if the dividend premium is high. They also find supporting evidence for the catering theory with a significantly negative relationship between the announcement returns arising from dividend decreases and the dividend premium and a significantly positive relationship between the announcement returns arising from dividend increases and the dividend premium.

Although the catering theory of dividends is supported empirically in the US market, the evidence of dividend catering is mixed across countries. Ferris et al. (2006) examine whether the dividend disappearing is present in the United Kingdom. They find that the number of payers also falls from 75.9% to 54.5% over the period 1988–2002. After firm size and profitability are controlled, their results show a decline in the propensity of paying dividends over the subperiod 1998–2002. Interestingly, a shift in catering incentives is considered most likely explanations for the changes in dividend policy in the UK market from 1998 to 2002. In addition, Bogolebska (2023) also finds supporting evidence for the catering mechanism in Poland. However, von Eije and Megginson (2008) investigate cash dividends and share repurchases of firms listed in 15 EU members from 1989 to 2005 and find no systematic impact of a country-specific catering variable on dividend policy. This implies that catering fails to play an important role in European firms' dividend policy. With a sample of firms listed in six developed markets including the United States, Canada, the United Kingdom, Germany, France, and Japan from 1989 to 2002, Denis and Osobov (2008) also report no supporting evidence for the catering incentive. They find that unexpected reductions in the paying proportion are determined by newly listed firms which have low proportions of dividend initiations. Moreover, Ferris et al. (2009) investigate catering incentives with a large dataset of 24,298 observations collected from 23 countries between 1995 and 2004. They only find supporting evidence for catering incentives in the subsample of common law countries. Even when the effect of firm life cycle is controlled, catering incentives remain persistent. They explain that stockholders of firms incorporated in common law countries experience a wider range of rights and protections, and thus, they are more able to discipline managers who cannot cater to investor demand.

3.8 Tax Clientele Theory

3.8.1 Main Arguments

From a microeconomic perspective, a tax clientele is defined as a group of people who prefer a certain asset or transaction since they have similar tax status. From this definition, Brennan (1970) proposes tax clientele theory based on an after-tax capital assets pricing model to explain corporate dividend policy under the impact of taxes. From a financial perspective, a tax clientele includes a group of investors who have similar preferences toward dividend policy since they have similar explicit marginal tax rates. Litzenberger and Ramaswamy (1979) improve the original model by removing some assumptions. However, the two models consistently show that taxes make investors fail to receive optimal benefits. When dividends have a heavier tax burden than long-term capital gains, investors are more likely to purchase nonpayers and firms with low payout ratios. Under the tax discriminations against dividends, firms tend to restrict their dividends in order to increase their stock prices.

Moreover, different investors belong to different tax brackets; therefore, they have different levels of preferences toward dividends. Investors with relatively low (high) marginal tax rates for dividends over capital gains have high preferences toward dividends (capital gains) (Black & Scholes, 1974). Besides, investors are indifferent to dividends and capital gains if their marginal tax rates are identical.

3.8.2 Empirical Evidence

Pettit (1977) investigates how transaction costs and taxes influence individual investors' portfolios and finds supporting evidence for the tax clientele effect. Investors charged with low tax rates and investors with tax discriminations against capital gains prefer high dividend yield stocks. Testing the extended after-tax capital assets pricing model in the NYSE over the period from January 1936 to December 1977, Litzenberger and Ramaswamy (1979) document supporting evidence for the tax clientele hypothesis. In addition, Poterba and Summers (1984) realize that the period from 1955 to 1981 offers a promising opportunity to test the tax clientele theory in the United Kingdom since it experiences two radical changes and many minor reforms in dividend tax policy. Using daily data on a limited sample and monthly data on a broad sample, they find a significant impact of taxes on the equilibrium relationship between market return rates and dividend yields. Their findings are consistent with the tax clientele theory.

However, using the data from Pettit (1977), Lewellen et al. (1978) show a weak effect of marginal tax rates on dividend yields of investors' portfolios. In addition, Black and Scholes (1974) show that the differences between the expected return rates on high yield common shares and low yield common shares are not significant both before and after taxes. Miller and Scholes (1982) continue to test whether investors with a heavier tax burden on dividend receive higher risk-adjusted returns with higher dividend yields. They also find no empirical support for the theory. Other studies examine the relationship between tax policy and dividend policy when there are changes in tax regimes in the United States (Tax Reform Act of 1986) and Canada (Canadian Tax Reform). These changes supply natural experiments to test the tax clientele hypothesis. However, they also find mixed results (Bolster & Janjigian, 1991; Casey & Dickens, 2000; Means et al. 1992; Papaioannou & Savarese, 1994; Saadi & Chkir, 2008).

Chapter 4

Internal Environment and Dividend Policy

Abstract

This chapter analyzes how the internal environment determines corporate dividend decisions. First, dividend policy is influenced by strategic and financial issues. Corporate strategies are developed by top managers to achieve firms' missions, visions, and long-term goals while business strategies are designed by middle managers to maintain firms' competitive advantages. These strategies affect corporate dividend decisions through corporate performance and business operations. In addition, many financial characteristics are important determinants of dividend policy. Financial characteristics are classified into three groups, namely performance-related issues (e.g., firm profitability, free cash flow, and stock liquidity), leverage-related issues (e.g., debt ratio, asset tangibility, business risk, and firm size), and investment-related issues (e.g., investment opportunities and firm maturity). Firms with high profitability, free cash flow tends to pay more dividends. Stock liquidity may have a positive effect on dividend payments through lowering costs of equity; however, it may also have a negative effect through weakening the signaling motive. Moreover, firms with high debt ratio, low asset tangibility, high business risk, and small size face higher costs of external financing. Therefore, they have low incentives to pay dividends. When firms have more investment opportunities, they are more likely to restrict dividends and save cash for their investment projects and vice versa. Second, internal stakeholders may influence corporate dividend policy since their benefits are closely related to dividend decisions. Shareholders, directors, the chief executive officer, and employees have different characteristics, positions, and hold various proportions of shares. Therefore, they create pressures on dividend decisions to protect their wealth.

Keywords: Internal environment; internal management; strategic issues; financial issues; internal stakeholders; shareholders; directors; CEO; employees

Dividend Policy, 43–56

Copyright © 2024 Quoc Trung Tran

Published under exclusive licence by Emerald Publishing Limited

doi:10.1108/978-1-83797-987-520241006

4.1 Internal Management and Dividend Policy

4.1.1 Strategic Issues

The term "strategy" derives from a Greek word "strategos" which means "the art of the general" (Dyer et al., 2021). As a concept in the military, its definition is broadened and used commonly in business administration. From business perspective, strategy is a set of joint actions deliberately designed to accomplish particular goals. All firms need to develop their strategies in order to accomplish their goals, improve their competitive advantage, and enhance their sustainable performance. There are two common levels of strategy: corporate strategy and business strategy.

First, top managers design a corporate strategy to develop a firm in accordance with the firm's missions, visions, and long-term goals. A corporate strategy shows what businesses the firm targets on or wants to target on, and what it intends to do with selected businesses (Robbins et al., 2014). Three major types of corporate strategy include growth, stability, and renewal. Firms follow growth strategy when they intend to expand its business. They may grow by concentration, vertical integration, horizontal integration, and diversification approaches. In addition, stability strategy helps firms remain and sustain their current business. Besides, firms use renewal strategy when they face serious problems and thus need to improve their performance. Firms correct minor problems by a retrenchment and solve major problems by a turnaround (Robbins et al., 2014).

Second, middle managers design a business strategy to create and maintain their firms' competitive advantages in the industry (Dyer et al., 2021). This strategy mainly focuses on short-term goals like attracting customers, improving firm profitability and enhancing customer satisfaction. According to Porter (1980), firms can create their competitive advantage by four generic strategies including cost leadership, cost focus, differentiation, and differentiation focus. Cost leadership and differentiation are used for a broad market, while cost focus and differentiation focus are applied for a narrow market segment or a niche market. Moreover, Miles et al. (1978) and Raymond and Charles (2003) suggest four patterns of business strategy, namely prospector, defender, analyzer, and reactor. A prospector concentrates on innovation and development. A defender is satisfied with its current position in the market and tries to maintain the position over time. Actually, a defender is mature and has less space for innovation and growth; therefore, it focuses on profitability. An analyzer employs others' inventions and innovations to develop their products and improve their performance. A reactor fails to have a particular business approach. It only reacts to what happens in the market. Besides, corporate social responsibility (CSR) is a popular approach to develop corporate competitive advantage (Villiers & Ma, 2017). Modern customers are not only concerned about product characteristics but also how their manufacturers are responsible to the society.

Recently, academics have paid attention to the relationship between firms' strategies and their dividend decisions. Vasanthan Subramaniam and Wasiuzzaman (2019) investigate how corporate diversification strategy affects Malaysian firms. With a sample of 712 firms listed between 2010 and 2014, they find that firms following industrial diversification strategy tend to have lower payout ratios. When firms diversify their businesses across more industries, they fail to take advantage of economies of scale. However, they document that firms with geographical diversification have high dividend levels. They explain this positive relationship by the resource-based view. Geographically diversified firms can allocate their resources such as assets, information, and skills more efficiently through their internal capital markets. Consequently, they have higher levels of profitability and are more willing to pay dividends.

In addition, Cao et al. (2022) examine the relationship between business strategy and corporate dividend policy in the United States. They argue that prospectors and defenders have different dividend decisions due to their contrasting characteristics, but their effects on dividend policy are controversial. On the one hand, the former have lower incentives to distribute cash than the later. Innovation-oriented firms need more cash to finance their R&D investments and costly marketing activities for their highly differentiated products. Besides, prospectors face higher operational risks since R&D investments are riskier than normal investments. This makes them face higher costs of external financing, and thus, they are more likely to retain earnings instead of disgorging dividends. On the other hand, innovation-oriented strategy may reduce prospectors' willingness to pay dividends. Since R&D projects require great funds, prospectors need to use both internal and external financing. They tend to pay more dividends to signal outside investors so that they have better access to external funds with lower costs. Moreover, risky R&D investments drive investors to prefer dividends to capital gains. Investors are more likely to pressure innovation-oriented firms to pay dividends and value dividend payers higher. As a result, firms cater to their investors' demand by paying high dividend levels. With a sample of 90,241 firm-years from about 12,000 US firms from 1962 to 2019, Cao et al. (2022) find supporting evidence for the negative effect of innovation-oriented business strategy on dividend policy. Akindayomi and Amin (2022) document a consistent finding and explain it by cash flow volatility and financial covenants in the US market during the period 1992–2018. First, they show that prospectors have higher cash flow volatility than defenders. Innovative firms have more risky R&D investments that increase their cash flow volatility. Therefore, they tend to restrict their dividends in order to hold cash as a buffer against cash flow volatility. Second, they show that prospectors face stricter financial covenants that restrict their capacity to distribute cash to their shareholders. This is a reaction of creditors to protect their benefits when they recognize that prospectors concentrate on risky investments such as R&D projects and marketing campaigns. Moreover, Akindayomi and Amin (2022) find that the negative impact of innovation-oriented business strategy on dividend policy is stronger in growth firms, in firms with less chief executive officer (CEO) performance-based compensation sensitivity and after the financial crisis.

Moreover, Poretti and Blal (2020) examine how asset-light business strategy influences dividend decisions the hospitality industry. Asset-light strategy focuses on reducing ownership of assets to have little capital for business activities. Firms following this strategy try to transition their noncore assets and capabilities to their partners and concentrate on their core assets and capabilities. Asset-light strategy helps firms broaden their businesses faster since their development is not limited by their own assets. Poretti and Blal (2020) argue that asset-light strategy increases firm growth, and corporate managers have more available cash flows; therefore, firms have to pay more dividends to avoid their managers' opportunistic behaviors. Using a data of 399 observations of firms in the hospitality industry between 2006 and 2018, they find that asset-light strategy positively affects dividend policy of high-growth firms. Especially, when high growth firms have low institutional ownership, the effect is more pronounced. Institutional investors are commonly more effective than individual investors in controlling corporate managers and improve corporate governance. Low institutional ownership makes firms face more severe agency problem; therefore, they have higher incentives to pay dividends.

Furthermore, the extant literature shows that as a business strategy, CSR may influence corporate dividend policy in opposite ways (Cheung et al., 2018). On the one hand, socially responsible firms are less willing to pay dividends due to low cost of equity. According to El Ghoul et al. (2011), high CSR firms have two advantages: (1) They face lower nondiversifiable risk since future explicit claims from stakeholders are fewer and (2) they have larger investor base due to less information asymmetry (high disclosure standards) and investor preferences. These advantages help socially responsible firms face lower costs of equity, and thus, they tend to save cash for their investment projects rather than distribute dividends. On the other hand, CSR positively affects corporate dividend policy through high profitability, high incentive to reduce managers' opportunistic behaviors, and strong motive of signaling. First, CSR projects have positive net present value; therefore, socially responsible firms have higher earnings which result in higher dividend levels (Cheung et al., 2018). Second, managers have more access to cash when firms focus on CSR projects beside their main business investments. This is an opportunity for managers to expropriate shareholders through overinvestment in social and environmental projects. Consequently, firms tend to pay more dividends in order to restrict managers' expropriation of shareholders. Third, dividends are a signal of firms' capability to implement CSR activities; consequently, socially responsible firms are more likely to pay high dividends (Benlemlih, 2019). With a sample of 15,561 observations from 1,965 US firms over the period 1991–2010, Cheung et al. (2018) find that CSR implementation has a positive effect on corporate dividend policy. Several empirical studies also show supporting evidence for this positive effect in the United States (Benlemlih, 2019; Hendijani Zadeh, 2021; Sheikh, 2022b), Sri Lanka (Dewasiri & Abeysekera, 2022), Malaysia (Badru & Qasem, 2021), and China (Fonseka & Richardson, 2023). However, Saeed and Zamir (2021) find a negative relationship between CSR disclosures and corporate dividend decisions in eight developing countries including India, China, Indonesia, Pakistan, Malaysia, Korea, Turkey, and Russia from 2010 to 2018.

4.1.2 Financial Issues

Dividend policy reflects how a firm distributes its earnings back to shareholders and retains its earnings for future investment. Dividend decisions are one in three main groups of financial decisions. Therefore, corporate dividend policy is determined by financial characteristics. Empirical studies show that performance-related issues (profitability, free cash flow, and stock liquidity), leverage-related issues (debt ratio, asset tangibility, business risk, and firm size), and investment-related issues (investment opportunities and firm maturity) are important determinants of corporate dividend policy.

4.1.2.1 Performance-Related Issues

Performance-related issues including profitability, free cash flow, and stock liquidity reflect firms' ability to pay dividends. Current profit is the main source of dividend payment; therefore, highly profitable firms are more likely to pay dividends and have high payout ratios. Besides, firms with high profitability also face high pressure to pay dividends from investors who consider dividends as the bird in hand. Insiders may convince shareholders to accept a low payout ratio when their firms have low profitability, but they are less able to avoid investors' request for dividends when their firms are highly profitable. The positive effect of firm profitability on dividend policy is found in many countries like the United States (Aivazian et al., 2003; Fama & French, 2001), the UK (Kilincarslan, 2021), Saudi Arabia (Boshnak, 2021), Australia (Gyapong et al., 2021), India (Labhane & Mahakud, 2016), and MENA countries (Jabbouri, 2016).

In addition, free cash flow is the residual fund after a firm pays its operating expenses and investment expenditure. According to agency theory, free cash flow leads to agency costs. When firms have high free cash flows, managers tend to use cash for bad investment projects that are unprofitable but beneficial to them. In order to avoid this opportunistic overinvestment, shareholders force firms to mitigate free cash flows through dividend payment. In other words, firms with high free cash flows have high payout ratios (Adjaoud & Ben-Amar, 2010; Amidu & Abor, 2006; Sawicki, 2009).

Moreover, stock liquidity is the ease in trading a stock without reducing its price. Stock liquidity decreases cost of equity and thus increases firm value (Baker & Stein, 2004). When having lower costs of equity, firms tend to hold cash or use cash for their investment projects instead of paying dividends. Nguyen (2020) investigates how stock liquidity affects dividend policy with a sample of listed firms in Australia over the period 2000–2018. He finds that stock liquidity has a positive impact on dividend payout ratio. However, stock liquidity may also reduce firms' willingness to pay dividends. When having high stock liquidity, insiders have low incentives to signal outside investors. As a means of signaling, dividends are restricted in firms with high stock liquidity. With a sample of firms listed in the United States over the period 1963–2003, Suman Banerjee et al. (2007) show that stock liquidity negatively influences payout ratio.

4.1.2.2 Leverage-Related Issues

Levered firms can take advantage of the tax shield to increase their profitability which, in turn, increases payout ratio. However, firms with high debt ratios face high risk of default. Highly levered firms face more difficulties to raise external funds and higher costs of external financing. Therefore, they are more likely to retain earnings for their future investment projects instead of paying dividends. Jensen et al. (1992) find that debt ratio negatively affects corporate dividend decisions. Several studies show consistent results in both developed and emerging markets (Aivazian et al., 2003; Al-Malkawi, 2007; Jensen et al., 1992; Kowalewski et al., 2007; Mehdi et al., 2017; Thanatawee, 2011).

Moreover, firms' ability to raise external funds also affects their dividend decisions. In an imperfect capital market, transaction costs and information asymmetry make external funds become more expensive than internal funds. When firms pay dividends, they are more likely to raise external funds for their investment projects. The cost of dividend payment includes the cost to raise external funds. Therefore, firms have higher dividend levels if their external financing costs decrease. Asset tangibility, business risk, and firm size are proxies of external financing costs. First, tangible assets can be used as collaterals with firms that borrow money from creditors. Firms with more tangible assets have easier access to credit and lower costs of credit; therefore, they tend to pay more dividends. Second, firms with high business risk have to pay high costs of external financing since outside investors insist on high risk premiums. Consequently, business risk has a negative effect on dividend policy. Finally, large-sized firms have better reputation and management. These characteristics help them have easier access to the capital market and face lower costs of external funds. Therefore, larger firms have higher payout ratios (Chang & Rhee, 1990; Holder et al., 1998). The effects of asset tangibility, business risk, and firm size on dividend policy are empirically supported in many countries such as the United States (Chang & Rhee, 1990), the United Kingdom (Al Shabibi & Ramesh, 2011; Basil Al-Najjar & Hussainey, 2009), Canada (Adjaoud & Ben-Amar, 2010), Poland (Kowalewski et al., 2007), Thailand (Thanatawee, 2011), Jordan (Al-Malkawi, 2007), and Bangladesh (Mollah, 2001).

4.1.2.3 Investment-Related Issues
In principles, a firm divides its annual income into two parts: the earnings retained for investment and the dividend paid to shareholders. Consequently, corporate dividend policy is determined by investment opportunities and the availability of investment opportunities. First, investment opportunities are commonly measured by Tobin's Q and firm growth. Since external financing is more expensive than internal financing due to market frictions, firms with high investment opportunities tend to restrict their dividend policy to avoid external financing. The negative relationship between investment opportunities and corporate dividend policy are found in the United States (Alli et al., 1993; Chang & Rhee, 1990; Holder et al., 1998; Jiraporn et al., 2011), Canada (Baker et al., 2007) and Ghana (Amidu & Abor, 2006).

Second, firm maturity affects dividend decisions through the availability of investment opportunities. Particularly, investment opportunities are less available in mature firms than young firms. Therefore, firms with high maturity tend to have excess cash which leads to higher payout ratios (DeAngelo & DeAngelo, 2006; Grullon et al., 2002). Empirical studies show positive impacts of firm maturity on both the likelihood to pay dividends and the dividend magnitude across countries (Brockman & Unlu, 2009; Denis & Osobov, 2008; Koo et al., 2017; Labhane, 2018a; Labhane & Mahakud, 2016).

4.2 Internal Stakeholders and Dividend Policy

4.2.1 Shareholders

Shareholders tend to pursue their own benefits. Shareholders in a group have similar characteristics, preferences, and behaviors. Shareholder structure reflects how rights and obligations are distributed among shareholders and thus determines corporate dividend policy. Shareholders are commonly split into the following pairs of groups: large shareholders and minority shareholders, insiders and outsiders, institutional shareholders and individual shareholders, the state and nonstate shareholders, foreign shareholders and local shareholders, and family shareholders and nonfamily shareholders.

First, large shareholders are individuals and organizations whose ownership reaches a certain percentage of shares as stipulated in the law. The common threshold to define large shareholders is 5%. The number of large shareholders and their shareholdings reflect ownership concentration.

Ownership concentration is high when a small number of large shareholders hold a large proportion of shares. According to agency theory, corporate managers tend to expropriate shareholders due to the separation of corporate ownership and control. Highly concentrated ownership provides large shareholders with more power to monitor and control managers effectively (Shleifer & Vishny, 1986). Consequently, firms with high ownership concentration pay more dividends to reduce free cash flows available to their managers. With a sample of 2,147 observations from 326 Indian firms between 2010 and 2017, Arora and Srivastava (2019) find that ownership concentration has a positive effect on corporate dividend decisions. Although high ownership concentration helps major shareholders reduce managers' opportunistic behaviors, it may also give major shareholders an opportunity to expropriate minority shareholders. Majority shareholders use their voting rights to restrict dividends and hold more cash for investment projects that serve their own interest. With a sample of 1,000 US firms from 1974 to 1980, Rozeff (1982) finds that ownership dispersion is negatively related to dividend payout ratio. This implies a positive relationship between ownership concentration and dividend policy. Moreover, using data of 14,155 from 1,431 Japanese firms between 1995 and 2007, Harada and Nguyen (2011) document that firms with high ownership concentration have low dividend payout ratios. Other studies also find supporting evidence for this negative relationship in Australia (Gyapong et al., 2021), Latin America (Gonzalez et al., 2017), and East Asian and Gulf Cooperation Council countries (Mehdi et al., 2017).

Second, insiders are obliged to run a firm in order to maximize its value. However, insiders may hold no shares or a certain proportion of shares. Therefore, there is a conflict of interest between insiders and other shareholders due to this separation of corporate control and ownership. Prior empirical studies show that the effect of insider ownership on dividend policy is controversial. On the one hand, when insiders hold a large proportion of shares, their benefits are more consistent with those of other investors. Consequently, they are more likely to implement their obligations and restrict their opportunistic behaviors. From a dividend policy perspective, firms with high insider ownership tend to reduce their free cash flows by paying more dividends. With a sample of 2,475 observations from the US firms over the period 2002–2013, Balachandran et al. (2019) find a positive impact of insider ownership on payout ratio. On the other hand, insiders holding a large percentage of shares may take advantage of their voting rights to expropriate other shareholders. Although other shareholders may insist on dividend payment, they decide to retain more earnings in order to serve their own benefits instead of distributing dividends. Their voting rights are also supported by their information advantage. Therefore, other shareholders cannot significantly affect their decisions. Alli et al. (1993), Holder et al. (1998), and Rozeff (1982) consistently show that insider ownership has a negative effect on corporate dividend policy in the United States. Similar empirical evidence is also present in Hongkong (Chen et al., 2005), Jordan (Al-Malkawi, 2007). In addition, the relationship between insider ownership and dividend policy may be represented by an inverse U-shaped curve. When insiders have a small proportion of shares, their voting rights are not enough to support their opportunistic behaviors. Therefore, they serve their own benefits by maximizing firm value. Their firms are more likely to pay dividends in order to mitigate free cash flows. Nevertheless, when their ownership reaches a particular level that is enough to support their decisions, they have high incentives to expropriate outside investors by restricting dividends. Using a sample of 4,028 observations from nonfinancial firms listed in 10 Asian countries from 2011 to 2014, Kim et al. (2020) find supporting evidence for the inverse U-shaped relationship between insider ownership and corporate dividend policy.

Third, institutional shareholders are more capable of monitoring and controlling managers than individual shareholders due to their advantages in experience, technology, skills, and information. When institutional investors have higher proportion of shares, their voice is stronger in corporate governance, and thus, managers face higher pressure to decrease free cash flows. In other words, institutional investors drive firms to pay more dividends. Short et al. (2002) examine how institutional ownership affects dividend policy of 211 listed firms in the United Kingdom from 1988 to 1992. They document that firms with high institutional ownership have high payout ratios. This relationship can be explained by both institutional investors' ability to control managers and tax preference for dividend payment. The role of institutional investors in reducing agency costs through dividend policy is also documented in the United States (Chang et al., 2016; Crane et al., 2016), India (Jacob & Jijo Lukose, 2018) and Jordan (Bataineh, 2021).

Fourth, the state or the government is a special shareholder. Government agencies hold shares of a joint-stock corporation since it is important to the government's economic and social policies. In transition economies, most firms with state ownership are originally 100% state-owned. In order to protect and expand its benefits, the government tends to grant favorable treatments and privileges to firms with state ownership. In many countries, the government controls and regulates the financial system strictly, and many banks are state-owned. Therefore, the government can support firms with state ownership to obtain bank credit easily and reduce costs of external financing (Cong et al., 2018; Megginson et al., 2014; Shailer & Wang, 2015). When having this soft-budget constraint, firms with state ownership face lower marginal costs of dividend payment, and thus, they tend to have higher dividend levels. With a sample of 13,116 observations from 1,024 Chinese firms listed between 1998 and 2008, Wang et al. (2011) find that state ownership positively influences both the likelihood to pay and the magnitude of dividends. Besides, Goyal et al. (2020) compare dividend policy of privatized and nonprivatized firms across 26 countries over the period 1990–2013 and also find that state ownership is positively related to dividend decisions. Many empirical studies show supporting evidence for this positive relationship in Jordan (Al-Malkawi, 2007), Vietnam (Tran et al., 2022), and Latin America (Gonzalez et al., 2017). However, state ownership has a disadvantage in corporate governance. While a corporation without state ownership faces an agency problem between shareholders and managers only, a state-owned firm faces a "double principal-agent problem." Elected politicians are not owners of state resources; they are only delegated to manage state resources by citizens. Therefore, they are less active in monitoring managers, and managers of a state-controlled firm have double incentives to conduct opportunistic behaviors (Gugler, 2003). This mechanism implies that managers of state-owned firms tend to retain earnings instead of paying dividends. Basil Al-Najjar and Kilincarslan (2016) document that state ownership has a negative impact on corporate dividend policies in Turkey.

Fifth, foreign investors play an important role in corporate governance although most countries have regulations on foreign ownership cap – the maximum percentage of shares that foreign investors are allowed to hold in a firm. On the one hand, foreign investors are more effective than local investors since they have more investment experience and technology. When foreign investors hold more shares, they have a stronger voice to monitor managers. Therefore, firms with higher foreign ownership tend pay more dividends to reduce free cash flows available to their managers. Jeon et al. (2011) use a sample of 5,583 observations from firms listed in Korea over the period 1994–2004 to investigate how foreign investors affect corporate dividend policy. They find that foreign investors initially prefer dividend payers; then, they drive firms to pay after having substantial shareholdings. Cao et al. (2017) also show consistent evidence in China. On the other hand, foreign investors have less information about local business environment than local investors. If this weakness exceeds the mentioned strength, foreign investors are less effective than local investors in corporate governance. As a result, firms with high foreign ownership have low payout ratios. Baba (2009) shows that foreign ownership is negatively associated with the likelihood to pay dividends. Lam et al. (2012) document that foreign ownership has negative effects on both the probability of dividend payment and payout ratio in China.

Finally, family investors have various patterns of behaviors when making financial decisions. Family controlled firms tend to nominate family members as managers, and thus, they face lower agency costs. However, families may also exploit their positions to expropriate other shareholders. Consequently, family ownership may have a positive or a negative relationship with corporate dividend decisions. Setia-Atmaja (2010) show that family controlled firms have high payout ratios while Attig et al. (2016), Setiawan et al. (2016), and Wei et al. (2011) find an opposite relationship.

4.2.2 Board of Directors

A corporation has many shareholders. Since they cannot gather to make business decisions on their own, they elect a group of people to represent their benefits. This group is called as a board of directors. The board of directors hires executives who have the expertise to run their corporation and ensure that these executives act to maximize shareholders' interest. Directors' rights and obligations are stipulated in legal documents and corporate bylaws. Board members or directors commonly discuss and make important decisions such as: setting missions, strategies and goals, hiring and firing the management, monitoring and controlling the management, providing important resources, making important investment decisions, proposing dividend policy, leading acquisitions and mergers. Consequently, the board's characteristics affect corporate dividend decisions.

First, board size may have a positive or a negative effect on dividend policy. On the one hand, board members are in charge of monitoring managers; therefore, a large board helps a firm strengthen its corporate governance. Facing strong corporate governance, corporate managers are less likely to conduct opportunistic behaviors. Consequently, firms with larger boards tend to pay more dividends in order to reduce its free cash flow. The positive relationship between board size and dividend policy is documented in the United States (Benjamin & Biswas, 2019; Thompson & Adasi Manu, 2021), China (Ain et al., 2021) and India (Roy, 2015). On the other hand, a firm with more directors may face weak corporate governance if the directors fail to cooperate and focus on its goals.

Second, a board includes both inside directors and outside directors (independent directors). Independent directors are not executives and fail to have a material or pecuniary connection with the firm. In most countries, the presence of independent directors is mandatory since the government wants to protect minority shareholders. Independent directors have both advantages and disadvantages in their contribution to corporate governance. On the one hand, independent directors are more effective than inside directors in corporate governance since their decisions are not determined by any conflicts of interest. Therefore, firms with more independent directors have stronger corporate governance and thus pay more dividends. Kaplan and Reishus (1990) investigate how independent directors affect the US firms' performance and find that firms with dividend reduction have about 50% of probability higher than firms without dividend reduction to have additional outside directorships. With a sample of 944 public companies in the United States, Sharma (2011) shows that board independence has a positive effect on the probability of dividend payment. Borokhovich et al. (2005), Jie Chen et al. (2017), and Thompson and Adasi Manu (2021) find supporting evidence for the positive relationship between board independence and dividend policy. On the other hand, independent directors fail to improve and even weaken corporate governance if they participate in the board as stooges. Since the legal regulations require firms to have a certain proportion of independent directors in the board, large shareholders find incapable independent directors to meet the requirement and maintain the power of inside directors. Moreover, independent directors have less information on business activities than inside directors. Therefore, outside directors have little contribution in the decision-making process. This mechanism implies that firms with more independent directors have weaker corporate governance, and thus, they are less likely to disgorge cash in the form of dividends. Roy (2015) and Setia-Atmaja (2010) show a negative impact of board independence on dividend policy.

Third, female directors have more contribution to corporate governance than male directors; therefore, the gender structure of the board also determines corporate dividend policy. Many scholars find that women are more trustworthy, virtuous, hardworking, and risk-averse than men (Chonko & Hunt, 1985; Faccio et al., 2016; Pucheta-Martínez & Bel-Oms, 2016). Therefore, female directors can help firms reduce managers' opportunistic behaviors more effectively. Firms with more female directors have stronger corporate governance, and thus, they have higher payout ratios. Benjamin and Biswas (2019) and Jie Chen et al. (2017) find a positive relationship between the proportion of female board members and dividend policy in the United States. Gyapong et al. (2021) and Ain et al. (2021) show consistent results in Australia and China, respectively.

4.2.3 Chief Executive Officer – CEO

A CEO is the highest ranking manager in a firm. In principles, a firm employs a CEO with appropriate managerial skills and experience to manage its business activities. Rights and obligations of a CEO are also presented in both legal documents and corporate bylaws. Since CEOs are one of the most important decision-makers in their firms, corporate financial decisions may reflect their characteristics such as attitude, gender, marital status, power, tenure, duality, and turnover.

Overconfident CEOs tend to be optimistic about the success of their investment opportunities. When having high investment expenditure, their firms are less willing to pay dividends (Schrand & Zechman, 2012). However, overconfident CEOs also want to show their managerial skills; therefore, they have high incentives to signal outside investors through dividend payment. Moreover, overconfident CEOs may be overoptimistic about their ability to raise external funds. Consequently, firms with overconfident CEOs have high dividend payout ratios (Dinh Nguyen et al., 2021). Furthermore, Caliskan and Doukas (2015) investigate how CEOs' risk preferences affect corporate dividend policy. With a sample of 2,117 observations listed in the United States over the period 2006–2011, they find that firms pay more dividends when their CEOs are more risk-averse.

Female CEOs are more risk-averse and less likely to conduct opportunistic behaviors (Faccio et al., 2016; Ullah et al., 2020). These two characteristics may lead to two opposite impacts on dividend policy. On the one hand, female CEOs' risk aversion motivates them to hold more cash and thus their firms are less willing to pay dividends (Zeng & Wang, 2015). On the other hand, female CEOs' honesty restricts their expropriation of shareholders by diverting cash into unprofitable projects. Consequently, firms with female CEOs tend to pay more dividends.

Besides, CEO marital status is also a determinant of corporate dividend policy. Married CEOs are more risk-averse due to two main reasons. First, they are more concerned about their job security and stability due to higher commitment consumption for their family. When making decisions, their families are relevant reference agents. Therefore, they are more likely to pursue risk-averse business activities. Second, the biological characteristics of married CEOs make them more risk-averse. For example, married men have less testosterone which supports risk-taking behaviors (Hossain et al., 2023). Using a sample of 14,362 observations from 2,008 US listed firms during the period 1993–2008, Hossain et al. (2023) find that firms with single CEOs have lower payout ratios.

Moreover, CEOs have incentives to expropriate shareholders due to the separation of corporate ownership and control; however, their ability to conduct opportunistic behaviors relies on their power. Powerful CEOs make corporate governance become less effective, and they have more opportunities to expropriate shareholders. Hence, their firms have lower dividend levels. Nevertheless, outsiders also recognize weak corporate governance in firms with powerful CEOs. Therefore, firms with powerful CEOs face higher costs of external financing. In order to build good reputation, firms tend to pay more dividends. Sheikh (2022a) examines the effect of CEO power on the dividend paying decision with a sample of 25,308 observations from US firms during the period 1992–2016. He finds that firms with powerful CEOs are more likely to pay dividends.

In addition, CEO tenure and CEO duality also reflect CEO power. When a CEO has a longer tenure or takes the chair, they have stronger power in corporate decisions. Therefore, like CEO power, CEO tenure and CEO duality may affect corporate dividend policy in two opposite ways. McGuinness et al. (2015) find that CEO tenure has a positive effect on dividend policy. However, Abor and Fiador (2013) show that CEO duality is negatively related to dividend decisions.

Furthermore, CEO compensation is a means to mitigate the agency problem between CEOs and their firms. When CEOs have more compensation, they have higher incentives to maximize shareholders' wealth. Therefore, they pay more dividends to reduce free cash flows instead of holding cash for overinvestment. Minnick and Rosenthal (2014) and White (1996) find that executive compensation positively affects dividend decisions in the United States. Ding et al. (2021) show a consistent result in Australia.

4.2.4 Employees

Corporate managers develop strategies and plans, but they fail to implement them directly. Instead, employees execute strategies and plans through their daily business activities. Their implementation ability determines how successfully a firm can sustain its competitive advantage and achieve strategic goals. Therefore, employees are important strategic resources (Garel & Petit-Romec, 2021; Saeed, 2021). However, there are conflicts of interest between firms and their employees. Firms tend to minimize their costs in order to maximize shareholders' wealth, while employees insist on higher levels of salary and other benefits such as job safety, insurance, and pension plans. Therefore, firms have to consider these employer–employee conflicts when they make financial decisions, especially when they distribute earnings to shareholders.

Employees understand that an individual bargaining power fails to affect their managers' decisions. Consequently, they gather in a collective organization called as labor union to have stronger voices in negotiations. A labor union is established by employees to protect their rights and benefits relating to their jobs. This organization negotiates with managers to ensure that employees have better working conditions and benefits. However, firms cannot satisfy all requests from their employees' collective bargaining. Unionized firms also use their financial decisions to strengthen their bargaining power. They may increase their financial leverage and decrease their cash reserves in order to avoid the expropriation from labor unions (Ahmad & Kowalewski, 2021; Bronars & Deere, 1991; Klasa et al., 2009; Shin et al., 2018). In addition, DeAngelo and DeAngelo (1991) show that unionized firms report low earnings before union negotiations. Cullinan and Bline (2003), D'Souza et al. (2000) document that firms intentionally use accounting methods with high flexibility to hide positive aspects of their performance so that they have stronger bargaining power against labor unions' wage demands. When the wealth is low, labor unions cannot ask for many benefits. This avoidance mechanism implies that firms tend to pay more dividends when they face high pressures from labor unions.

On the other hand, firms may be active to satisfy their employees by adopting employee friendly practices. According to Saeed (2021), employee friendly practices may have two opposite effects on corporate dividend policy. First, employee friendly practices lead to high dividend payouts. These practices help firms attract and retain the best employees who, in turn, make significant contribution to their strategic goals and performance. Fair employee treatment strengthens employees' commitment and loyalty to their firms and reduce employee turnover which leads to additional recruitment and training costs. Therefore, employee friendly practices help firms improve their productivity. Besides, a good employer–employee relationship results in a moral capital that protects firms from environmental uncertainty; therefore, their cash flows are more stable (Godfrey et al., 2009).

When firms have high employee loyalty, productivity, and cash flows, they have better reputation in the capital market. Consequently, they have better access to external funds and incur lower costs of external financing. However, employee friendly practices may also raise shareholders' concern about their benefits. Fair employee treatment represents a strong relationship between managers and employees who have incentives to expropriate shareholders' wealth (Faleye & Trahan, 2011). Therefore, shareholders tend to mitigate this risk by reducing free cash flows available to corporate managers. These mechanisms consistently drive firms to pay more dividends. Second, employee friendly practices have a negative effect on dividend policy due to managerial entrenchment. Labor unions are a threat for managers' careers. If managers fail to deal with labor unions' pressures, they are more likely to be replaced. Furthermore, their entrenchment activities are closely monitored by labor unions if they fail to satisfy employees' demands. Consequently, corporate managers have high incentives to conduct employee friendly policies in order to have a "quiet life" (Bertrand & Mullainathan, 2003). In other words, employee friendly practices provide corporate managers with more opportunities and flexibility to expropriate shareholders. This reduces both the likelihood to pay dividends and the dividend magnitude. With a sample of 6,071 observations from 862 firms listed in 17 emerging markets, Saeed (2021) finds that firms with strong employee friendly policies have low dividend payout ratios. This finding supports the managerial entrenchment mechanism.

Chapter 5

Industry Environment and Dividend Policy

Abstract

This chapter analyzes how the industry environment determines corporate dividend decisions. First, common participants in the product market are competitors, suppliers, and customers. These micro-stakeholders create competitive pressures on firms and thus affect their current and future performance. Competitors influence dividend decisions through three mechanisms, namely predation threat, corporate governance, and imitation. Predation threat reduces firms' incentives to pay dividends when facing high rivalry. Competition helps firms improve corporate governance. However, strong corporate governance may increase or decrease dividend payments since dividend policy may be the outcome of strong corporate governance or the substitute for weak corporate governance, respectively. Besides, firms tend to imitate their industry peers in dividend policy. Second, as a financial policy, dividend policy is also affected by participants in the financial market like investors, creditors, and auditors. These financial stakeholders' behaviors are important to stock prices. Due to the agency problem, creditors have high incentives to restrict firm's dividend payments in order to protect their benefits. On the other hand, creditors are effective external monitors who help firms improve their corporate governance. Outside investors affect corporate dividend policy through their valuation. Firms pay more dividends if investors prefer dividends to capital gains. Auditors play the role of a third-party monitor, and thus, they help firms reduce managers' expropriation of shareholders and improve the quality of accounting information. Furthermore, we also investigate dividend policy of regulated industries in both financial sector (banking, insurance, and real estate) and utilities sector (energy, telecommunications, and transportation).

Keywords: Industry environment; competitors; suppliers; customers; investors; creditors; auditors; dividend policy

Dividend Policy, 57–66
Copyright © 2024 Quoc Trung Tran
Published under exclusive licence by Emerald Publishing Limited
doi:10.1108/978-1-83797-987-520241007

5.1 Product Market Participants and Dividend Policy

A product industry is a group of all firms supplying similar products and services. According to Pearce and Robinson (1985), the product industry environment is defined as general competition conditions in an industry. In addition, Grant (1991) postulates that the product industry environment is the firm's relationship with its competitors, suppliers, and customers. Remarkably, when investigating why some industries have higher levels of profitability than others, Porter (1979) finds that the structure of an industry drives the industry and determines firms' ability to create profits. The industry structure is shaped by five forces including existing competitors, potential entrants, suppliers, buyers, and substitute products. These forces are close to all firms in the industry and influence their ability to satisfy customers which, in turn, affects their profitability. When a firm faces pressures from these forces, its managers have to take them into consideration. Dividend decisions rely on corporate performance and other financial decisions like investment and financing. Therefore, product market participants play an important role in corporate dividend policy.

5.1.1 Competitors

Competitors include existing rivals and new entrants. Existing firms compete in an industry to obtain more market shares. Their common rivalry tools include new product development, quality improvement, service enhancement, price discounts, and advertisements (Porter, 2008). Firms without improvement cannot survive while other firms continuously improve their business operations. Their competition leads to limits of profitability in the industry. Rivalry among existing firms is high when the industry has high degree of concentration, high heterogeneity of competing incumbents, high overcapacities, high exit barriers, high fix costs, low product differentiation, and low industry growth (Porter, 2008). In addition, an industry with high profitability is attractive to new entrants which have new capabilities. These new firms try to obtain more market shares and thus create pressures on existing firms' prices and costs. According to Porter (2008), although the industry is attractive, the number of new entrants relies on entry barriers. Common entry barriers include economies of scale, existing firms' cost advantages, distribution channels, capital requirements, switching costs, government policy to restrict new entrants, and retaliation. When entry barriers are high, existing competitors face less pressures from new firms. The effect of competitors on dividend policy may be explained by predation threat, agency problem, and imitation (Babar & Habib, 2021).

5.1.1.1 Predation Threat-Based Theory

Predation threat-based theory states that firms' cash reserves determine their ability to compete successfully against their existing competitors and prevent potential competitors from entering their industry (Bolton & Scharfstein, 1990; Telser, 1966). Firms with sufficient internal liquidity are more flexible in their reactions to their competitors' predatory actions. If their internal funds are insufficient, they fail to seize profitable investment opportunities and thus lose their market shares to their competitors (Alimov, 2014). As a result, firms facing high rivalry from existing competitors are less likely to pay dividends since they tend to save more cash in order to maintain their competitive strength in the product market. Hoberg et al. (2014) investigate how product market fluidity affects dividend policy of the US firms over the period 1997–2008. Fluidity reflects how competitors change the product space around a firm. They find that product market fluidity has a negative effect on firm propensity to pay dividends and a positive effect on corporate cash holdings. These effects are stronger when firms have difficulties in raising external funds.

Furthermore, prior studies show that market power is also a determinant of corporate dividend policy. Market power is a firm's ability to manipulate market prices by influencing other product market participants such as competitors, suppliers, and customers. Firms with strong market power are less affected by the product market and their investors face less information uncertainty (Ramezani & Moosavi, 2015). Therefore, strong market power reduces business risk and thus drives them to pay more dividends. Booth and Zhou (2015) investigate how market power affects dividend policy in the US manufacturing firms from 1976 to 2006. They find that firms with stronger market power are more likely to pay dividends and have higher payout ratios. Ramezani and Moosavi (2015) also document a positive effect of market power on payout ratio in Iran over the period 2009–2013.

5.1.1.2 Agency-Based Theory

Agency-based theory posits that rivalry among existing competitors is an effective substitute for corporate governance. According to Machlup (1967), in a perfect competition market, firms have no significant managerial slacks as they cannot survive without cost minimization. Competition makes corporate managers fail to slack off. Consequently, they have to work hard in order to achieve their firms' financial goals which help them maintain their positions. According to Hart (1983) and Shleifer (1985), information asymmetry between corporate managers and shareholders is less severe when firms face strong product market competition. Shareholders can easily use rivals' performance as a benchmark for their firms, and thus, their information is not limited to what is disclosed by managers. Moreover, Schmidt (1997) argues that when the intensity of competition increases, firms with high costs face high default risk and liquidation risk. This makes corporate managers try to serve their firms instead of conducting opportunistic behaviors in order to save their jobs (Pahi & Yadav, 2022). Consistently, Shleifer and Vishny (1997) show that high competitive pressures restrict corporate managers' incentives to invest in unprofitable projects. In other words, competition is effective in decreasing agency costs of free cash flow. Fee and Hadlock (2000) show that competition leads to higher CEO turnover. Furthermore, Karuna (2007) documents that managerial incentives are greater when firms face intense competition in their industry.

Although several studies show a consistently positive impact of product market competition on corporate governance, the relationship between product market competition and corporate dividend policy can be explained by two opposite mechanisms which rely on the role of corporate governance in corporate dividend decisions. On the one hand, strong corporate governance pressures managers to reduce their expropriation of shareholders, and thus, their firms tend to pay more dividends. In other words, high payout ratios are the outcome of strong corporate governance. On the other hand, when corporate governance is weak, firms tend to use dividends as a compensation for shareholders' agency costs. Therefore, high payout ratios are the substitute of weak corporate governance (Grullon & Michaely, 2007).

Grullon and Michaely (2007) investigate the effect of product market competition on corporate dividend policy in the US market between 1972 and 2001. Using a sample of 42,859 observations from manufacturing firms, they document that firms in high competition industries tend to pay more dividends than those in low competition industries. This finding supports the outcome mechanism. He (2012) examines the role of product market competition in mitigating the conflict of interest between controlling and minority shareholders in Japanese firms. With a sample of 35,462 observations over the period 1977–2024, he finds that competition has a positive effect on dividend payout ratio, a positive effect on the likelihood of dividend increase, and a negative effect on dividend omission. Besides, the relationship between firm-specific agency problems and payout ratios becomes weaker in industries of high competition. Kao and Chen (2013) investigate how product market competition influences corporate dividend decisions in Taiwan. They posit that legal protection of shareholders is weak in Taiwan; therefore, minority shareholders face high agency costs. This institutional environment may support the substitute mechanism rather than the outcome mechanism. Their results show that product market competition positively affects corporate dividend policy (the outcome mechanism is supported) in highly competitive industries. However, product market competition negatively influences dividend decisions (the substitute mechanism is supported) in industries of low competition. With a sample of 1,142 listed in India over the period 2001–2018, Pahi and Yadav (2022) also show that firms have higher probability of dividend payment when they face less competition. Kang and Kim (2021) examine the relationship between product market competition and corporate dividend policy in two groups of dividend payers: high payout ratios and low payout ratios. They find that the relationship is positive in the former but negative in the latter. These findings can be explained that high payout firms focus more on their reputation, and thus, they tend to pay more dividends as a reaction to high competition. However, low payout firms concentrate more on their survival. This makes the substitute mechanism more effective. Moreover, Zhou et al. (2013) analyze the impact of import competition on dividend policy in the US market. They document that import competition increases uncertainty in corporate performance, and thus, firms facing intense import competition are less likely to pay dividends.

5.1.1.3 Imitation-Based Theory

Economic theory shows that individuals or organizations in a peer group tend to have similar decisions since they imitate each other (Adhikari & Agrawal, 2018). According to Lieberman and Asaba (2006), this imitation is not only explained by rivalry-based mechanism but also information-based mechanism. The former posits that firms follow their competitors since they want to maintain their competitiveness or reduce rivalry. The latter states that firms follow others since their peers are believed to have information advantage. Although the two mechanisms are based on different motivations, both of them may explain why firms imitate their competitors which are also members of their peer group. Graham and Harvey (2001) show that CEOs consider how other firms conduct their financial policies when making financial decisions for their own firms.

Adhikari and Agrawal (2018) are the pioneer researchers investigating the effect of peer pressure on corporate dividend policy. With a sample of firms listed in the United States from 1965 to 2010, they find that firms imitate their industry peers in dividend policy. The peer effect is stronger when product market competition is more intense and information uncertainty is lower. Moreover, they also document that firm size and age determine the extent of imitation. Firms are more likely to imitate the dividend levels of industry peers which have similar size and age. Especially, this sensitiveness is higher for small and young firms. Furthermore, motivated by a real-life story about General Electric (GE) and Westinghouse (WHS), Grennan (2019) examines how corporate dividend policy reacts to peer pressure. According to O'Sullivan (2006), although WHS had lower levels of profitability than GE, it still followed GE's dividend payments in lock-step for many decades. From 1970 to 1990, WHS had 10 increases in its dividend levels, and most of them were conducted after GE introduced dividend increases. The magnitude of two firms' dividend increases is also equal. In order to finance its dividend imitation, WHS had to increase its financial leverage. This made the firm face severe financial distress in the 1990s. Based on this story, Grennan (2019) defines dividend peer effect as the behavior to change dividend decisions in consistent with the prevalence of the similar behavior in peer groups. Using data from the United States over the period 1975–2001, Grennan (2019) finds supporting evidence for the peer influence on corporate dividend payment. Peer pressures drive firms to decrease the time period between two dividend changes by about 4.5 months and raise their dividend levels by 16%. However, the peer influence is only effective with dividend increases. Besides, later studies also document the peer influence in China (Yan & Zhu, 2020) and Taiwan (Lee, 2020).

5.1.2 Suppliers and Customers

A firm's customers and suppliers also determine its profit potential. When suppliers have stronger voices in negotiations, they create more pressures on the firm. Their bargaining power is strong if they account for a large proportion of the firm's input, the firm's input is differentiated, the availability of substitute inputs is low, the firm faces high switching costs, they have a large contribution to the firm's product quality, or the threat of forward integration is high (Porter, 2008). In addition, customers' bargaining power is strong if they constitute a large proportion of the firm's output, the firm's product is not differentiated, substitute products are available, they face low switching costs, they have a large contribution to the firm's product quality, or the threat of backward integration is high (Porter, 2008).

Customers/suppliers may use their bargaining power to affect their partners' dividend policy through two channels: shielding wealth and corporate governance. On the one hand, firms use dividends as a means to avoid their customers'/suppliers' expropriation. According to Dasgupta and Sengupta (1993) and Subramaniam (1996), firms use their financial leverage in order to shield a part of their wealth away from their suppliers. Extending this mechanism, Kale and Shahrur (2007) posit that financial leverage plays an important role in firms' negotiations with their customers/suppliers and it helps firms reduce pressures from them. Firms tend to increase their debt ratios when they face strong customer/supplier bargaining power. Using a sample of firms from the Compustat database over the period 1984–2003, they find that customer/supplier concentration has a positive relationship with financial leverage. Consequently, firms may follow a similar behavioral pattern when they make dividend decisions under pressures from their customers/suppliers. Specifically, customers/suppliers are likely to take advantage of their bargaining power to expropriate the wealth from their partners. Therefore, firms tend to pay more dividends to shelter their surplus from their customers'/suppliers' expropriation when the bargaining power of their customers/suppliers is strong. On the other hand, customers/suppliers may take advantage of their bargaining power to improve their partners' corporate governance. According to Johnson et al. (2010), a principal customer plays the role of a monitor and certifier for its suppliers; therefore, it can mitigate information asymmetry between its suppliers and their investors. Cremers et al. (2008) also posit that customers and suppliers are able to control a firm strictly by many requirements. For instance, they may require the firm to disclose financial information regularly. Consistently, Patatoukas (2012) finds that when firms have a small number of large customers, their performance is better. These customers monitor them and help them improve operational efficiency. When customers/suppliers have strong bargaining power, their monitoring and certifying activities are more effective. Therefore, firms' managers have fewer opportunities to expropriate their shareholders when their firms have customers/suppliers with strong bargaining power. Wang (2012) argues that customers'/suppliers' monitoring and certifying activities can substitute for dividends to reduce free cash flow. In other words, firms have low payout ratios when their customers/suppliers have strong bargaining power. With a sample of 94,651 observations from firms listed in the United States from 1981 to 2006, Wang (2012) finds supporting evidence for the certification mechanism.

Moreover, the relationship between a firm and its suppliers/customers also affects corporate dividend decisions. A firm has supplier–customer relationships if it sells products to a small number of customers or it buys inputs from a small number of suppliers. Prior research shows that the effect of supplier–customer relationship on corporate dividend policy can be explained by financial distress (Wang, 2012). Customer–supplier relationships increase relationship-specific investment that makes firms face financial distress costs. Titman (1984) and Titman and Wessels (1988) posit that when a firm sells its products, its liquidation make its customers incur switching costs. Especially, if its products are unique, the switching costs are much higher due to specific investments. In addition, a firm facing high liquidation risk is less likely to care about product quality. This makes its customers switch to other firms and thus incur switching costs. Moreover, Banerjee et al. (2008) posit that when a firm sells its products to a small number of big customers, the relationship between the firm and its customers becomes bilateral. The firm's assets are specific to its customers since it has to invest in assets and customize its products to serve them. Therefore, customers' liquidation risk is important to the firm. Its big concern is how to redeploy its dedicated assets when its customers are liquidated. In other words, customer-supplier relationships make firms conduct relationship-specific investments which increase financial distress costs. Therefore, firms are less likely to pay dividends in order to improve their liquidity and avoid the negative impact of financial distress on firm value.

5.2 Financial Market Participants and Dividend Policy

Firms operate not only in a product market but also in a financial market where they obtain external funds. Financial market participants such as creditors, investors, and auditors have financial resources and professional expertise. Therefore, they may pressure or support firms in their business activities. When corporate managers make dividend decisions, they have to consider their financial status and their relationship with other participants in the financial market.[1]

5.2.1 Creditors

According to Jensen and Meckling (1976), there is a conflict of interest between shareholders and creditors. The former uses the latter's financial resources, and a moral hazard is present. Firms tend to have opportunistic behaviors to serve their shareholders' benefits at creditors' expenses. Therefore, creditors recognizing this moral hazard need to monitor and control their debtors in order to protect their own interest. A common protection means is a financial covenant – a contract between a creditor and a debtor. Financial covenants stipulate rights and obligations of the two parties, especially the debtor's obligations to guarantee the creditor's benefits. For example, the debtor has to disclose information about its financial health and restrict its dividend payment (Gârleanu & Zwiebel, 2009; Tran, 2019c). Investigating the relationship between dividend policy adjustments

---

[1]In this chapter, we only focus on how financial market participants' characteristics and preferences affect dividend policy. The effects which are created by legal regulations are presented in Chapter 6 – Macro-environment and dividend policy.

and financial distress in 80 NYSE firms from 1980 to 1985, DeAngelo and DeAngelo (1990) find that most of them have to execute financial covenants in the same year when they decrease dividends. Moreover, with a sample of 10,936 firm-quarter observations from 622 firms, Bulan and Hull (2013) show that firms are more likely to reduce their dividends in the next quarter it they have loan covenant violations in the previous quarter. Additionally, they also find that dividend cuts are determined by both the financial constraint and the conflict between shareholders and creditors.

In addition, creditors are considered as external supervisors which help firms monitor managers' activities. Professional creditors like banks have sufficient skills, technology, and information to improve their borrowers' governance mechanisms. Firms with strong corporate governance face low bankruptcy risk, and thus, they are more able to pay off their debt. According to Allen et al. (2012), corporate governance and financial covenants are complementary mechanisms to restrict dividend payment. Strong corporate governance reduces the gains from precommitting to costly dividends. With a sample of 73,342 observations from 21,901 firms over the period 1983–2006, they find that firms have lower payout ratios when they rely more on bank financing.

5.2.2 Outside Investors

Firms are valued by outside investors. Therefore, when firms make dividend decisions, their value relies on how outside investors these dividend decisions. In other words, outside investors create pressures on corporate dividend policy. Outside investors' characteristics and preferences may determine corporate dividend policy through three channels: threat of takeover, short-term trading, and demand for dividend payment. First, when a firm recognizes that it is likely to be the target of a takeover attempt, it tends to pay more dividends. A dividend increase leads to higher stock price and thus the acquiring firm cannot afford the bid (Driver et al., 2020). Second, a firm increases its dividends as reaction to high stock liquidity. When its stock liquidity increases, more transient investors focus on its stocks to chase current profits. This makes the firm suffer short-term market pressure. Therefore, it pays more dividends so that investors hold its stock longer or attract long-holding investors (Driver et al., 2020). Third, corporate dividend policy focuses on satisfying investors' demand for dividends. When outside investors assign higher value to payers and high payout firms, firms have higher propensity to pay dividends and payout ratios (Baker & Wurgler, 2004b; Li & Lie, 2006).

Investigating dividend policy of firms listed in the United Kingdom from 1977 to 2012, Driver et al. (2020) find supporting evidence for two channels including threat of takeover and short-term trading. Besides, many empirical studies also document the demand for dividend payment channel in the United States (Baker & Wurgler, 2004b; Li & Lie, 2006), Middle Eastern, and North African countries (ElBannan, 2020).

5.2.3 *Auditors*

According to Jensen and Meckling (1976), firms have to pay bonding costs to independent third parties in order to mitigate agency problems. Auditing firms are one of the most important independent outsiders since they guarantee the accuracy and correctness of financial reports. Audited financial reports are considered as the most reliable source of information about a firm. Many stakeholders use their information to make decisions. Auditing firms play the role of external monitors and thus improve corporate governance. Consistently, Fan and Wong (2005) examine the role of audit firms in East Asian emerging markets. They find that firms with high agency costs have high incentives to hire Big 5 auditing firms. Choi and Wong (2007) also show that the role of Big 5 audit firms in corporate governance is stronger in countries of poor shareholder rights. Big 5 are the five largest audit firms in the world in terms of revenue. Large audit firms are more reliable and trustworthy in their auditing services since they have better expertise and higher incentives to maintain their reputation.

Mitton (2004) investigates how corporate governance affects corporate dividend policy in emerging market and finds a positive effect of audit quality on dividend decisions. Particularly, firms are audited by Big 4 audit firms have higher payout ratios. With a sample of 1,438 observations form firms listed in Australia over the period 2005–2011, Farooque et al. (2021) document that firms using Big 4 auditors have higher payout ratios. This can be explained that Big 4 auditors help firms improve their corporate governance, and thus, they are more likely to reduce their free cash flows by paying dividends. However, Lawson and Wang (2011) argue that auditor monitoring is a substitute for dividends which are paid to reduce agency costs of equity. Using data from the US firms between 2003 and 2008, they show that auditor monitoring has a negative effect on corporate dividend policy.

5.3 Dividend Policy in Regulated Industries

Studies in corporate financial decisions mostly focus on unregulated industries since their firms are active and flexible in making these decisions. However, firms in regulated industries face many strict constraints; therefore, their financial decisions are not attractive to academics. Typical regulated industries are from financial sector (banking, insurance, and real estate) and utilities sector (energy, telecommunications, and transportation). These industries have widespread and strong effects on households' life and firms' business activities; therefore, the government monitors and controls them strictly in order to maintain economic and social development. Besides, financial firms also have a different financial structure compared with industrial firms. Financial firms mainly use outsiders' funds for their business activities; consequently, their balance sheets show much higher debt ratios (Kent Baker & De Ridder, 2018).

Dividend distribution reduces equity ratio, increases debt ratio, and transfers risk from shareholders to creditors. If a financial firm or a utilities firm goes bankrupt, the public and the government have to incur high costs to deal with its consequences. Therefore, the government commonly has regulations to restrict regulated industries' dividend payment and make them maintain a secure level of capital ratio. Especially, the global financial crisis 2007–2009 raises policymakers' attention to dividend restriction in the banking industry. Undercapitalized and risky banks have to face strict control of their dividend policy. Consistently, the Basel III Accord also stipulates that banks are allowed to pay dividends if they meet requirements of minimum capital ratios. Their dividend levels are not higher than the thresholds of the capital conservation and countercyclical buffers (Ashraf et al., 2016). Moreover, policymakers also use common equity-based capital requirements to force banks to increase their common equity. When preferred equity and debt are not allowed to increase common equity, banks tend to retain more earnings and thus have lower dividend levels (Ashraf et al., 2016).

Chapter 6

Macro-Environment and Dividend Policy

Abstract

This chapter analyzes how the macro-environment determines corporate dividend decisions. First, political factors including political uncertainty, economic policy uncertainty, political corruption, and democracy may have two opposite effects on dividend decisions. For example, firms learn democratic practices to improve their corporate governance, but dividend policy may be the outcome of strong corporate governance or the substitute for poor corporate governance. Second, firms in countries of high national income, low inflation, and highly developed stock markets tend to pay more dividends. A monetary restriction (expansion) reduces (increases) dividend payments, as economic shocks like financial crises and the COVID-19 may negatively affect corporate dividend policy through higher external financial constraint, economic uncertainty, and agency costs. On the other hand, they may positively influence corporate dividend policy through agency costs of debt, shareholders' bird-in-hand motive, substitution of weak corporate governance, and signaling motive. Third, social factors including national culture, religion, and language affect dividend decisions since they govern both managers' and shareholders' views and behaviors. Fourth, firms tend to reduce their dividends when they face stronger pressure to reduce pollution, produce environment-friendly products, or follow a green policy. Finally, firms have high levels of dividends when shareholders are strongly protected by laws. However, firms tend to pay more dividends in countries of weak creditor rights since dividend payments are a substitute for poor legal protection of creditors. Furthermore, corporate dividend policy changes when tax laws change the comparative tax rates on dividends and capital gains.

Keywords: Macro-environment; political; economic; social; environmental; legal; dividend policy

Dividend Policy, 67–84
Copyright © 2024 Quoc Trung Tran
Published under exclusive licence by Emerald Publishing Limited
doi:10.1108/978-1-83797-987-520241008

6.1 Political Factors and Dividend Policy

6.1.1 Political Uncertainty

Political stability is an important goal of a political system. Political stability contributes to creating a predictable and stable macro-environment in which firms are less concerned about changes in government policies. However, there are many conflicts between political parties, governmental organizations, civil organizations, businesses, and citizens. These conflicts are threats toward political stability. Political risk is defined as unexpected consequences arising from political changes or actions (Kobrin, 2022). Political risk increases uncertainty in financial markets, and thus, market participants' perceived risk is higher (Pástor & Veronesi, 2012). Prior studies show that political risk has two opposite effects on corporate dividend decisions.

On the one hand, Huang et al. (2015) argue that political risk may negatively affect corporate dividend policy through two mechanisms. First, political risk makes firms face higher costs of external financing. Uncertainty caused by political changes or actions increases outside investors' risk perception; therefore, they raise risk premia to compensate the additional perceived risk. When firms incur higher costs of external funds, they tend to reduce their cash dividends in order to save internal funds for future investment. Second, corporate managers perceiving political uncertainty tend to recognize that they face higher cash flow risk since a firm's cash flow is exposed to both idiosyncratic and aggregate shocks (Huang et al., 2015). This makes managers become more conservative in their dividend decisions, and thus, their firms have lower payout ratios. Huang et al. (2015) initially investigate how political risk affects corporate dividend policy in 35 countries between 1990 and 2008. There are 99 global political crises over the research period. They document that international political shocks increase investors' uncertainty perception and make firms incur higher costs of external funds. Remarkably, their findings show that political risk reduces payers' incentives to pay dividends and nonpayers' incentives to initiate dividend payments. These effects are more pronounced for multinational firms. In addition, Lei et al. (2015) analyze the relationship between political uncertainty and dividend policy in China over the period 2004–2010. They posit that a change of a municipal party chief causes political uncertainty. Consistently, they find that political risk makes firms more prudent in their dividend payments. Nonpayers facing high political risk have lower probability to initiate dividends. Besides, political risk also reduces payers' dividend levels. State-owned firms are more sensitive to political risk in their dividend decisions than private firms. Furthermore, ElBannan (2020) examines how political transitions caused by the Arab Spring protests affect corporate dividend policy in 11 countries in the Middle East and North Africa (MENA) region. He documents that when firms are influenced strongly by these political transitions, they have lower propensity to distribute dividends after the crisis period.

On the other hand, Farooq and Ahmed (2019) postulate that political risk may drive firms to pay more dividends through three mechanisms including signaling, substitution of shareholder protection, and cash reduction. First, political risk increases information asymmetry between insiders and outsiders. This makes the adverse selection problem become more severe, and firm value decreases. Therefore, firms tend to increase their dividends as a signal to outside investors about their performance quality in order to maintain their shareholders' wealth. Moreover, dividend distribution is also a signal of their managers' good faith. Second, when information asymmetry increases, firms face more pressures from minority shareholders. The poor information environment strengthens their "bird in hand" motive. High dividend payments are a substitute for weaker shareholder protection caused by political risk. Finally, political risk increases managerial conservatism. Corporate managers are willing to reduce capital expenditure when facing high uncertainty (Bernanke, 1983; Panousi & Papanikolaou, 2012). In order to maintain their job safety, they only increase their investment when the uncertainty level is lower. Choi et al. (2022) show that firms have lower levels of investment when they are more exposed to political risk. Lower investment leads to higher cash reserves, and thus, firms are more likely to pay dividends to disgorge cash. Farooq and Ahmed (2019) investigate how the US firms make dividend decisions during the presidential election years (high political risk) and nonelection years (low political risk). They find that firms tend to have higher payouts in the election years. Besides, the market value of high dividend payers is higher than that of low dividend payers. Consistently, Ahmad et al. (2023) also document a positive effect of firm-level political risk on dividend payouts in the United States.

6.1.2 Economic Policy Uncertainty

Economic policy uncertainty is defined as uncertainty arising from government activities that influence the economic environment. According to Attig et al. (2018), economic policy uncertainty is different from macroeconomic uncertainty, event-related uncertainty, and firm-level uncertainty. First, while macroeconomic uncertainty is caused by macroeconomic issues (e.g., economic growth, inflation, unemployment, and foreign exchange), economic policy uncertainty arises from government policies that change the economic environment. Second, while event-related uncertainty is caused by socioeconomic shocks (e.g., political elections and economic crises), economic policy uncertainty is not based on these event periods. Third, firm-level uncertainty is from the internal management activities, while economic policy uncertainty is beyond firms' control.

Like political risk, economic policy uncertainty may also determine corporate dividend policy through uncertainty with two opposite mechanisms. Attig et al. (2018) conduct a pioneer study to investigate the effect of economic policy uncertainty on dividend policy across 19 countries. They find that firms tend to pay more dividends when they face high levels of economic policy uncertainty. Their further analysis shows that this relationship is moderated by both internal and external corporate governance factors. Collectively, their results imply that firms pay dividends to reduce agency costs when facing high economic policy uncertainty. However, using data of 517 nonfinancial firms listed in China from 2007 to 2015, Sarwar and Hassan (2021) document that firms are more likely to stop paying dividends during the period of high economic policy uncertainty. Similarly, Tran (2020) finds that the US bank holding firms tend to restrict their dividend payments when facing high economic policy uncertainty over the period 2001–2015.

6.1.3 Political Corruption

Political corruption is defined as government officials' behaviors to use public power for their own interest (Jain, 2001). Although corrupt behaviors are conducted by public officials, individuals and organizations may contribute to the proliferation of political corruption by their willingness to pay bribes. Political corruption can have a negative impact (sand the wheel) or a positive impact (grease the wheel) on business activities. Firms have to incur higher costs in a corrupt environment. Firms pay bribes to avoid red tape and obtain public services. This payment dampens firm performance. However, a corrupt environment may also be an opportunity for firms to improve their competitive advantages. Firms are willing to pay bribes to have better access to scarce resources, win public tenders, and have lower tax burdens (Wei & Kaufmann, 1999; Xu et al., 2017).

Political corruption may affect corporate dividend policy in two opposite ways. On the one hand, political corruption has a negative effect on dividend policy through three mechanisms including external financing, cash trading, and managerial entrenchment. According to Bekaert et al. (2011) and Jain et al. (2017), political corruption makes financial markets less transparent and more segmented. When financial markets are less efficient, firms have to incur higher costs of external financing and transaction costs (Baxamusa & Jalal, 2014; Du et al., 2020). This drives firms to retain more cash since they need to save enough cash for emerging investment opportunities and avoid transaction costs. In other words, political corruption reduces firms' incentives to pay dividends through increasing external financing costs. In addition, firms in highly corrupt environment may trade cash for specific benefits. They are willing to pay bribes to corrupt officials if bribery helps them obtain preferences and favorable treatments from the government. Thakur and Kannadhasan (2019) and Tran (2020) consistently show that firms in countries of high corruption tend to have higher levels of cash. When bribery can create competitive advantages, the availability of cash to pay bribes plays an important role in business. Consequently, high corruption results in low propensity to pay dividends. Moreover, corporate managers have high incentives to take advantage of corrupt environment to expropriate their shareholders. Since bribes are unofficial payments, corporate managers are more flexible to save and pay cash to corrupt officials (Tran, 2019b). This mechanism weakens shareholders' ability to control managers' liquidity decisions. Therefore, managers exploit this opportunity to accumulate cash for overinvestment and avoid shareholders' pressure to disgorge cash. In other words, political corruption provides corporate managers with an opportunity to restrict dividend payments.

With a sample of 608 firms listed in 13 African countries from 1996 to 2011, Yensu and Adusei (2016) find that firms in countries of high corruption have lower payout ratios. Dong et al. (2022) use data of 33,293 observations from listed firms in China over the period 1990–2017 to investigate how local corruption affects dividend policy. Consistently, they find a negative relationship between local corruption and dividend decisions.

On the other hand, political corruption may have a positive impact on corporate dividend policy through shielding and bird-in-hand mechanisms. First, firms tend to reduce their liquidity to avoid corrupt officials' extraction. Firms intentionally lower their cash levels to show corrupt officials that they fail to have enough resources for paying bribes. If corrupt officials strongly pressure them to pay bribes, they may go bankrupt. Therefore, corrupt officials are less likely to ask them for bribery and wait until their liquidity is better. Xu and Li (2018) find a positive relationship between local corruption and cash reserves in China. In other words, firms in a corrupt environment shield their liquid assets by increasing their dividend levels. Second, political corruption increases uncertainty in financial markets and weakens investors' ability to monitor managers. Consequently, shareholders perceiving these disadvantages tend to pursue the bird-in-hand viewpoint. They are more likely to insist on dividend payments, and thus, corporate managers have to pay more dividends to satisfy their shareholders. With a sample of 199,333 observations from firms listed in 46 countries and territories during the period 2001–2016, Tran (2019b) shows that firms in high corruption countries have higher likelihood of dividend payment and larger dividend magnitude. Moreover, Hossain et al. (2021) and Tran (2021) also document that local corruption positively affects dividend decisions in Vietnam and the United States, respectively.

6.1.4 Democracy

Democracy is commonly defined as a political system in which power belongs to people. According to Cheibub and Przeworski (1999) and Trantidis (2016), in a democratic society, the government is accountable to people, and this account-ability is assured by competitive elections. Democracy is one of the fundamental conditions to create a level playground for all firms and individuals in the society. According to Nguyen and Tran (2022), firms in a democratic environment can face lower costs of debt financing and learn democratic procedures to improve their corporate governance. These two mechanisms affect their dividend policies in two opposite ways.

First, democratization leads to lower costs of debt financing since it improves economic efficiency, borrowers' performance, and reduces information asymmetry in financial markets (Delis et al., 2020). Democracy reduces uncertainty and guarantees predictable market expectations about macro-environment factors. Therefore, economic efficiency is higher, and creditors tend to request lower risk premia. Furthermore, a democratic society has effective checks and balances that enhance market expectations. These create more investment opportunities and improve borrowers' performance. Besides, civil liberties in a democratic environment facilitate information flows, improve information transparency, and thus mitigate information asymmetry between creditors and borrowers. When firms have lower costs of debt financing, the marginal cost of dividend distribution is lower. Consequently, firms in a democratic environment tend to have higher payout ratios.

Second, in a democratic society, firms are able to learn democratic procedures from political institutions to improve their corporate governance (Gomez & Korine, 2005). Three main democratic practices are enfranchisement, power separation, and representation (De Tocqueville, 1988). Firms apply enfranchisement by facilitating their shareholders to execute their voting rights. Shareholders can use their voting rights to participate in making important decisions. In addition, firms practice power separation by allocating power to different organizations and individuals such as the board of directors, the management, and the internal auditing committee. These organizations and individuals are independent so that they can control each other. Moreover, firms employ representation by supporting shareholders to choose their representatives. Shareholders can use their voting rights to nominate directors and execute their rights through their representatives. Minority shareholders also have their representatives to protect their rights. Collectively, firms in a democratic environment have strong corporate governance. Therefore, firms face less pressure to disgorge cash from their investors, and thus, they save more cash for future investment. In other words, democracy leads to lower dividend payouts. Consistently, Chen and Yang (2017) show that democratization makes firms increase their cash holdings across 67 countries.

Nguyen and Tran (2022) initially investigate how democracy affects corporate dividend decisions. Using a sample of 228,628 firm-years across 37 countries, they find that firms in highly democratic countries have lower probability to pay dividends and dividend magnitude. Moreover, the negative relationship is more pronounced under poor (strong) protection of shareholders (creditors). Their further analysis also shows that democracy reduces likelihood to initiate dividends. Besides, with a sample of 229,636 observations from firms listed in 50 countries from 1991 to 2010, Guedhami et al. (2017) also find a consistent result. Their findings show that firms have higher probability of dividend payment and payout ratios when they are located in countries of low political freedom.

6.2 Economic Factors and Dividend Policy

6.2.1 National Income

National income is the total amount of income made in an economy within a period of time. In other words, it is the net outcome of all economic activities conducted in a country. The common measures of national income are gross domestic product (GDP), GDP per capita. National income reflects the quality of business environment in a country. Most countries with high national income have developed transparent and predictable economic environment. Firms in these countries face less uncertainty and lower financing costs. This implies that firms in countries of high national income are less concerned about raising funds to finance their investment projects, and thus, they are more likely to pay dividends. With a sample of 149,568 observations from 16,440 firms listed in 35 countries from 1987 to 2017, Chang et al. (2020) find that GDP per capita has a positive relationship with corporate dividend policy. Consistently, Yaseen (2019) documents that living standards have a positive effect on dividend payouts across 56 countries.

Moreover, GDP growth rate is also a determinant of dividend decisions. When national income increases, consumers are more willing to pay for goods and services. This increases firm profitability, and firms tend to pay more dividends. Tran et al. (2017) find a positive relationship between GDP growth rate and dividend policy across 41 countries. The effect of GDP growth rate on dividend decisions is weaker under the impact of the global financial crisis. However, an economy with high GDP growth rate also generates more investment opportunities for firms. Therefore, they have high incentives to restrict their dividends in order to save cash for their investment expenditure. Das (2017) shows that economic growth and dividend payout have a negative relationship in India.

6.2.2 Inflation

Inflation is defined as an increase in the overall price in the economy over a certain period of time. Inflation is commonly measured by the consumer price index (CPI). High inflation implies that goods and services become more expensive nominally. According to Basse et al. (2011), high inflation increases corporate dividend policy due to two reasons. First, when an economy experiences high inflation, firms' nominal income is higher. Consequently, shareholders and investors expect higher payout ratios. This drives firms to increase their dividend levels. Second, corporate managers may follow optimal levels of real dividends. Under high inflation, their real dividends are lower than the optimal levels. Therefore, they tend to increase dividend payments to maintain their firms' real dividends at the optimal levels.

Basse et al. (2011) investigate how inflation affects corporate dividend policy in the United States from Q1/1993 to Q4/2009. They find a positive relationship between inflation and dividend distribution. Baker et al. (2018) conduct a mail survey to analyze different explanations for dividend policy in India. Their findings also show support to the positive effect of inflation on dividend decisions.

6.2.3 Stock Market Development

Stock market is a channel through which firms issue debt and/or equity securities to obtain external funds. Developed stock markets have transparent information, high market liquidity, and a wide range of financial assets. The effect of stock market development on corporate dividend policy may be determined by pecking order theory or signaling theory. First, the pecking order theory states that firms prefer internal to external funds. Due to information asymmetry between insiders and outsiders, internal financing is cheaper than external financing. In developed stock markets, information is more transparent and available to outside investors. Therefore, firms have better access to external funds and lower costs of external financing. This decreases marginal costs of dividends, and thus, firms tend to pay more dividends. Shao et al. (2010) find that stock market development has a positive impact on dividend policy across 21 countries.

Second, the signaling theory posits that firms pay dividends as a signal of their quality to outside investors in order to reduce information asymmetry. Well-developed stock markets require firms to disclose information and monitor them effectively. Therefore, information asymmetry is restricted, and firms have low incentives of using dividends to signal to outside investors. Twu (2012) examines how stock market development influences the propensity to pay dividends across 31 countries around the world. They find that firms in well-developed stock markets have lower propensity to pay dividends, lower payout ratios, and higher propensity to omit dividends. Bae et al. (2012) and Esqueda (2016) also find supporting evidence for the positive relationship between stock market development and dividend policy across countries.

6.2.4 Monetary Policy

Monetary policy is an economic policy conducted by the central bank to manage the overall money supply in an economy. When monetary policy is implemented effectively, the economy can successfully achieve major macroeconomic goals (e.g., high economic growth, low unemployment, stable foreign exchange rate, low and stable inflation). There are two opposite types of monetary policy. First, a contractionary policy is conducted to reduce the overall money supply. It helps the government slow economic growth in the booming period and reduce inflation. Second, an expansionary policy is conducted to increase the overall money supply. It helps the economy recover from a recession and enhance economic growth. Common tools of monetary policy include reserve requirement, discount rate, and open market operation.

A monetary policy can influence individuals and firms in an economy through four channels including interest rate, credit, asset price, and exchange rate (Mishkin, 1995). First, the interest rate channel transmits a monetary policy by changing the long-term real interest rate. For example, a contractionary policy increases the short-term nominal interest rate. According to the expectations hypothesis of the term structure, the long-term nominal interest rate increases when the short-term nominal interest rate is higher. However, nominal prices are sticky. This makes the long-term real interest rate increase, and firms face higher costs of external financing. Second, the credit channel transmits a monetary policy by determining the availability or terms of new credit. For instance, a monetary contraction reduces the supply of bank loans. Firms face many difficulties to finance their business activities if they rely heavily on bank credit and have no perfect substitute. Third, the asset price channel is present when a monetary policy changes the value of assets such as equity and collateral in the economy. This channel is effective if bond, equity, and real estate markets are developed and important in the economy. For example, a decrease in increase in short-term interest rate caused by a monetary contraction leads to a decline in real estates if the real estate market plays an important role in the economy. When they use their real estate as a collateral to raise external funds, they receive less. In other words, a contradictory policy restricts firms' access to external funds. Finally, the exchange rate channel transmits a monetary policy by changing the value of domestic currency. For instance, a monetary contraction increases the value of domestic currency. This leads to higher prices of exports, lower prices of imports, and higher inflation.

As an important macroeconomic policy, monetary policy affects corporate dividend policy through its transmission channels, especially interest rate, credit, and asset price. These three channels directly determine firms' access to external funds and costs of external financing. However, the credit channel may be the most effective channel in economies with underdeveloped and bank-based financial systems (Yang et al., 2017). When the central bank conducts an expansionary (a contractionary) policy, firms have better (worse) access to credit and lower (higher) external financing costs. Therefore, they are more (less) willing to pay dividends. Pandey and Bhat (2007) find that a monetary restriction reduces both the likelihood to pay dividends and the payout ratio in India. Investigating the effect of monetary policy on Vietnamese firms' dividend policy, Tran et al. (2019) document that money supply has a positive effect on dividend decisions including the choice to pay, payout ratio, and dividend adjustment speed.

6.2.5 Financial Crises

A financial crisis is an exogenous economic shock to business activities. According to Mishkin (1992), a financial crisis is considered as a disruption to financial markets which makes financial markets fail to channel funds from lender–savers to borrower–spenders efficiently. On the one hand, a financial crisis may negatively affect corporate dividend policy due to higher external financial constraint, economic uncertainty, and agency costs. Under a financial crisis, financial markets become less efficient and bank credit dries up; therefore, firms' access to external funds is restricted (Arslan et al., 2006). In addition, a financial crisis leads to higher uncertainty in the business environment. This stimulates firms' precautionary motive to reserve cash (Lian et al., 2011). Moreover, a financial crisis makes firms face lower returns on their investment projects. This implies that the marginal costs of shareholder expropriation are also lower. Therefore, corporate managers have higher incentives to conduct opportunistic behaviors, and their firms face higher agency costs of equity (Johnson et al., 2000). Consistently, Hauser (2013) investigates the propensity to pay dividends in the United States during the global financial crisis and finds that firms are less likely to distribute dividends over the crisis period 2008–2009. Hilliard et al. (2019) show that firms that pay dividends in 2007 tend to reduce or omit their dividend payments in 2007 when they have higher risk-adjusted returns in 2009. Their findings imply that firms adjust their dividend policy to save more cash when they are aware of the coming crisis.

On the other hand, a financial crisis may positively influence corporate dividend policy through three mechanisms including agency costs of debt, shareholders' bird-in-hand motive, and substitution of weak corporate governance and signaling motive. In stable economic conditions, firms have incentives to restrict their dividend payments so that they can obtain more funds from creditors. However, these incentives are weaker when external funds are less available under the impact of a financial crisis. Therefore, firms tend to pay more dividends. Besides, when facing high uncertainty in the business environment, shareholders are more likely to be driven by the bird-in-hand motive. They tend to prefer dividends to capital gains and thus pressure firms to disgorge cash. Furthermore, firms may increase their dividend payments as a substitute for weaker corporate governance caused by a financial crisis in order to maintain their firm value. Moreover, since dividends are a means to signal outside investors about firms' future prospects, they are reluctant to reduce dividends during crisis period. They even take this opportunity to build their reputation by increasing dividend payments. Tran et al. (2022) examine how the global financial crisis affects dividend policy of Vietnamese firms with a sample of 5,489 observations over the period 2007–2017. They find that firms have higher likelihood to pay dividends and payout ratios over the crisis period 2008–2009.

6.2.6 COVID-19 Pandemic

COVID-19 pandemic is an unprecedented economic and social shock in human history. There were about 194 million infections and 4.5 million deaths from its outbreak to the end of 2021. Theoretically, the mechanisms through which the pandemic affect corporate dividend policy are similar to those of a financial crisis. Investigating how COVID-19 influences dividend decisions of about 1,400 dividend payers in the US market, Krieger et al. (2021) show that 213 paying firms reduce dividend levels, and 93 firms omit dividend payments in the second quarter of 2020. Moreover, dividend cuts spread across both financial and nonfinancial industries. Consistently, Pettenuzzo et al. (2023) find that there are an unprecedented number of firms suspending dividend payments under the impact of COVID-19. Xu et al. (2023) also document a negative effect of COVID-19 on dividend policy in China. Moreover, Ali (2022) shows that the majority of firms in the G-12 countries still have stable or higher payout ratios during the pandemic despite higher percentage of dividend cuts and omissions.

6.3 Social Factors

6.3.1 Culture

Culture is defined as a set of values, norms, and practices recognized and shared by members of a community (Hofstede, 1984). People from the same culture tend to have similar attitudes and behaviors. People from different countries have different views and behavioral patterns since they learn and perceive different culture values. In a corporation, cultural values determine its financial decisions through their impacts on its stakeholders like managers, shareholders, creditors, peer groups. Particularly, prior research shows that national culture affects corporate dividend policy mainly through managers' and shareholders' attitudes and behaviors.

6.3.1.1 Hofstede's Cultural Dimensions

The most popular cultural measures are suggested by Hofstede. Hofstede (1984) surveyed employees of the International Business Machines (IBM) Corporation in 40 countries to investigate their work-related culture. He found that their cultural values could be grouped into four dimensions: uncertainty avoidance (attitude toward unpredictable prospect), power distance (attitude toward discrimination in social relationships), masculinity (attitude toward achievements), and individualism (attitude toward the role of an individual in an organization). Then, Hofstede (1990) adopted Confucian cultural values to create the fifth dimension and then called it as long-term orientation. In addition, Hofstede et al. (2010) analyzed data from the World Values Survey and added the sixth dimension named as indulgence (attitude toward restriction of wants and needs). The value of each dimension varies from 0 to 100. Higher values imply stronger attitudes.

Uncertainty avoidance dimension represents how people are concerned about uncertainty and ambiguity. People in countries of high uncertainty avoidance are less likely to take risk (Hofstede, 1984). They tend to prefer the bird in their hands to the bird in the bush. Therefore, uncertainty avoidance culture drives shareholders to force corporate managers to disgorge cash. However, corporate managers in high uncertainty avoidance culture tend to accumulate high levels of cash for future investment opportunities. When shareholders' pressure is stronger than managers' precautionary motive, firms have high payout ratios and vice versa. Bae et al. (2012) investigate the relationship between national culture and dividend policy across 33 countries from 1993 to 2004 and find that uncertainty avoidance has a negative effect on dividend levels. Aggarwal and Goodell (2014) also document a consistent effect with a sample of 82 countries over the period 2010–2011. Nevertheless, Chang et al. (2020) show that uncertainty avoidance culture positively affects corporate dividend policy across 35 countries over the period 1987–2017.

Power distance dimension describes how people expect and agree on the inequality of power in the society. In countries of high power distance, shareholders and subordinates tend to respect corporate managers' decisions. They are less likely to question managers or ask them to justify their decisions (Cohen & Nelson, 1992). Consequently, corporate managers in high power distance culture have more power in making dividend decisions. Due to the agency problem, managers have high incentives to reserve cash for their overinvestment instead of paying dividends. Consequently, power distance has a negative impact on dividend policy. Consistently, Aggarwal and Goodell (2014), Bae et al. (2012), and Chang et al. (2020) document supporting evidence for this negative relationship.

Masculinity dimension represents how people focus on outcomes and performance. People in a masculine community are highly goal-oriented. They try to achieve their goals and evaluate others by material achievements (Hofstede, 1984). Masculinity culture drives people, especially men, to pursue power, wealth, and status quickly (Park, 2003). Therefore, managers in countries of high masculinity tend to accumulate cash to finance investment opportunities that may provide them great achievements. However, masculinity culture also stimulates shareholders' bird-in-hand motive. Shareholders in countries of high masculinity want to obtain dividends quickly instead of waiting for capital gains in the future. From a theoretical perspective, when the pressure from shareholders is stronger than the role of managers, firms pay more dividends and vice versa. Empirical studies show a negative relationship between masculinity and dividend policy (Aggarwal & Goodell, 2014; Bae et al., 2012; Chang et al., 2020). This implies that managers' cultural views empirically dominate dividend policy.

Individualism describes how people focus on their own interest instead of the collective interest. People in countries of high individualism are more likely to care about their own rights, success, and autonomy (Hofstede, 1984). Consequently, individualism drives managers to pursue their own benefits instead of shareholders' wealth. When managers have high incentives to expropriate shareholders, they tend to reserve more cash for overinvestment in unprofitable projects. However, shareholders in highly individualistic culture also pay more attention to their own interest, and thus, they tend to prefer dividends to capital gains. Therefore, they create more pressures on managers to obtain higher levels of dividends. Bae et al. (2012), Byrne and O'Connor (2017), and Chang et al. (2020) show that individualism has a positive impact on corporate dividend policy across countries.

Long-term orientation represents how people concentrate on long-term devotion and commitment. People in countries of high long-term orientation respect patience, thrift, and self-reliance (Bae et al., 2012; Hofstede, 1984). They are willing to sacrifice a small benefit in present to obtain a larger benefit in the future. Therefore, shareholders in high long-term orientation societies are less likely to insist on dividend payments. They are willing to sacrifice current dividends to have capital gains in the future. In addition, corporate managers in high long-term orientation countries are more concerned about their careers and have better commitments with their firms. This drives corporate managers to hold more cash for profitable investment opportunities. Consequently, long-term orientation culture is negatively related to corporate dividend decisions. Consistently, Bae et al. (2012) and Khambata and Liu (2005) empirically show that firms in countries of high long-term orientation have lower dividend levels.

6.3.1.2 Schwartz's Culture Dimensions

Schwartz (1992) proposed that national culture was described by seven cultural dimensions, namely conservatism, intellectual autonomy, affective autonomy, egalitarianism, hierarchy, mastery, and harmony. Schwartz (1994) modified his original dimensions by two changes. First, he used a new name "embeddedness" for "conservatism." Second, he combined two original dimensions including intellectual autonomy and affective autonomy to have a new dimension named as autonomy. These new six cultural dimensions are organized into three pairs including autonomy versus embeddedness, hierarchy versus egalitarianism, and mastery versus harmony. Schwartz's autonomy versus embeddedness are similar to Hofstede's individualism versus collectivism, respectively. Autonomy focuses on intellectual inspiration (e.g., creativity and innovation) and affective inspiration (e.g., happiness and satisfaction), while embeddedness concentrates on collective values. In addition, hierarchy and egalitarianism reflect power distance. Hierarchy emphasizes power, paternalism, and social order, but egalitarianism respects equality and social justice. Moreover, mastery and harmony describes how people interact with the environment. Mastery refers to changing and mastering the environment, while harmony appreciates environment protection. Mastery respects independence, ambition, and success, while harmony emphasizes peace, dependence, and adaptability (Schwartz, 1994; Shao et al., 2010).

According to Shao et al. (2010), conservatism positively affects corporate dividend policy through three channels: reducing agency problem, strengthening shareholders' bird-in-hand motive, and increasing managers' signaling incentive. First, conservatism appreciates collective values and maintains positive interactions. Therefore, managers in countries of high conservatism have lower incentives to conduct opportunistic behaviors which reduce their firms' value. When their firms have free cash flows, managers are more likely to pay dividends instead of diverting free cash flows into unprofitable projects. Shareholders in countries of high conservatism also prefer managers' self-disciplining dividend decisions which support a good relationship between them. Second, conservative culture focuses on security, specifically family security which increases shareholders' bird-in-hand motive. Shareholders insist on dividend payments instead of waiting for future gains from investment projects which are financed by retained earnings. Third, people in conservative countries have high incentives to create and protect their public images. This drives firms to use dividend payments as a signal in order to build up their good images and reputation. Consequently, conservative culture supports high levels of dividends. Moreover, Shao et al. (2010) argue that mastery has a negative effect on dividend policy. People in mastery countries appreciate independence and success. When shareholders respect managers' independence in their decisions, they are less likely to monitor and control managers' behaviors. This is an opportunity for managers to expropriate shareholders by accumulating more cash to finance unprofitable investment projects which provide them benefits instead of paying dividends. Besides, when managers and shareholders focus on success, they have high incentives to restrict dividends and retain more earnings for future investment. With a sample of 27,462 observations from firms listed in 21 countries over the period 1995–2007, Shao et al. (2010) empirically show that conservatism and mastery positively and negatively influences dividend decisions, respectively.

6.3.1.3 Social Capital

At the societal level, social capital is considered as norms and networks which enhance mutual trust, support, and solidarity (Coleman, 1988). Social capital helps people have better collaboration and behaviors (Rupasingha et al., 2006). According to Davaadorj (2019), social capital may determine corporate dividend decisions through the board's behavior (the direct channel) and cost reduction (the indirect channel). First, people in communities of high social capital tend to be more altruistic. When board members are altruistic, they are more likely to cater to investors' "bird-in-hand" demand for dividend payments. Therefore, firms in high social capital areas have higher payout ratios. Second, social capital reduces both agency cost and capital cost. Since social capital supports good and responsible behaviors, managers in high social capital communities have lower incentives to conduct opportunistic behaviors. When corporate managers focus more on serving shareholders' interest, they face lower pressure to pay dividends from shareholders. Therefore, firms in high social capital areas have lower dividend levels. Moreover, social capital enhances social trust, collaboration, and information transparency; consequently, it decreases cost of capital. When firms face lower financing costs, they tend to pay more dividends.

Davaadorj (2019) investigates the relationship between social capital and dividend policy across counties in the US market over the period 1991–2014. With a final sample of 44,047 observations from 5,943 unique firms in 64 industries, he finds that county social capital positively affects dividend decisions, and this effect is more pronounced in firms with poor corporate governance. In addition, Qin et al. (2022) examine how social trust as a form of social capital determines dividend payout policy in China. Using a sample of 24,086 firm-year observations, they find that firms in high social trust areas have lower payout ratios, and this negative relationship is stronger for firms with less information transparency and poor corporate governance.

6.3.2 Religion

Religion is a communication between people and controlling forces which they trust and worship such as gods or supernatural entities. Religion encompasses organized beliefs, rules, and practices (e.g., sermons, rituals, prayer, meditation, and trances). Religion encourages people to conduct good behaviors and avoid bad behaviors. Most religion emphasizes and teaches their followers humane and ethical values like honest, compassion, forgiveness, sacrifice, and love. Chintrakarn et al. (2019) argue that shareholders in high religiosity regions are more risk-averse. Since returns from dividends are more certain than those from capital gains, shareholders prefer dividends to capital gains. Chintrakarn et al. (2019) investigate how religious piety affects corporate dividend policy across the US counties over the period 1992–2010. They find that firms located in counties high in religious piety tend to pay more dividends. With a sample of 33,293 observations from 1998 to 2017, Dong et al. (2022) also document that firms located in Chinese provinces with more religious sites have higher payout ratios.

In addition, many empirical studies show that different religions affect corporate dividend policy. Ucar (2016) posits that firms with different religious affiliations are different in their dividend levels since different religions have different levels of attitude toward risk-aversion. Investigating how local religion influences corporate dividend policy across the US counties, he finds that firms in Protestant counties have higher likelihood to pay and initiate dividends and have higher dividend yields than those in Catholic counties. Moreover, Cao et al. (2016) examine how Buddhism and Taoism determine dividend decisions in Chinese listed firms from 2003 to 2013. They argue that both Buddhism and Taoism emphasize and teach their followers compassion. According to Buddha's advice, charity is considered as the greatest consolation in life. The concept of "karma" also instructs Buddhism's followers to share their wealth in order to have better consequences in the future. Moreover, *Tao Te Ching* – the most important book of Taoism – advises the sage to live for other people and devote his wealth to them. In addition, firms in regions of Buddhism and Taoism tend to have employees, suppliers, and customers who are influenced by their religious values and practices. When firms are located in an environment of heavy Buddhism and Taoism, they are more likely to share wealth to shareholders. Using data of 10,127 observations from firms located across 31 Chinese provinces, Cao et al. (2016) document that Buddhism and Taoism drive firms to pay more dividends. In addition, Ben-Nasr and Ghouma (2022) investigate how Islam affects corporate dividend policy. They posit that Shariah – a collection of Islamic laws containing Muslims' religious and secular practices – has two opposite effects on dividend decisions through investment and financing constraints. On the one hand, Shariah restricts investment opportunities, and thus, Shariah-compliant firms are more likely to pay dividends. On the other hand, when interest-bearing financing is banned, firms have to retain more earnings to finance their investment instead of paying dividends. Using data of 13,249 observations from firms listed in 17 Islamic countries, they show that Shariah-compliant firms have higher payout ratios than non-Shariah-compliant firms. Imamah et al. (2019) also find a consistent result in Indonesia over the period 2012–2016.

6.3.3 Language

According to the Sapir–Whorf theory, the structure of a language determines its speakers' way of thinking, and thus, different languages create various patterns of thoughts and behaviors (Whorf, 1956). Based on this theory, a language may affect people's thoughts and behaviors through the way it grammatically references to the future. A language is strong in referencing the future if its speakers use the future tense to describe future activities. A language is weak in referencing the future if its speakers do not have to use the future tense to mark future events. Instead, they can use the simple present tense to reference the future. From a psychological perspective, the future becomes less important to speakers when they must use the future tense which broadens the psychological gap from the future. By contrast, using the simple present tense makes people feel that future events are closer (Dahl, 2000; Thieroff, 2000).

Consequently, Nishikawa et al. (2021) argue that investors speaking strong future-time reference languages are less concerned about future returns from capital gains than current returns from dividends. Similarly, managers speaking strong future-time reference languages are less likely to hold precautionary cash and have higher incentives to cater investors' demand for dividends. With a sample of 331,547 observations from firms headquartered across 46 countries, Nishikawa et al. (2021) find that firms have higher payout levels when they are headquartered in countries of strong future-time reference languages. He and Zhang (2022) also show a consistent result across 19 countries.

6.4 Environmental Factors

In the modern society, people are more aware of environmental protection since the world is facing many environmental problems in recent decades. As a result, firms face stronger pressure to reduce pollution and produce environment-friendly products. When firms are more likely to take environmental responsibility and environmental risk, they tend to retain more earnings in order to invest in new environment-efficient machines, plants, and equipment (Chen & Silva Gao, 2012). Moreover, they also need to save more precautionary cash which is available for unexpected environmental problems. Chapple et al. (2013) show that firms have lower future earnings and cash flows when they conduct measures to reduce environmental pollution. Using a data of 15,632 observations from firms listed in China, Hu and Chang (2022) find that firms in high air-pollution cities have lower dividend levels. Consistently, their findings show that this effect is weaker in firms with ISO 14001 certificates.

In addition, climate change is one of the most serious environmental problems threatening the future of human life; therefore, controlling carbon dioxide emissions – the major cause of greenhouse effect – is considered as a corporate responsibility. According to Balachandran and Nguyen (2018), when firms are more fossil fuel-intensive, they are highly exposed to carbon risk. Their future carbon performance relies on many uncertain factors like antipollution legislations, the ability to comply with carbon control policy, and managers' views on carbon control. Besides, fossil fuel–intensive firms also incur additional carbon-related management and accounting costs. Investigating how carbon risk influences corporate dividend policy in Australia from 2002 to 2013, Balachandran and Nguyen (2018) document that firms in the highest-emitting industries have lower likelihood to pay dividends and payout ratios after Kyoto Protocol ratification. Furthermore, Li et al. (2023) show that polluting firms have lower payout ratios when the Chinese government adopts a green credit policy.

6.5 Legal Factors

6.5.1 Shareholder and Creditor Protection Laws

According to La Porta et al. (1998), the rights attached to securities rely on the legal regulations in which they are issued. Different legislations have different views and practices to protect the rights of shareholders and creditors. Therefore, corporate financial decisions are also determined by shareholder and creditor rights. Analyzing legal protection of shareholders and creditors across 49 countries, La Porta et al. (1998) find that common laws are stronger than civil laws in protecting investors. Among civil law countries, French civil law countries are the poorest in investor protection, followed by German civil law and Scandinavian civil law countries.

La Porta et al. (2000) initially investigate how shareholder protection laws influence corporate dividend policy. They develop two opposite hypotheses, namely the outcome hypothesis and the substitute hypothesis. The former describes dividend payments as the outcome of shareholder protection. Strong shareholder rights force managers to serve shareholders' wealth effectively, and thus, managers tend to pay more dividends instead of using them for unprofitable projects. The latter posits that dividend payments are paid to shareholders who have to suffer weak legal protection. In other words, dividends are the substitute for poor shareholder protection. Many empirical studies show that firms in countries of strong shareholder rights have higher probability to pay dividends and large dividend magnitude across countries (Bae et al., 2012; Chang et al., 2020; La Porta et al., 2000). Moreover, Brockman and Unlu (2009) argue that creditors have high incentives to insist on additional control rights in the relationship with their debtors when they are poorly protected by laws. One of the tools which creditors use to protect themselves is stipulating debtors' obligations to restrict dividend payments in debt covenants. In other words, dividend restriction is a substitute for weak legal protection of creditors. Byrne and O'Connor (2017), Tran (2019c), and Tran et al. (2017) find that firms tend to have lower payout ratios when they are incorporated in countries of poor creditor rights around the world. In addition, Shao et al. (2013) show that there is an interaction between corporate dividend decisions to execute shareholder and creditor rights. Firms are more likely to serve shareholders by increasing dividends when creditors are strongly protected. However, firms tend to reduce dividends in order to satisfy creditors when shareholders are adequately protected. Furthermore, Tran et al. (2017) find that legal protection of shareholders and creditors is less effective in dividend policy after the global financial crisis. This can be explained that the crisis creates opportunities for managers to expropriate shareholders through lowering investment opportunities and expected returns. Moreover, it also reduces firms' motives to serve creditors since firms face external financial constraint caused by high uncertainty and inefficient financial markets.

6.5.2 Securities Laws

According to Brockman et al. (2014), insider trading laws also play an important role in corporate dividend decisions. Insider trading is the outcome of high information asymmetry and agency costs. Insiders have more information than outside investors, and they take this information advantage to conduct insider trading behaviors. When insider trading laws are weak, outside investors face more advantages, and thus, they tend to assign lower value to firms. Therefore, firms have to use their dividend payments in order to reduce information asymmetry and show fair treatment to outside investors. With a sample of 32,503 observations from 24 countries over the period 1994–1997, Brockman et al. (2014) find that firms in countries of weak insider trading laws have higher dividend distribution propensity, payout ratios, and dividend smoothing. Besides, dividends receive higher market value under weak insider trading laws.

In addition, international enforcement of securities laws may affect cross-listed firms' dividend policy. International investors are less likely to have cross-border investment due to information disadvantage, environment uncertainty, capital account restriction, and agency problems (Silvers, 2021). When governments sign agreements to enforce their securities laws across countries, these frictions and barriers are controlled and reduced. Chen et al. (2022) postulate that international enforcement of securities laws determine corporate dividend decisions through the outcome and the substitute mechanisms. First, agreements to enforce their securities laws help firms improve their corporate governance and thus pay more dividends from free cash flows. Second, dividend payments may be a compensation for weak corporate governance. Therefore, firms tend to have lower payouts when corporate governance is stronger under the impact of international enforcement of securities laws. Chen et al. (2022) empirically show that foreign firms cross-listed in the US market pay more dividends when their home governments sign a Multilateral Memorandum of Understanding Concerning Consultation and Cooperation and the Exchange of Information. This effect is stronger in firms of weak corporate governance, countries of poor external governance, and countries of low information transparency.

6.5.3 Tax Laws

As an income of investors, dividends are commonly taxable. Many prior empirical studies show that a change in dividend tax drives firms to change their dividend policy. Pattenden and Twite (2008) show that firms are more likely to initiate dividends, raise payout ratios, and increase dividend reinvestment plans after the Australian government introduces dividend imputation in 1987. Wang and Guo (2011) also find that Chinese firms tend to pay more dividends when a dividend tax cut comes into force in 2005. Buchanan et al. (2017) document that the US firms have more dividend initiations and higher payouts before dividend tax rates increase.

Chapter 7

Business Environment and Dividend Smoothing

Abstract

This chapter introduces dividend smoothing, presents theories to explain dividend smoothing behavior, and analyzes how different levels of business environment affect dividend smoothing. First, dividend smoothing describes a mechanism in which a firm is reluctant to reduce dividends and only increases dividends when its earnings increase permanently. In practice, dividend smoothing behavior is found in both developed and developing countries. Firms in developed countries are more likely to smooth dividends than those in developing countries. Second, although Miller and Modigliani (1961) posit that investors are indifferent between stable and unstable dividend payments in a perfect environment, market frictions in the real world make stable and unstable dividends have different effects on firm value. Three common frictions are information asymmetry, agency problem, and investors' demand for income smoothing. Due to information asymmetry between insiders and outsiders, firms tend to smooth their dividends to signal outside investors about their quality. In addition, dividend smoothing may be the substitute for weak corporate governance and/or the outcome of free cash absorption behavior. Besides, dividends are more convenient for investors' consumption; therefore, firms are more likely to smooth dividends in order to satisfy investors' demand for smooth income. Finally, as a special dividend decision, dividend smoothing is also affected by an internal micro (industry) and macro-environment. Dividend smoothing theories are the behind mechanisms to explain these effects.

Keywords: Business environment; dividend smoothing; information asymmetry; income smoothing; internal environment; industry environment; macro-environment

Dividend Policy, 85–98
Copyright © 2024 Quoc Trung Tran
Published under exclusive licence by Emerald Publishing Limited
doi:10.1108/978-1-83797-987-520241009

7.1 What Is Dividend Smoothing?

7.1.1 Introduction

In a pioneer study, Lintner (1956) surveys corporate managers about dividend policy in the United States and finds that firms tend to follow stable dividend levels. Corporate managers believe that investors assign premia to firms with stable dividends or gradual increases in dividend payments. Therefore, firms tend to pay a dividend which is equal to those paid in prior years even when their current earnings are lower. In addition, about two-thirds of surveyed firms set a target payout ratio and adjust their dividends at a standardized speed to reach in the long run. These behaviors are defined as dividend smoothing. In other words, firms following the dividend smoothing mechanism rarely reduce their dividends and only increase their dividends when their income increases permanently. Later surveys in the United States also show that firms still try to smooth their dividends (Baker et al., 1985; Pruitt & Gitman, 1991). Remarkably, Brav et al. (2005) survey 384 financial executives. About 90% of respondents think that dividend cuts lead to negative consequences.

Based on the results of his survey, Lintner (1956) suggests a partial adjustment model to describe how firms smooth their dividend payments. The target dividend per share of firm i in year t ($TD_{i,t}$) is determined by the earnings per share of firm i in year t ($E_{i,t}$) and the target payout (TP) ratio as follows:

$$TD_{i,t} = TP_i * E_{i,t} \qquad (7.1)$$

Every year, firms partially adjust its dividend per share toward the target level with a certain adjustment speed.

$$D_{i,t} - D_{i,t-1} = \alpha_i + \beta_i * (TD_{i,t} - D_{i,t-1}) + u_{i,t} \qquad (7.2)$$

Where: $D_{i,t}$ is the dividend per share of firm i in year t; $D_{i,t-1}$ is the dividend of firm i in year $t-1$. α is a constant. β is the dividend adjustment speed. Its value varies from 0 to 1. When β is higher, dividends go less smoothly.

Eq. (7.2) can be written as follows:

$$D_{i,t} - D_{i,t-1} = \alpha_i + \beta_i * TD_{i,t} - \beta_i * D_{i,t-1} + u_{i,t} \qquad (7.3)$$

Replacing $TD_{i,t}$ in Eq. (7.3) by Eq. (7.1) gives:

$$D_{i,t} - D_{i,t-1} = \alpha_i + \beta_i * TP_i * E_{i,t} - \beta_i * D_{i,t-1} + u_{i,t} \qquad (7.4)$$

Fama and Babiak (1968) posit that the process to create the annual earnings per share is as follows:

$$E_{i,t} = (1 + \delta_i) * E_{i,t-1} + e_{i,t} \qquad (7.5)$$

Where $e_{i,t}$ is a serially independent error term. The target divided per share is still: $TD_{i,t} = TP_i * E_{i,t}$. However, they assume that dividends fully adjust to the expected earnings change $\delta * E_{i,t-1}$ and partially adjust to the remainder:

$$D_{i,t} - D_{i,t-1} = \alpha_i + \beta_i * [TP_i * (E_{i,t} - \delta_i * E_{i,t-1})] + TP_i * \delta_i * E_{i,t-1} + u_{i,t} \qquad (7.6)$$

Fama and Babiak (1968) show that the Lintner's model may have a stronger predictive power if the first lag of earnings per share is added. Dividends are distributed from corporate earnings; therefore, dividend payments convey useful information about firm performance. A stable dividend policy may be determined by two mechanisms: smoothing and signaling. According to Chen and Wu (1999), an important difference between them is the information content they imply. In the smoothing mechanism, dividends rely on the expected future earnings that are based on available information. Therefore, dividend changes indicate corporate managers' prediction of subsequent earnings. However, in the signaling mechanism, dividends provide outside investors with information about the expected future earnings that they cannot have access to. In other words, the smoothing mechanism posits that current dividends are determined by managers' forecasts of future income, while the signaling mechanism posits that dividend changes imply unexpected changes in future income.

7.1.2 Dividend Smoothing in Practice

Empirical studies show that dividend smoothing is popular in developed markets. Aharony and Swary (1980) investigate quarterly dividend payments in 149 industrial firms in the United States from the first quarter of 1963 to the last quarter of 1976 and find that there are 2,968 cases of no change among 3,399 cases of dividend payments (equivalent to 87.3%). Loderer and Mauer (1992) and Nissim and Ziv (2001) also show that the US firms have about 80% of no change cases in quarterly dividend payments from 1960s to 1980s. With a sample of 900 large industrial firms listed in the United States from 1946 to 1968, Fama (1974) finds supporting evidence for the dividend smoothing mechanism. Other studies also show that firms tend to smooth their dividends in the United States (Basse et al., 2011; Basse & Reddemann, 2011; Chateau, 1979), the United Kingdom (Kilincarslan, 2021; Lasfer, 1996; Renneboog & Trojanowski, 2007), Australia (Gugler, 2003), Japan (Dewenter & Warther, 1998), Hong Kong (Chemmanur et al., 2010), and Korea (Jeong, 2013). Firms in Japan, Hong Kong, and Korea have lower dividend adjustment speed than those in the United States (Chemmanur et al., 2010; Dewenter & Warther, 1998).

In developing markets, firms are less likely to concentrate on dividend smoothing; their dividends per share increase or decrease along with earnings (Wang et al., 2011). Glen (1995) shows that firms in developing markets try to reach a target payout ratio without caring about short-term volatility. Examining dividend policy in the Istanbul Stock Exchange (Turkey) from 1985 to 1997, Adaoglu (2000) finds that firms fail to follow the dividend smoothing mechanism, and their dividend payments, all changes in earnings. Wang et al. (2011) also document that there is a lack of payout smoothing in China over the period 1998–2008. However, with a sample of firms listed in South Africa during the period 1995–2011, Sibanda (2014) shows that dividend smoothing is still useful to estimate firms' target payout ratios, although firms are less likely to pay dividends. Al-Najjar (2009) finds that Jordanian firms also follow the dividend smoothing mechanism, and their dividend adjustment speed is higher than those in more developed countries. Examining dividend smoothing behavior with a sample of 5,298 Chinese and Taiwanese firms between 1996 and 2015, Hoang and Hoxha (2021) find that Chinese firms follow the dividend smoothing mechanism, but Taiwanese firms' dividends are strongly sensitive to changes in their earnings.

7.2 Dividend Smoothing Theories

Dividend smoothing theories concentrate on explaining what frictions drive firms to smooth their dividend payments. According to Leary and Michaely (2011), there are three common frictions including information asymmetry, agency problem, and investors' demand for income smoothing.

7.2.1 Information Asymmetry-Based Theories

Coarse signaling: According to the classical signaling theory, corporate dividend payments completely reflect firms' prospects and thus completely eliminate the information asymmetry between insiders and outside investors (Bhattacharya, 1979; John & Williams, 1985). This signaling mechanism fails to explain why firms smooth their dividend payouts when their earnings are serially associated. Therefore, Kumar (1988) suggests a new modified signaling model which is named as coarse signaling model to explain dividend smoothing behavior. Then, it is extended by Guttman et al. (2010) and Kumar and Lee (2001). Unlike the classical theory, the coarse signaling theory argues that dividend payments only reflect the broad quality of firms' future prospects instead of changing one-to-one with them. Firms pool with each other when possible prospects fall within a range. Firms smooth their dividends to signal the broad quality of their range. They are more likely to smooth dividends when their range is wider. When dividend smoothing is driven by the coarse signaling motive, dividend smoothing is more prevalent in firms with severe information asymmetry. Comparative statics show that firms have higher incentives to smooth dividends when they face higher cash flow volatility (Kumar, 1988), higher equity risk (Kumar & Lee, 2001), higher investment opportunities, and shorter investment horizon (Guttman et al., 2010).

External financing constraints: Due to information asymmetry between insiders and creditors, firms may face difficulties in raising external funds under the adverse selection mechanism. When external financing is costly, it tends to hold more cash for precautionary savings. Therefore, they are less likely to pay dividends even if they have high earnings. Moreover, firms with external financing constraints also need to signal creditors about their quality; therefore, they are reluctant to cut dividends. These mechanisms lead to dividend smoothing (Leary & Michaely, 2011).

Shareholder preferences: Brennan and Thakor (1990) argue that share repurchases are not a costless alternative to dividends, if investors have to pay significant costs to collect information and share repurchases are not pro rata.

Uninformed investors tend to prefer dividends. When information acquisition is endogenous and a majority of shares are held by uninformed investors, small payouts are conducted through dividends, while intermediate and large payouts are conducted through share repurchases. Consequently, dividend is less likely to reflect the changes in earnings. Dividend payments are smoother than earnings instead. When uninformed investors hold more shares, dividend smoothing is more pronounced (Leary & Michaely, 2011).

7.2.2 Agency-Based Theories

Corporate governance substitute: Due to the separation of ownership and control, corporate managers tend to expropriate shareholders by diverting free cash flows into unprofitable investment projects. Dividend payments help firms reduce free cash flows which are available to managers. Therefore, when a firm has weak corporate governance, its shareholders insist on a smooth stream of dividends to reduce agency costs (Lambrecht & Myers, 2010). In addition, corporate managers may be reluctant to cut dividends and have high incentives to smooth dividends in order to show outside investors their accountability (Guedhami et al., 2017). This helps the firm build up its reputation and prestige which are important for raising external funds and improving firm value.

Free cash absorption: According to Amihud and Lev (1981) and Jensen and Meckling (1976), corporate managers are concerned about their career, and thus, they tend to make decisions in order to maintain their positions. Corporate managers have incentives to report adjusted outcomes instead of real outcomes to shareholders in order to reduce the risk of being fired. When their firms have good performance, they underreport so that they can overreport when their firms have bad performance. Therefore, corporate managers tend to smooth dividends as a means to maintain their job safety (Fudenberg & Tirole, 1995). Moreover, shareholders obtain information about their firms' profitability based on current cash flows; however, one of managers' obligations is keeping cash holdings at a reasonable level to avoid premature liquidation (DeMarzo & Sannikov, 2008). When firms have high cash flows, shareholders realize high profitability and expect high dividend levels. However, high cash flows also increase optimal levels of cash reserves; therefore, increases in cash holdings absorb the changes in cash flows. This leads to smoothed dividends.

7.2.3 Income Smoothing Theory

According to Miller and Modigliani (1961), in a perfect environment without taxes and transaction costs, dividends and capital gains are perfect substitutes. However, Shefrin and Statman (1984) find that many individuals prefer dividends to cash, and this preference is not only determined by taxes. They posit that dividends are more convenient for investors' consumption. Investors use income from dividends for their consumption but fail to dip into capital. Since investors tend to smooth their consumption, they expect and pressure firms to smooth dividend payments (Baker et al., 2006). Individual investors have high incentives to smooth consumption; therefore, firms with more individual investors are more likely to smooth dividends.

7.3 Internal Environment and Dividend Smoothing

7.3.1 Internal Management

7.3.1.1 Strategic Issues

In a modern economy, corporate social responsibility (CSR) is a new business strategy which helps firms improve their reputations and gain competitive advantages. CSR may affect dividend smoothing behavior through both agency and signaling channels. First, CSR is an opportunity for corporate managers overinvest their firms' resources in social, environmental, and philanthropic projects since they obtain both financial and nonfinancial benefits (e.g., gifts, reputations, and new networks) from these projects (Brown et al., 2006). Recognizing this opportunistic behavior, shareholders tend to restrict CSR programs at an optimal level that has no room for overinvestment and maximizes firm value (Ye & Zhang, 2011). Dividend payments are a means for corporate managers to show their responsibility to shareholders. Therefore, socially responsible firms are more likely to smooth their dividends and avoid cutting dividends. Second, dividends signal outside investors about firms' prospects. Dividend smoothing shows that firms are fair and ethical in wealth distribution. Besides, it also indicates that socially responsible firms can allocate their resources well despite CSR projects. With a sample of 22,839 observations from 3,040 firms listed in the United States over the period 1991–2012, Benlemlih (2019) finds that firms with higher CSR scores have higher levels of dividend smoothing than firms with lower CSR scores. The latter adjust dividends more quickly than the former.

Innovation is also an emerging business strategy that creates competitive advantages and economic benefits. However, innovation leads to more severe information asymmetry since research and development (R&D) projects are not comparable and even confidential. Outsiders fail to collect enough information about their productivity and value which are used to compare them with those of other firms. In some cases, innovative projects are not released to avoid industrial espionage. Furthermore, innovation increases agency costs. R&D projects are commonly risky, unpredictable, long-term, and multistage; therefore, corporate managers have more opportunities to expropriate shareholders in innovative firms (Block, 2012). Dividend smoothing is a means to reduce both information asymmetry and agency costs. Consequently, highly innovative firms have high incentives to smooth their dividends. With a sample of 863 observations over the period 2005–2018, Gounopoulos et al. (2021) find that innovation has a positive effect on dividend smoothing in the United States. Moreover, Labhane and Mahakud (2018) show that firms affiliated with a business group smooth dividends more in India. This can be explained that affiliation with a business group makes firms face more severe information asymmetry. Group-affiliated firms make their decisions not only based own their own benefits but also their group's interest. Therefore, outside investors can collect information and predict behaviors of a stand-alone firm more easily than those of group-affiliated firms.

7.3.1.2 Financial Issues

As an important financial decision, dividend payments are determined by leverage-related and investment-related issues. First, dividend payments reduce internal funds and thus make firms rely more on external funds. Therefore, financial slack and flexibility may affect dividend smoothing. Firms with high financial slack face the underinvestment problem and have low demand for external funds. They have low incentives to signal outsiders by smoothing dividends. With a sample of 720 firms listed in the United States from 1980 to 1998, Bhabra et al. (2002) show that firms smoothing dividends have lower levels of financial slack than those without dividend smoothing. Jeong (2013) and Nowak et al. (2021) also find that financial slack has a positive effect on the speed of dividend adjustment in Asian countries. This finding implies that financial slack makes dividends move less smoothly. Moreover, firms with high financial flexibility can raise external funds easily; therefore, they are less likely to cut their dividends since this behavior leads to negative reactions from the market (Kalay, 1980). These firms also have incentives to signal outside investors in order to take advantage of their unused debt capacity. As a result, they smooth dividends more. Fliers (2019) investigate how financial flexibility influences dividend smoothing of 571 firms in the United States over the period 1986–2013 and find a positive relationship between financial flexibility and dividend smoothing. Besides, corporate managers consider risk when they make decisions in dividend smoothing. Risky firms tend to smooth their dividends in order to show outside investors that they have low systematic risk (Guttman et al., 2010). This helps them reduce external financing costs. Consistently, Labhane (2018b) documents that firms with low financial leverage and high risk have more stable dividend payments. Investigating dividend smoothing behavior in seven Asian countries (China, Indonesia, Korea, Malaysia, the Philippines, Taiwan, and Thailand) between 2000 and 2015, Nowak et al. (2021) find that risk is an important determinant of dividend smoothing.

Second, firms with more investment opportunities need to send signals to outsiders about their future prospects (Bhabra et al., 2002). On the other hand, they need to improve their reputation and image so that they have lower financing costs. Therefore, firms tend to maintain their dividends at a specific level. Labhane (2018b) examines determinants of dividend smoothing in India from 1994 to 2013 and finds a positive relationship between investment opportunities and dividend stability. Moreover, firms which are cash cows have few investment opportunities. Hence, they may face a severe agency problem since their managers have good conditions to expropriate shareholders. This encourages firms smooth dividends to reduce agency costs. García-Feijóo et al. (2021) and Leary and Michaely (2011) consistently show that cash cows have low levels of dividend adjustment speed in the United States. In other words, their dividends move more smoothly.

7.3.1.3 Other Firm-Specific Characteristics

Firm size is an important determinant of corporate financial decisions since large and small firms have different levels of resources. Large firms face less serious information asymmetry between insiders and outsiders; therefore, their information is more available. Besides, large firms are well-organized and monitored by many parties; therefore, their corporate governance is stronger than small firms. Consequently, large firms have low incentives to smooth their dividends. Many empirical studies show a negative relationship between firm size and dividend stability in the United States (Bhabra et al., 2002), Korea (Jeong, 2013), and India (Labhane, 2018b). In addition, older firms have more public information, and thus, they are less likely to signal outsiders by dividend smoothing (Javakhadze et al., 2014; Leary & Michaely, 2011).

7.3.2 Internal Stakeholders

7.3.2.1 Shareholders

Shareholders' ability to affect corporate decisions depends on their voting rights and characteristics. When a small number of shareholders hold a large proportion of shares, corporate managers are strictly monitored and disciplined by large shareholders. Therefore, firms with high ownership concentration have strong corporate governance and have low incentives to smooth dividends. Javakhadze et al. (2014) show that ownership concentration has a negative impact on dividend smoothing across 24 countries over the period 1999–2011. Consistently, Michaely and Roberts (2012) find that public firms with diffused ownership smooth dividend less in the United Kingdom from 1993 to 2002. However, ownership concentration also leads to higher risk for minority shareholders. Controlling blockholders may take advantage of their voting rights to expropriate minority shareholders. Consequently, firms with concentrated ownership tend to show fair treatment of minority shareholders by smoothing their dividend payments. Examining how ownership concentration affects dividend smoothing in six Latin American countries, Tigero et al. (2023) document that firms with high ownership concentration have more stable dividends. Jeong (2013) also finds a positive effect of ownership concentration on dividend stability in Korea.

In addition, various groups of shareholders have different characteristics that determine dividend smoothing. State-controlled firms have poor corporate governance since they face a "double agency problem" (Gugler, 2003). The final owners of a state-controlled firm are citizens. However, citizens fail to make important decisions in the firm directly. Instead, they elect a group of politicians who play the role of owners on their behalf. These politicians are not real owners; therefore, they are less active and effective in disciplining managers. Consequently, state-controlled firms tend to keep their dividends stable since dividend smoothing is a substitute for weak corporate governance. Gugler (2003) analyzes how ownership structure affects dividend policy of 214 firms listed in the Austrian stock market from 1991 to 1999 and find that state-controlled firms are reluctant to reduce their dividends.

Moreover, many studies compare dividend smoothing behavior of state-controlled and family-controlled firms. The latter tend to face less severe conflicts of interest between shareholders and managers since family shareholders closely monitor and control managers. Gugler (2003) shows that family-controlled firms are less likely to smooth dividends than state-controlled firms in Austria. On the other hand, family-controlled firms face another kind of interest conflict. As blockshareholders, family shareholders may take advantage of their voting rights to expropriate minority shareholders. Therefore, they need to show outsiders about their fair treatment of shareholders in order to maintain stock prices. This drives them to follow stable dividend payments. He et al. (2012) compare dividend stability of 90 state-controlled firms and 166 family-controlled firms in Hong Kong. They document that the latter smooth dividends more than the former.

7.3.2.2 Board of Directors
The board of directors is an important corporate governance mechanism. The quality of corporate governance relies on its characteristics (e.g., size and structure). On the one hand, a large board may help a firm improve its corporate governance since its managers are monitored and controlled closely. On the other hand, a large board may weaken a firm's corporate governance if board members cannot cooperate and work well as a team. Dividend smoothing is a compensation for weak corporate governance; consequently, the effect of a large board on a firm's incentive to smooth dividends depends on the role of the board in corporate governance. Ali et al. (2019) find that board size has a positive relationship with dividend stability in Pakistan from 2005 to 2015.

In addition, the presence of independent directors improves corporate governance. Independent directors commonly have necessary expertise and are objective in their activities; therefore, they are more effective than related directors in monitoring managers. This implies that firms with high board independence are less likely to smooth dividends. Consistently, García-Feijóo et al. (2021) show that board independence has a negative impact on the speed of dividend adjustment in the United States from 1999 to 2014.

7.3.2.3 Chief Executive Officer – CEO
CEO is the most important decision-maker in a firm. Therefore, CEOs' characteristics such as ownership, tenure, social capital, and overconfidence determine how their firms smooth dividends. First, CEOs' benefits are more aligned with shareholders' wealth when they hold a high proportion of shares. Holding more shares reduces CEOs' incentives to use dividend smoothing as a substitute for poor corporate governance. James et al. (2017) investigate the relationship between CEO ownership and dividend smoothing of the US firms during the period 1995–2008. They find that CEO delta (the sensitivity of CEO wealth to stock price) – a proxy of CEO ownership is positively related to dividend adjustment speed. In other words, CEO ownership has a negative effect on dividend stability.

Second, when a CEO's tenure is longer, they are more likely to signal investors about their capability and the firm's prospect in order to maintain their position. Therefore, CEOs with longer tenure may choose dividend smoothing as a means of signaling. Fuller (2001) shows that both CEOs' tenure with their firms and their tenure as CEOs have positive effects on dividend smoothing in the United States from 1989 to 1993.

Third, social capital is vital to a CEO's career success. From the signaling perspective, managerial social capital may decrease a firm's incentive to signal outsiders by smoothing dividend payments. High social capital CEOs have board and supportive networks which are commonly based on information transparency and trust. Consequently, outsiders have much information about them and have less adverse selection. Besides, social capital is an important ability in business. CEOs with high social capital can employ their personal connections to obtain resources, preferences, and information advantage for their firms. Therefore, CEOs with high social capital are less concerned about their job safety. Furthermore, social capital also helps CEOs obtain external funds with lower costs. Collective firms with lower information asymmetry, career concerns, and financing costs are less likely to smoothing dividends. On the contrary, from the agency perspective, firms have lower external financing costs due to their CEOs' social capital have high propensity to smooth dividends. Easy and cheap access to external funds may face high pressure from their shareholders to maintain a stable stream of dividends which are believed as a means to reduce agency costs. Investigating how managerial social capital influences dividend smoothing in 843 US firms from 1999 to 2014, García-Feijóo et al. (2021) find supporting evidence for the positive effect of managerial social capital on dividend smoothing.

Finally, CEO overconfidence may have two opposite effects on dividend stickiness. On the one hand, overconfident CEOs tend to believe that the market undervalue their firms despite available information (Deshmukh et al., 2013). Therefore, they are less likely to send signals to outside investors through dividend payments. When their firms have high earnings, they are less likely to increase dividends. When facing low income, they are likely to cut dividends in order to save funds for future projects. This leads to downward dividend stickiness. On the other hand, overconfident CEOs tend to be overoptimistic about their capability and performance. They are keen on smoothing dividend to show their ability. Furthermore, they believe that success is the outcome of their talent, but failure is from bad luck (Gervais & Odean, 2001). A decrease in income is considered as a temporary phenomenon. They still maintain dividend payments in spite of low income. When income increases, they are keen on increasing dividends corresponding to their overestimated future prospects. Consequently, their firms have a higher degree of dividend stickiness. With a sample of 6,658 observations from the US firms over the period 1990–2017, Lin and Yu (2023) document that CEO overconfidence results in downward dividend stickiness.

7.4 Industry Environment and Dividend Smoothing

Firms face several pressures from different participants in the product market. Main participants such as existing competitors, customers, and suppliers considerably affect their dividend smoothing. When firms have aggressive competitors, their managers concentrate more on maximizing shareholders' wealth (Raith, 2003). Moreover, corporate managers in a highly competitive industry have to compete sharply for obtaining external funds. This drives them to smooth dividends more since dividend smoothing implies a decrease in agency costs. Javakhadze et al. (2014) show that industry competition has a positive relationship with dividend smoothing across 24 countries.

Besides, a firm's dividend smoothing behavior is also affected by industry peers' dividend policy. On the one hand, peer pressure may drive a firm to smooth dividends more (less) when dividend smoothing is a common (rare) behavior of its competitors. On the other hand, a firm may use dividend smoothing to make it different from competitors and create its own competitive advantage. It is more (less) keen on smoothing dividends, while industry peers are less (more) likely to conduct this policy. Syed et al. (2018) find that the US firms tend to employ dividend smoothing as a means to build up their reputation. Their findings show that firms which have lower or no reputational concerns are less likely to smooth dividends. Chen et al. (2022) investigate how firms react to dividend smoothing behavior of their peers in China from 2003 to 2020 and find that firms' dividend smoothing decisions follow the competition policy instead of the imitation policy.

In addition, customer–supplier relationships may determine dividend smoothing behavior through two mechanisms: financial distress and certification. On the one hand, when firms have close customer–supplier relationships, they have to concentrate on relationship-specific investments (Banerjee et al., 2008). This makes them face higher financial distress. In order to reduce financial distress, firms tend to save more cash and thus restrict their dividends. In other words, firms are less able to maintain a stable stream of dividends due to financial distress. On the other hand, a large customer can monitor and control its suppliers' managers effectively since it has access to managerial information (Wang, 2012). The integration between the principal customer and its suppliers is a certification and thus reduce information between suppliers' managers and outside investors. When facing less severe information asymmetry, suppliers have low incentives to smooth dividends. With a sample of 94,651 firm-year observations in the United States from 1981 to 2006, Wang (2012) empirically documents that customer–supplier relationships have a negative effect on dividend stability.

Furthermore, firms in regulated industries have to strictly follow legal regulations; therefore, their dividend smoothing mechanisms are different from those of unregulated firms. Examining dividend policy of 106 firms in the European electricity industry between 1986 and 2010, Bremberger et al. (2016) find that cost-based regulated firms smooth dividends more than incentive-regulated firms. This can be explained that the former tend to have stable performance and thus pay stable dividends over time. The latter are more dynamic in their business activities, and thus, their income has many fluctuations. Consistently, using a large sample of banks in the United States and the European Union from 1998 to 2016, Koussis and Makrominas (2019) show that banks facing high regulatory pressure smooth dividends more. Felimban et al. (2022) also document that financial firms have more stable dividend payments than nonfinancial firms in the Gulf Cooperation Council countries during the period 1994–2016.

7.5 Macro-Environment and Dividend Smoothing

7.5.1 Political Factors

Political freedom reflects the government quality. Firms in countries of weak political freedom face high government expropriation and thus have poor corporate governance (Stulz, 2005). Therefore, they tend smooth dividends as a substitute for weak corporate governance (Leary & Michaely, 2011). However, Guedhami et al. (2017) find a positive effect of political freedom on dividend smoothing across 50 countries from 1991 to 2010. This result can be explained that firms in countries of weak political freedom have high incentives to avoid severe state expropriation by reducing their liquidity. They try to disgorge cash as much as possible through dividend payments instead of signaling outsiders about their fair treatment or the future prospects. In other words, firms in poor political freedom environment are less likely to smooth dividends.

In addition, political corruption may affect dividend smoothing behavior through increasing costs of doing business, weakening corporate governance, and raising incentives of sheltering liquid assets. Firms in a corrupt environment pay bribes as grease money or protection money. Regardless of bribery purposes, they have to incur higher cost of doing business since bribes are additional payments. These illegal payments provide corporate managers with more flexibility in liquidity policy, and thus, they tend to exploit this opportunity to expropriate shareholders. Besides, when political corruption is widespread, firms have high incentives to reduce their liquid assets in order to avoid corrupt officials' rent-seeking. The corporate governance channel implies a positive relationship between political corruption and dividend smoothing, while the other two channels indicate an opposite relationship. With a large sample of 22,040 foreign subsidiaries established by the US multinational firms between 2005 and 2016, Tahir et al. (2020) find that these subsidiaries in countries of high corruption tend to adjust quickly toward optimal dividend repatriation. In other words, political corruption has a negative effect on smoothing dividend repatriation.

7.5.2 Economic Factors

Monetary policy influences corporate decisions to smooth dividends through external financing. On the one hand, from the liquidity perspective, an expansionary (contradictionary) policy may increase (decrease) firms' incentives to smooth dividends since they are more (less) flexible in liquidity policy. Pandey and Bhat (2007) show that Indian firms have higher speed of dividend adjustment when monetary policies are restricted during the period 1989–1997. This implies that restricted monetary policies lead to high dividend instability. On the other hand, from the signaling perspective, an expansionary (contradictionary) policy may drive firms to smooth dividends less (more) since they face lower (higher) costs of external financing. Consistently, Jeong (2013) finds that interest rates positively affect dividend stability in Korea.

Moreover, a financial crisis is an exogenous shock to dividend smoothing behavior. It increases external financial constraint, agency costs, and information asymmetry (Tran, 2019a; Tran et al., 2017). Rhee and Park (2018) investigate how the global financial crisis influences dividend smoothing in Korean firms. They document that the speed of dividend adjustment in the postcrisis period is higher in the precrisis period. In other words, the crisis decreases dividend stability. This can be explained that the external financial constraint makes firms less flexible in their liquidity policy, and thus, they are less likely to smooth dividends. Consistently, with a sample of 1,178 firms listed in the United Kingdom from 2008 to 2017, Kilincarslan (2021) shows that despite having a stable stream of dividends from 2008 to 2012, the level of dividend stability in the period 2013–2017 is higher. Besides, the COVID-19 pandemic also leads to an economic shock due to social distancing and supply chain interruptions. Cejnek et al. (2021) find that the COVID-19 also creates interruptions in dividend smoothing. However, this breakdown is less serious when firms have high cash flows.

7.5.3 Social Factors

Culture values govern people's attitude and behavior; therefore, national culture also determines how firms smooth dividends (Javakhadze et al., 2014). First, people in high power distance culture respect and accept inequality in their social relations. This implies that they are less likely to expect a uniform distribution of wealth. Consequently, firms in high power distance countries have low incentives to smooth dividend payments. Second, people in individualistic culture tend to focus on their personal achievements and success. Dividend smoothing is a means to show managers' ability in allocation of resources. Therefore, individualism leads to more stable dividend payments. Third, uncertainty avoidance culture appreciates and emphasizes stability and certainty. This drives firms to maintain a smooth stream of dividends. Fourth, long-term orientation culture respects traditional and historical connections. They prefer predictable and steady policy. As a result, firms in long-term orientation culture are more likely to smooth dividends. Finally, masculinity emphasizes material achievements, power, and control. These characteristics tend to support dividend smoothing which represents an effective control and predictability. Analyzing the effects of Hofstede's culture dimensions on dividend smoothing in 24 countries between 1999 and 2011, Javakhadze et al. (2014) find that cultural individualism, masculinity, uncertainty avoidance, and long-term orientation positively influence dividend stability, while power distance has a reverse impact.

7.5.4 Environmental Factors

When people are more aware of environment protection and sustainable development, firms have to meet environmental requirements and expectations from various stakeholders. First, climate change is a popular problem challenging governments, firms, and individuals around the world; therefore, firms are more concerned about climate risk. Chasiotis et al. (2022) argue that climate risk may have two opposite impacts on dividend smoothing. On the one hand, it strengthens corporate managers' precautionary motive, and thus, they tend to hold more cash. This increases firms' financial slack which, in turn, facilitate a stable stream of dividends. On the other hand, climate risk decreases both internal and external financing abilities (Huang et al., 2018). When firms face high climate risk, they need more investment capital for adaptation projects and incur high costs of external financing. With a sample of firms listed in 10 countries from 2005 to 2019, Chasiotis et al. (2022) find a negative relationship between climate risk and dividend stability.

In addition, many governments conduct green credit policy in order to encourage and pressure firms to reduce pollution. This policy restricts polluting firms' access to external financing. Therefore, polluting firms are less likely to smooth dividends when green credit policy is effective. Li et al. (2023) examine the effect of green credit policy on dividend stability in China. They find that polluting firms smooth dividends less after the Chinese government adopts the green credit policy in 2012.

7.5.5 Legal Factors

Generally, legal protection of shareholders is an important determinant of corporate financial decisions. Dividend smoothing is considered a substitute of weak corporate governance. Therefore, strong shareholder rights reduce firms' incentive to smooth dividends. Javakhadze et al. (2014) empirically show that legal protection of shareholders make dividends go less smoothly in 24 countries. Particularly, firms in common law countries are less likely to engage in dividend smoothing than those in civil law countries. Moreover, Tigero et al. (2023) document that firms incorporated in countries of mandatory dividend payments have lower propensity to smooth dividends than those in countries of flexible dividend payments.

In addition, tax laws also significantly determine corporate dividend behavior. In a classical tax system, shareholders face double taxation for the income from dividends. Therefore, firms tend to distribute small payouts via dividends. In other words, firms have high incentives to smooth dividends when the government follows the classical tax system. Shinozaki and Uchida (2017) find supporting evidence for this mechanism when they examine dividend smoothing behavior in about 6,000 firms across 28 countries. Consistently, Labhane (2018b) shows that Indian firms smooth dividends more when the government imposes high tax rates for dividends. Besides, firms have higher propensity to smooth dividends in Hong Kong than in the United States since the former has no tax discrimination between dividends and capital gains (Chemmanur et al., 2010).

Chapter 8

Dividend Policy and Stock Price

Abstract

As a financial policy, dividend policy significantly affects firm value. This chapter analyzes how stock prices react to dividend decisions. First, a dividend payment is an extraction of value; therefore, stock price theoretically drops by the dividend amount on the ex-dividend day. In practice, the price drop and the dividend magnitude are not equal because of tax clientele, short-term trading, and market microstructure. Investors are indifferent in trading stocks before and after stocks go ex-dividend if they obtain equal marginal benefits from the two trading times. The difference in tax rates on dividends and capital gains leads to the gap between the price drop and the dividend amount. Moreover, if transaction costs are considerable, investors have high incentives to short-sell stocks until they cannot obtain more profits. The final outcome of this short-term trading is the difference between the price drop and the dividend amount. Furthermore, market microstructure factors such as limit orders, bid-ask spread, and price discreteness also create this gap. Second, dividend announcements convey valuable information to outsiders. When firms announce increases (decreases) in dividends, their stock prices tend to increase (decrease). Third, dividend policy is negatively related to stock price volatility. This negative relationship is explained by duration effect, rate of return effect, arbitrage realization effect, and information effect. Empirical evidence for this relationship is found in many countries. Finally, dividend smoothing is also considered as a signal about firms' future earnings. Consequently, firms with stable dividends have higher market value. In other words, dividend stability has a positive effect on stock prices.

Keywords: Dividend policy; stock price; ex-dividend day; tax clientele; short-term trading; microstructure; dividend announcement; stock price volatility

Dividend Policy, 99–112

Copyright © 2024 Quoc Trung Tran

Published under exclusive licence by Emerald Publishing Limited

doi:10.1108/978-1-83797-987-520241010

8.1 Stock Price Behavior on the Ex-dividend Day

In a perfect environment, dividend policy is not relevant to shareholder wealth. Stock prices should fall precisely by the dividend magnitude on the ex-dividend day. However, the price drop on the ex-dividend day is not equal to the dividend amount in practice due to various frictions including tax clientele, short-term trading, and market microstructure.

8.1.1 Tax Clientele Mechanism

8.1.1.1 Main Arguments

A tax clientele is a group of investors who have particular preferences for a financial asset or transaction due to their similar tax status. Elton and Gruber (1970) initially use the tax clientele effect to explain the behavior of stock price on the ex-dividend day. In other words, the ex-day behavior of stock price is determined by marginal stockholders' tax rates.

In practice, the government imposes taxes on both capital gains and dividends. On the one hand, when investors sell their stocks before the ex-dividend day, they fail to receive dividends. They have to pay personal income tax for capital gains from selling their stocks on or after the ex-day. On the other hand, when investors hold their stocks until the ex-dividend day, they pay personal income tax for dividends. They expect a lower price level for their stocks because of their dividend retention. Regardless of tax policy, the selling time is irrelevant to investors' wealth when the marginal benefits from selling stocks before, on, and after the ex-day are equal.

$$P_c - t_g(P_c - P_o) = P_e - t_g(P_c - P_o) + D(1 - t_d) \qquad (8.1)$$

Where: P_c is the stock price on the last cum-day. P_e is the expected stock price on the ex-dividend day. P_o is the price at which stocks are bought. t_d is the marginal tax rate on dividends. t_g is the marginal tax rate on capital gains. D is the dividend magnitude.

Rearranging Eq. (8.1), we obtain:

$$\frac{P_c - P_e}{D} = \frac{1 - t_d}{1 - t_g} \qquad (8.2)$$

The price drop to dividend ratio $(P_c - P_e)/D$ is determined by the difference between marginal tax rates on dividends and capital gains. If the marginal tax rate on dividends is higher than the marginal tax rate on capital gains, the price drop on the ex-dividend day is smaller than the dividend magnitude (i.e., the price drop to dividend ratio is smaller than one). On the contrary, the difference in stock prices is higher than the dividend amount if the marginal tax rate on dividends is lower than the marginal tax rate on capital gains.

Jerry (1980) extends the Elton–Gruber analysis with abnormal trading volume around ex-dividend days. He argues that delaying or advancing a transaction due to tax-related reasons is costly. Therefore, high tax bracket investors who want to advance selling their stocks tend to sell on the cum-dividend day, while high tax bracket investors who want to postpone a purchase of stocks tend to buy on the first day when stocks go ex-dividend. Based on these arguments, they posit that some positive abnormal trading volume should be observable on the ex-dividend day and the day before, while negative abnormal trading volume should appear on other days. Moreover, Michaely and Vila (1995) extend Elton and Gruber's analysis by developing a dynamic tax-induced clientele model. They posit that investors with preferential taxation of dividends tend to hold and buy stocks before the ex-day, while investors with tax disadvantages on dividends tend to sell stocks on cum-dividend days and buy them back on the ex-day. As a result, investors trade with each other around the ex-dividend day due to their different valuation of dividends. In this model, dividend yields and tax heterogeneity indicate gains from tax arbitrage trading activities, while risk and transaction costs prevent these activities. In equilibrium, the price drop to dividend ratio is shaped by the average investors' preference for dividends to capital gains, rather than by a single group of investors.

8.1.1.2 Empirical Evidence

Elton and Gruber (1970) investigate the relationship between relative tax bracket and dividend yield in the US market by sorting the research sample into deciles by dividend yield and calculate the average ratio of price drop to dividend for each group. Their findings show that the mean is 0.778, and the ratio is positively related to dividend yield. The former is consistent with the US tax policy. The latter is in line with the presence of tax clientele effect. Investors with low relative tax brackets are more likely to hold low yield stocks. Using Elton and Gruber's model, Barclay (1987) investigates the ex-dividend behavior of stock price in the US market before the enforcement of the federal income tax over the period 1900–1910. They document that the price drop is, on average, equal to the full dividend value during the pretax period. In addition, Lamdin (1993) examines how stock price changes on the ex-dividend day before and after the US Tax Reform Act of 1986. This Act increases the tax rate on capital gains. Using data from 1982 to 1991, they show that the price drop to dividend ratio is lower in the postreform period than the prereform period.

In addition, Whitworth and Rao (2010) analyze how changes in the US tax policy affect ex-dividend stock pricing during the period 1926–2005. They find that the price drop ratio and the ex-dividend day return are associated with the dividend amount and the tax rate on capital gains. Corporate income tax rates are more effective in explaining the ex-day price changes in the group of high-dividend yield stocks, while personal income tax rates are more effective in the low-dividend yield group. The positive association between the price drop ratio and dividend yield is more pronounced when the difference between tax rates on dividends and capital gains is larger. Investigating the ex-dividend stock price behavior for special dividends in the United States over the period 1960–2012, Chowdhury and Sonaer (2016) find that the price drop to dividend ratio is lower than one. The ex-day returns are significantly positive and not fully eliminated by arbitrage activities. This finding is consistent with the tax clientele mechanism. Graham et al. (2003) take the opportunity of decimalization of price quotations from 1/8s and 1/16s to decimals in the US stock market to test the microstructure hypothesis. However, they find that abnormal stock returns on the ex-dividend day increase in both the 1/16 and decimal pricing periods, relative to the 1/8 period. This implies there is no supporting evidence of the price discreteness effect and transaction costs theory. They show that a decrease in the capital gains tax rate can explain the change in abnormal returns.

Moreover, there are many empirical studies supporting the tax clientele mechanism in non-US stock markets. Booth and Johnston (1984) extend this line of research to Canadian stock market where the tax policy of dividends over capital gains is absolutely different from the tax system in the US stock market. They estimate the price drop ratio for four separate tax periods (i.e., 1970–1971, 1972–1976, 1977, and 1978–1980) and find that the price drop ratio on the ex-dividend day is not equal to zero or one. This implies that taxes have significant effects on investor preferences for dividends over capital gains. Besides, the behavior of the price drop ratio on the ex-dividend day under different tax regimes supports the argument that individuals of effectively low dividend tax brackets are marginal traders in the stock market. Moreover, Kato et al. (1995) argue that investigation of stock price and trading volume behavior around the ex-dividend day in Japan can provide more understandings on the tax clientele effect since the Japanese stock market is different from the US market in terms of tax code (i.e., short-term and long-term trading activities are imposed with the same tax rate, and there is significant change in tax policy in the tax reform of 1988) and the means of information dissemination. With a comprehensive empirical analysis of the ex-dividend day stock price behavior, they find that prices increase on the ex-dividend day, and the effects of taxes on the ex-day stock price behavior seem to be secondary. Stock returns around the ex-dividend day are dominated by the fiscal year-end effect.

Furthermore, Milonas et al. (2006) choose the Chinese stock market where cash dividends are either taxable or nontaxable based on their magnitude, comparative to the annual interest to examine the ex-dividend day behavior of stock price. After neutralizing potential factors which can affect the stock price behavior, they find that the ex-dividend price drop to dividend ratio of nontaxable stocks is not significantly different from one, while that of taxable stocks is significantly less than one. For stocks with high-dividend yield, the price adjustment relies on the effective dividend tax rate. These overall findings support the tax clientele hypothesis. Investigating the ex-dividend trading behavior of institutional equity funds in Australia from January 2, 1995 to December 31, 2001, Ainsworth et al. (2016) find that institutional investors' trading behavior around the ex-day are driven by taxes, transactions costs, and the cum-day price run-up. Muñoz and Rodriguez (2017) estimate the price drop after 578 dividend payments in Chile during the period 1999–2012 and find that a major decrease in dividend tax leads to higher dividend value. Ainsworth et al. (2018) show that dividend payers with a tax credit attract ex-dividend arbitrage in Australia. Dividend capture makes stock prices increase before the ex-dividend day. Then, they turn to decrease during the ex-dividend period. Consistently, Ainsworth and Lee (2023) posit that only certain investors can exploit the tax credit. They show that individual investors who obtain the highest benefit aggressively purchase stocks before the ex-dividend day and then sell them aggressively in the ex-dividend period. These trading activities determine ex-dividend pricing. Besides, other studies also find the tax clientele is effective in the ex-day stock behavior in many countries and territories such as Finland (Hietala, 1990), Italy (Michaely et al., 1995), Germany (McDonald, 2001), the Netherlands (Florentsen & Rydqvist, 2002), Sweden (Daunfeldt et al., 2009), and Taiwan (Chen et al., 2013).

However, tax clientele is not the only mechanism to explain the ex-dividend behavior of stock price. Using data of the US firms from July 2nd, 1962 to December 31st, 1980, Eades et al. (1984) show that preferential tax treatment fails to explain the ex-day abnormal returns. Consequently, the price drop to dividend ratio cannot be used to estimate marginal tax rates on dividends and capital gains. Contrary to the tax clientele mechanism, they show that abnormal returns appear on days rather than the ex-dividend day. In addition, with a sample of 1,124 US firms having at least 30 ex-dividend days from August 1993 to October 2012, Ainsworth et al. (2020) find that most implied tax rates fail to fall within reasonable taxation bounds. This implies that the tax clientele is not the only mechanism to explain the stock price behavior on the ex-dividend day.

8.1.2 Short-Term Trading Mechanism

8.1.2.1 Main Arguments
In Elton and Gruber's model, marginal investors are long-term investors. Their decisions of buying or selling are irrelevant to dividends; therefore, transaction costs are considered as fixed costs and fail to affect the equilibrium. Nevertheless, Kalay (1982) argues that many investors are still having different preferences for selling and buying time due to transaction costs, although the tax clientele effect is not present (e.g., equal income tax rates for dividends and capital gains). When transaction costs are significant, investors are likely to make profits from short-selling. Particularly, investors tend to short-sell their stocks before the ex-dividend day and then purchase them back in the ex-dividend period if the gap between the price drop minus the dividend amount is higher than total trading costs.

$$(1 - t_o)(P_c - P_e - D - \alpha P) > 0 \tag{8.3}$$

Where t_o is the tax rate on ordinary income, α is the expected transaction costs of a round-trip transaction and $P = (P_c + P_e)/2$.

However, if the price drop minus the dividend amount is lower than total trading costs, investors have high incentives to purchase stocks before the ex-dividend day and sell them in the ex-dividend period.

$$(1 - t_o)[D - (P_c - P_e) - \alpha P] > 0 \tag{8.4}$$

According to Kalay (1982), a profit is realized only if it is not exploited by arbitrage activities. As a result, the condition of nonprofit opportunities is presented as follows:

$$|D - (P_c - P_e)| \le \alpha P \qquad (8.5)$$

After rearranging Eq. (8.5), we get:

$$1 - \frac{\alpha P}{D} \le \frac{P_c - P_e}{D} \le 1 + \frac{\alpha P}{D} \qquad (8.6)$$

Accordingly, the nonprofit opportunity range of $(P_c - P_e)/D$ is negatively proportional to dividend yield, and stockholders' marginal tax rates cannot be estimated from the price drop to dividend ratio. If transaction costs are zero, the value of $(P_c - P_e)/D$ will be limited to unity. When the ratio varies within the allowable range, there is presence of arbitrageur.

8.1.2.2 Empirical Evidence

Lakonishok and Vermaelen (1986) argue that trading volume around the ex-dividend day also provides information on marginal investors on the ex-day. Their findings show that trading volume increases considerably on days around the ex-dividend day. This increase tends to be stronger for high-yield, active stocks, and over the period after the launch of negotiable brokerage commissions. In addition, they find that abnormal returns are positive before ex-dividend days and negative after ex-dividend days, and abnormal increases in stock prices are positively related to dividend yield. These results are supporting evidence for transaction cost theory. Investigating short-term trading before and after ex-dividend days on the New York Stock Exchange (NYSE) from 1964 to 1985, Karpoff and Walkling (1988) find that ex-day returns are impacted by arbitrage trading and positively related to transaction costs. Arbitrageurs are marginal investors in stocks with high-dividend yield, while arbitrage trading is not present with low-yield stocks and before negotiated commissions. Moreover, Karpoff and Walkling (1990) confirm that dividend capture trading plays an important role in dividend puzzle, and the explanation of ex-day returns is more complex than indicated by Elton and Gruber's tax-induced hypothesis. Ex-dividend day returns of stocks with dividend capture reflect arbitrageurs' marginal transaction costs, while those without dividend capture may reflect long-term investors' marginal tax rates.

Supporting evidence for the short-term trading mechanism is mainly from the US market. Boyd and Jagannathan (1994) develop an equilibrium model based on three stylized facts: (1) transaction costs are significant, (2) there are different groups of traders (i.e., taxable individuals, tax-favorable dividend capturing traders, and tax-neutral arbitrageurs) with various transactions costs and/or tax brackets, and (3) high-yield stocks experience dividend capture. They argue that when the price data include a mixture of observations of different traders, the relationship between dividend yield and the ex-dividend price drop is not linear and find supporting evidence of this prediction. Moreover, after eliminating low-dividend observations, they find that the proportion of data points at which short-term trading to capture dividend is appearing to increase. Naranjo et al. (2000) re-examine and extend the study of Eades et al. (1984) by focusing on the inter-temporal behavior of stock returns on the ex-day for high-yield stocks which are potentially attractive to corporate dividend capture. They find that abnormal ex-day returns are, on average, uniformly negative during the years after the launch of negotiable commission rates, and the variation of time in ex-day returns over the negotiable commission rates period is in line with the tax-based dividend capture hypothesis. Returns on ex-days are more negative when the tax advantage to short-term trading is greatest and more positive when transaction costs and risk of dividend capture increase. However, Chowdhury and Sonaer (2016) use large special dividends paid over the period 1960–2012 to examine whether tax clientele or short-term trading is effective in explaining the ex-dividend day price drop. They document that the price drop is lower than the dividend magnitude on the ex-day, and the ex-dividend day returns are positive. There findings show that the tax clientele effect is stronger than the short-term trading effect in explaining this stock behavior.

Furthermore, Castillo and Jakob (2006) investigate the ex-day behavior of stock prices on the major Chilean exchange and find that the price drop is, on average, equal to only 81.5% dividend amount. With the absence of discreteness, they test the dividend clientele effects with five subsamples classified by dividend yield but find no significant relationship between the price drop to dividend ratio and dividend yield. In addition, they use regression analysis to investigate the effect of dividend yield on the price drop ratio and the ex-day abnormal return, but there is no consistent evidence with the tax hypothesis. This is explained that the dividend payment requirement stipulated by the Chilean government makes the dividend clientele effect less prevalent. Consequently, they suggest that transactions costs for short-term traders may ultimately be the friction restricting the price adjustment on the ex-dividend day in Chile. Moreover, Dasilas (2009) find that the data collected from the Athens Stock Exchange over the period from 2000 to 2004 are a good laboratory to investigate the reaction of stock prices on the ex-dividend day due to its special dividend distribution mechanism: (1) dividends are paid annually instead of quarterly or semiannually, (2) according to corporate laws 2190/1920 and 148/1967, the minimum amount of dividend shall be paid from the taxed corporate profits, (3) dividends are exempt from personal taxes over the research period, (4) commission costs are deregulated and tick size is significantly small, and (5) opening stock prices are deducted artificially by the dividend amount on the ex-day. Their results show that stock prices fall less than the dividend amount on the ex-day, and the behavior of both abnormal returns and abnormal trading volume around the ex-dividend day supports the presence of short-term trading. Besides, Haesner and Schanz (2013) investigate stock price behavior on the ex-dividend day in Germany when its tax system switches from a full imputation to a classical system in 2001. While the tax clientele mechanism predicts that the price drop ratio and the trading volume are lower after the reform, they show high trading volume around the ex-day and low value of net dividends.

8.1.3 Microstructure Mechanism

8.1.3.1 Main Arguments

Dubofsky (1992, 1997) proposes the limit order adjustment model to explain ex-dividend day behavior of stock price based on the regulations in the NYSE. If bid and ask prices are constant during intra-ex-day trading and market orders on the ex-dividend day have equal probability to be a buy order or a sell order which is filled at the ask price PA_e or the bid price PB_e on the last cum-dividend day, respectively, then the average closing price on the ex-day P_e is calculated as $(PA_e + PB_e)/2$, and the stock's mean return is as follows:

$$\overline{R} = \frac{\frac{PA_e + PB_e}{2} + D - P_c}{P_c} \tag{8.7}$$

Where P_c is the mean closing price on the cum-dividend day. P_e is the mean closing price on the ex-dividend day. D is the cash dividend paid per share.

In a perfect capital market, the difference between PA_e and PB_e and their corresponding cum-dividend levels are precisely equal to the dividend amount; therefore, R is equal to zero. Nevertheless, stocks are trade at 1/8 increments, but dividend amounts are commonly not multiple increments of eighths. According to Rule 118, all limit buy orders existing on the exchange are compulsorily reduced by the amount of paid dividend. If resulting prices are not equal to a multiple of a tick, prices of limit buy orders will be reduced to the next tick. Meanwhile, limit sell orders are not subject to the price adjustment mechanism. Price adjustment of limit orders leads to less than one price drop to dividend ratio.

Moreover, Frank and Jagannathan (1998) develop a microstructure model to explain ex-day puzzle based on the spread between bid price and ask price. Studying behavior of stock price on ex-days on the Hong Kong stock market which has no taxes on both dividends and capital gains and no market makers until 1993, they find that price drop to dividend ratio is about a half. The mean value of dividend per share is HK $0.12, while that of the price drop on the ex-dividend day is only HK $0.06 per share. To explain this phenomenon, they propose an investor behavior model in which there are two types of prices in the stock market including the price for buying (i.e., ask price) and the price for selling (i.e., bid price). In the bid-ask bounce model, rational investors who have decided to purchase stocks would prefer to conduct their behavior on the ex-day instead of on the last cum-day (i.e., they would rather delay their trading activity by a day) due to costs arising from dividend collection. However, market makers who collect dividends with lower cost buy stocks before the ex-day and resell them on the ex-day. Consequently, most transactions are conducted at the cum-dividend bid price and the ex-dividend ask price. This bid-ask spread implies that the price drop is smaller than the dividend magnitude on the ex-dividend day. Using the data on share prices, dividends, and ex-dividend dates of 351 firms provided by the Pacific Basin Capital Markets Research Center in the period from January 1980 to December 1993, Frank and Jagannathan (1998) find supporting evidence of the bid-ask bounce hypothesis.

In addition, Bali and Hite (1998) posit that stock price behavior on the ex-dividend day is determined by price discreteness since dividends are commonly small. Frank and Jagannathan (1998) develop a simple model of trading activities around the ex-day with the prediction that the price drop tends to be smaller than the dividend amount but greater than or equal to the difference between the dividend amount and one tick. According to the price discreteness hypothesis, if stock prices are restricted to discrete ticks and dividends are continuous, dividend amounts are always rounded down to ticks next to dividends. This adjustment makes ex-day price drops lower than dividend amounts in most cases. If tick size is larger, price drop ratio will be higher. Using data from the American Stock Exchange (AMEX) over the period from July 2nd, 1962 to December 31st, 1994, they find supporting evidence for the price discreteness hypothesis.

8.1.3.2 Empirical Evidence
Efthymiou et al. (2021) re-examine how the limit order adjustment affects stock price on the ex-dividend day in three stock exchanges including NYSE, National Association of Securities Dealers Automated Quotations Stock Market (NAS-DAQ), and AMEX. If the limit order adjustment is effective as suggested by Dubofsky (1992, 1997), the asymmetric limit order adjustment in accordance with the regulations of NYSE and AMEX is enough to generate the ex-day abnormal return. However, analyzing minute-by-minute trade and quote data, they find that the limit order bias has a strong effect on the overnight ex-day return, but later it is considerably eliminated through active trading until the end of the ex-day. In other words, the effect of the opening limit order bias on the ex-day price drop discrepancy is eroded before the ex-day ends. This finding implies that the limit order adjustment is less effective in explaining the ex-day price drop discrepancy.

In addition, Jakob and Ma (2004) conduct direct empirical tests of the price discreteness hypothesis and the limit order adjustment hypothesis with the data from the NYSE between January 1993 and December 2001. The two models are tested with all three tick size regimes during the research period. Five major findings are reported as follows: (1) For the most commonly paid dividends, the likelihood that the price drop in the ex-day is the tick above is just equal to the likelihood that the ex-day price drop is the tick below the dividend, (2) regression results show that the average price drop is different from the tick below the dividend, (3) under three tick size regulations, the average difference in bid price between the cum-day and the ex-day is larger than the average dividend, which is larger than the average difference in ask price between the cum-day and the ex-day, (4) the opening bid-ask bounce is larger on the ex-day than on the cum-day, and (5) there is no significant decrease in the difference between the dividend amount and the average price drop when the tick size is decreased. All of these findings support the price discreteness model and is not consistent with the limit order adjustment model.

Besides, Al Yahyaee et al. (2008) examine the ex-dividend reaction of stock prices in the Oman stock market which is characterized as follows: (1) Either dividends or capital gains are taxable, (2) stock prices are decimalized, (3) dividends are paid annually, and (4) the data are available to investigate the bid-ask bounce hypothesis. Under this institutional environment, lower than one price drop to dividend ratio is not caused by taxes and price discreteness. In line with prior studies, they find that the price drop is smaller than the dividend amount and the ex-day return is significantly positive. However, when they examine the behavior of abnormal trading volume around the ex-day, there is no supporting evidence of the short-term trading hypothesis. Then, they take the market microstructure effect into account, and they find that the ex-dividend price drop is not significantly different from the dividend magnitude. Mortal et al. (2017) show that the price drop to dividend ratio of the NASDAQ is smaller than one and it is also smaller than the ratio of the NYSE. Investigating a group of firms which go voluntarily from the NASDAQ to the NYSE, they document that these firms have higher price drop to dividend ratios after this movement. These findings imply that the market structure is a determinant of stock price behavior on the ex-dividend day. Dupuis (2019) investigates how liquidity affects stock price on the ex-dividend day in a tax-free market without common microstructure impediments and find that abnormal returns still exist. He also shows that liquidity is effective in explaining the ex-day price anomaly.

8.2 Stock Price Reaction to Dividend Announcement

In a corporation, insiders have full information about its operations, but outside investors face information disadvantage. This information asymmetry leads to outsiders' adverse selection and thus reduces economic efficiency. According to the signaling theory, dividend payments are a means to reduce information asymmetry between insiders and outside investors. Dividends signal outsiders about the firm's future prospects. A positive signal increases stock price, while a negative signal reduces stock price. Dividend announcements are considered as a positive signal if dividend payments are up to investors' expectations. Nevertheless, they are considered as a negative signal if dividends decrease.

In a pioneer empirical study conducted in the US market, Pettit (1972) shows that announcements of dividend changes convey valuable information, and thus investors use them to value stocks. Stock prices reflect most information implicit in dividend announcements as of the end of the announcement period. Charest (1978) examines stock returns around announcements of stock splits and dividend changes in the NYSE from 1947 to 1967. He finds that excess returns increase about 1% due to announcements of dividend increases. However, he fails to show whether the effect of dividend announcements is driven by contemporaneous income announcements. Then, Aharony and Swary (1980) separate the effect of earnings announcements and show that dividend announcements still affect abnormal returns. Particularly, dividend increases create about 1% increase in abnormal returns during the announcement period of over 2 days. With a sample of 131 initiators and 972 omitters, Healy and Palepu (1988) examine how dividend initiations and omissions convey information on earnings in the US market from 1969 to 1980. They document that initiators experience earnings increases before and after their dividend initiations, while omitters experience earnings decreases. Subsequent earnings changes have a positive relationship with dividend announcement returns. These findings indicate that outsiders perceive announcements of dividend changes as a real signal of firms' earnings prospects. Consistently, with a sample of dividend announcements from 1971 to 2016, Ham et al. (2020) show that dividend announcement returns are driven by permanent earnings. Moreover, Nguyen (2014) uses a sample of 688 dividend initiators in the United States over the period 1977–2010 to investigate how dividend initiation wave affects stock returns. They document that firms initiating dividends in a dividend initiation wave period have lower announcement returns than those initiating dividends outside the wave period. Besides, the former has better performance than the latter in the long run. Investigating the relationship between dividend payments and price momentum, Asem (2009) finds that losers' positive dividend-maintaining announcements receive investors' under-reaction.

In addition, stock prices' reaction to dividend announcements is also present in other countries and territories. Investigating dividend initiations of initial public offerings (IPOs) in the United Kingdom from 1983 to 1991, McCaffrey and Hamill (2000) document that excess returns are available around the event days. Felimban et al. (2018) use a sample of 1,092 dividend announcements from 299 US firms over the period 2010–2015 to analyze stock price reaction to dividend announcements in the Gulf Cooperation Council market. This is a special environment since taxes on capital gains and dividends fail to exist. They find that stock prices react slowly to announcements of dividend increases while they react significantly to announcements of dividend decreases in the short term. Kumar (2017) posit that the Company's Act 2013 is a good opportunity to investigate the relationship between dividend announcements and stock prices in India since the Act provides firms with more autonomy to declare dividends. With a sample of 4,868 dividend announcements from 2012 to 2014, he documents that announcements of dividend increases (decreases) result in higher (lower) stock prices. Firms without dividend changes have no significant changes in stock prices around the announcement day. Remarkably, excess returns are higher after the issuance of the Act. Besides, Dang et al. (2021) investigate the effect of dividend policy on firm value in Vietnam from 2006 to 2017 and find that dividend payout is positively related to stock prices. By contrast, nonpayers and payers with low payout ratios fail to have significant increases in their stock prices. The significant relationship between dividend announcements and stock prices is also found in Ireland (McCluskey et al., 2006), Cyprus (Travlos et al., 2001), Jordan (Al-Shattarat et al., 2018), India (Anwar et al., 2017; Chatterjee et al., 2021), and Nigeria (Ozo & Arun, 2019).

Moreover, some studies show that the effect of dividend announcements on stock prices relies on market efficiency and exogenous shocks. Rabbani (2017) examines how announcements of dividend changes influence stock prices of firms listed in Bangladesh and finds that firms increasing dividends have positive abnormal stock returns before the announcement period. This finding implies that information on dividend increases may be leaked before they are announced officially. Announcements of dividend decreases lead to negative abnormal returns on the event day and the postevent period. Andres et al. (2013) examine how surprises in dividend announcements influence stock prices since they argue that stock prices only react to these surprises in an efficient market. The dividend surprise is measured by the actual dividend minus the mean analysts' forecast. Using data from German firms between 1996 and 2006, they find that surprises in dividend announcements have a positive effect on cumulative abnormal returns, while announcements of dividend changes have no significant effect. This finding is in line with the signaling mechanism. Prakash and Yogesh (2021) use a sample of 174 dividend announcements in the Bombay Stock Exchange from 2018 to 2021 to investigate whether the COVID-19 pandemic affects the effect of dividend announcements on stock prices in India. They find that the negative relationship between dividend announcements and stock prices is stronger during the COVID-19 pandemic. This can be explained that investors tend to assign high value to dividends when firms face many difficulties in their operations during the crisis period. Dividend payments in the pandemic reflect firms' strong survival and development capabilities.

However, investors may still value stocks based on dividend announcements, although these announcements fail to reflect firms' future prospects. Fukuda (2000) investigates how dividend announcements signal outsiders about firms' quality in Japan from 1990 to 1994. With a sample of 348 dividend changes, he finds that stock prices increase (decrease) when dividend increases (decreases) are declared. However, earnings of dividend-increasing firms only grow before the event years and then decline after the event years. These findings imply that outside investors perceive dividend changes as a signal of firms' future prospects, but corporate managers change their dividends based on their confidence. When managers are overoptimistic (overpessimistic), they tend to announce dividend increases (decreases), and then outsiders believe in their information quality. Moreover, Ho and Wu (2001) re-examine the effects of dividend initiations and omissions on earnings in the United States from 1964 to 1995. Contrary to Healy and Palepu (1988), they find that after firms initiate dividends, their earnings fail to rise significantly and even decline in the next period. This can be explained that survivorship is likely to bias the signaling mechanism.

8.3 Dividend Policy and Stock Price Volatility

8.3.1 Theoretical Arguments

Stock price volatility is defined as fluctuations of stock prices over time due to instability, uncertainty, and risk (Phan & Tran, 2019). According to Baskin (1989), dividend policy theoretically has a negative relationship with stock price volatility through four mechanisms including duration effect, rate of return effect, arbitrage realization effect, and information effect. The first two mechanisms use dividends to measure the effectiveness of cash flow, while the last two mechanisms imply that corporate managers can affect stock price volatility actively.

First, the duration effect reflects how dividend payout or dividend yield reduces stock price volatility through "stock duration". High-dividend yields result in near-term cash flows. Like debt securities, stocks with high-dividend yields have shorter duration if dividend policy remains stable. The value of a short-term security is close to its par value, and thus its price is less affected by discount rates. In other words, prices of high-dividend yield stocks are less sensitive to changes in discount rates.

Second, the rate of return effect implies that firm value is determined mainly through the rate of return instead of the discount rate. Particularly, when firms have low payouts or dividend yields, investors tend to value them through their investment opportunities rather than their assets in place. Consequently, their stock prices are more sensitive to estimated rates of return over distant time periods.

Third, the arbitrage realization effect helps firms with high-dividend yields or payouts face less irrational underpricing. A mispriced stock cannot have excess returns if it fails to pay dividends and have opportunities to achieve its intrinsic under an efficient market. However, when an undervalued stock pays a liquidating dividend during the holding period, it creates a complete arbitragable profit to investors. If the stock has a high-dividend payout or dividend yield, the supranormal profit is more likely to be realized. Therefore, dividend policy reduces stock price volatility.

Finally, information effect is based on the signaling theory. Investors are more likely to consider dividends as an accurate signal of payers' future prospects if earnings announcements are followed by generous payouts. When investors' confidence is high, they value stocks with less irrational actions. In other words, high payout ratios reduce uncertainty in stock valuation and thus lead to lower stock price volatility. This implies that corporate managers can reduce stock price volatility by raising the target payout.

8.3.2 Empirical Evidence

Allen and Rachim (1996) use a sample of 173 firms listed in Australia over the period 1972–1985 to investigate how dividend policy affects stock price fluctuations. They find that there is a negative relationship between dividend payout ratio and stock price volatility, while dividend yield fails to have a significant effect on stock price volatility. Dewasiri and Banda (2015) document similar findings in Sri Lanka. However, Phan and Tran (2019) find a negative association between dividend yield and stock price volatility in the Vietnamese stock market over the period 2008–2015. In Malaysia, Zainudin et al. (2018) show that dividend policy strongly influences the volatility of industrial products' stock prices before and after the global financial crisis.

8.4 Dividend Smoothing and Stock Price

Baker and Farrelly (1988) conduct a survey to examine the behavior of dividend achievers. A firm is considered as a dividend achiever if it has at least 10 consecutive years of dividend increases. They find that dividend achievers mainly focus on dividend smoothing and its effect on stock price. Dividend smoothing is commonly used to reduce information asymmetry, compensate for weak corporate governance, and meet investors' demand (Leary & Michaely, 2011). In addition, dividend smoothing helps investors reduce the present value of their expected income tax liabilities (Rozycki, 1997). Therefore, investors tend to assign high value to firms with high-dividend stability.

Larkin et al. (2016) investigate how investors value firms with dividend stability in the United States from 1970 to 2012. They find that dividend smoothing has a positive effect on stock price, but the effect is little. Dividend smoothing has a strong impact on ownership structure. Dividend smoothing stocks are more attractive to institutional investors than retail investors. Karpavičius (2014) examines dividend smoothing in the United States from 1980 to 2009 and finds that firms with higher dividend stability have higher stock prices. In a cross-country study, Brockman et al. (2022) document that high-smoothing firms have higher values for dividends than low-smoothing firms. Besides, their findings also show that investors tend to increase dividend-smoothing premiums when shareholder rights are poor. This implies that dividend smoothing is a substitute for weak corporate governance. However, investigating the effect of dividend smoothing on firm value of 184 US firms during the period 1972−1977, Stevens and Jose (1992) find an opposite result. They explain that dividends may be artificially smoothed, and investors recognizing this behavior tend to increase the discount rate. Consequently, firm value fails to increase in spite of dividend stability.

References

Abor, J., & Fiador, V. (2013). Does corporate governance explain dividend policy in Sub-Saharan Africa? *International Journal of Law and Management, 55*(3), 201–225.

Adaoglu, C. (2000). Instability in the dividend policy of the Istanbul Stock Exchange (ISE) corporations: Evidence from an emerging market. *Emerging Markets Review, 1*(3), 252–270. https://doi.org/10.1016/S1566-0141(00)00011-X

Adhikari, B. K., & Agrawal, A. (2018). Peer influence on payout policies. *Journal of Corporate Finance, 48*, 615–637. https://doi.org/10.1016/j.jcorpfin.2017.12.010

Adjaoud, F. (1984). The information content of dividends. A Canadian test. *Canadian Journal of Administrative Sciences [Revue Canadienne des Sciences de l'Administration], 1*(2), 338–351. https://doi.org/10.1111/j.1936-4490.1984.tb00295.x

Adjaoud, F., & Ben-Amar, W. (2010). Corporate governance and dividend policy: Shareholders' protection or expropriation? *Journal of Business Finance & Accounting, 37*(5–6), 648–667. https://doi.org/10.1111/j.1468-5957.2010.02192.x

Aggarwal, R., & Goodell, J. W. (2014). Cross-national differences in access to finance: Influence of culture and institutional environments. *Research in International Business and Finance, 31*, 193–211. https://doi.org/10.1016/j.ribaf.2013.09.004

Aharony, J., & Swary, I. (1980). Quarterly dividend and earnings announcements and stockholders' returns: An empirical analysis. *The Journal of Finance, 35*(1), 1–12. https://doi.org/10.1111/j.1540-6261.1980.tb03466.x

Ahmad, M. F., Aziz, S., El-Khatib, R., & Kowalewski, O. (2023). Firm-level political risk and dividend payout. *International Review of Financial Analysis, 86*, 102546. https://doi.org/10.1016/j.irfa.2023.102546

Ahmad, M. F., & Kowalewski, O. (2021). Collective bargaining power and corporate cash policy. *International Review of Law and Economics, 68*, 106007. https://doi.org/10.1016/j.irle.2021.106007

Ahmed, H., & Javid, A. (2009). Dynamics and determinants of dividend policy in Pakistan (Evidence from Karachi stock exchange non-financial listed firms). *International Research Journal of Finance and Economics, 1*(25), 148–171.

Ain, Q. U., Yuan, X., Javaid, H. M., Zhao, J., & Xiang, L. (2021). Board gender diversity and dividend policy in Chinese listed firms. *Sage Open, 11*(1). https://doi.org/10.1177/2158244021997807

Ainsworth, A., Fong, K. Y., Gallagher, D. R., & Partington, G. (2016). Institutional trading around the ex-dividend day. *Australian Journal of Management, 41*(2), 299–323.

Ainsworth, A. B., Fong, K. Y. L., Gallagher, D. R., & Partington, G. (2018). Taxes, order imbalance and abnormal returns around the ex-dividend day. *International Review of Finance, 18*(3), 379–409. https://doi.org/10.1111/irfi.12155

Ainsworth, A., & Lee, A. D. (2023). Sharing the dividend tax credit pie: The influence of individual investors on ex-dividend day returns. *Journal of Financial Markets, 62*, 100740. https://doi.org/10.1016/j.finmar.2022.100740

Ainsworth, A., Lee, A. D., & Walter, T. (2020). Can firm-specific dividend drop-off ratios be used to infer shareholder marginal tax rates? *Accounting and Finance*, *60*(1), 507–534. https://doi.org/10.1111/acfi.12322

Aivazian, V., Booth, L., & Cleary, S. (2003). Do emerging market firms follow different dividend policies from U.S. firms? *Journal of Financial Research*, *26*(3), 371–387. https://doi.org/10.1111/1475-6803.00064

Akerlof, G. A. (1970). The market for 'lemons': Quality uncertainty and the market mechanism. *Quarterly Journal of Economics*, *84*(3), 488–500.

Akindayomi, A., & Amin, M. R. (2022). Does business strategy affect dividend payout policies? *Journal of Business Research*, *151*, 531–550. https://doi.org/10.1016/j.jbusres.2022.07.028

Al Shabibi, B. K., & Ramesh, G. (2011). An empirical study on the determinants of dividend policy in the UK. *International Research Journal of Finance & Economics*, *80*, 105–120.

Al Yahyaee, K., Pham, T., & Walter, T. (2008). Ex-dividend day behavior in the absence of taxes and price discreteness. *International Review of Finance*, *8*(3–4), 103–123. https://doi.org/10.1111/j.1468-2443.2008.00078.x

Al-Malkawi, H.-A. N. (2007). Determinants of corporate dividend policy in Jordan: An application of the tobit model. *Journal of Economic and Administrative Sciences*, *23*(2), 26. https://doi.org/10.1108/10264116200700007

Al-Najjar, B. (2009). Dividend behaviour and smoothing new evidence from Jordanian panel data. *Studies in Economics and Finance*, *26*(3), 182–197. https://doi.org/10.1108/10867370910974017

Al-Najjar, B., & Hussainey, K. (2009). The association between dividend payout and outside directorships. *Journal of Applied Accounting Research*, *10*(1), 15. https://doi.org/10.1108/09675420910963360

Al-Najjar, B., & Kilincarslan, E. (2016). The effect of ownership structure on dividend policy: Evidence from Turkey. *Corporate Governance: The International Journal of Business in Society*, *16*(1), 135–161. https://doi.org/10.1108/CG-09-2015-0129

Al-Shattarat, W. K., Al-Shattarat, B. K., & Hamed, R. (2018). Do dividends announcements signal future earnings changes for Jordanian firms? *Journal of Financial Reporting & Accounting*, *16*(3), 417–442. https://doi.org/10.1108/JFRA-03-2017-0021

Albouy, M., Bah, R., Bonnet, C., & Thévenin, D. (2012). The perception of dividends by managers: Do French CFOs differ from their North-American peers? *Bankers, Markets & Investors*, *116*, 52–64.

Ali, H. (2022). Corporate dividend policy in the time of COVID-19: Evidence from the G-12 countries. *Finance Research Letters*, *46*, 102493. https://doi.org/10.1016/j.frl.2021.102493

Ali, Z., Ullah, A., & Ali, A. (2019). Board structure and dividend smoothing: A case of Pakistani listed firms. *IBA Business Review*, *14*(2).

Alimov, A. (2014). Product market competition and the value of corporate cash: Evidence from trade liberalization. *Journal of Corporate Finance*, *25*(0), 122–139. https://doi.org/10.1016/j.jcorpfin.2013.11.011

Allen, L., Gottesman, A., Saunders, A., & Tang, Y. (2012). The role of banks in dividend policy. *Financial Management*, *41*(3), 591–613. https://doi.org/10.1111/j.1755-053X.2012.01207.x

Allen, F., & Michaely, R. (1995). Chapter 25 dividend policy. In V. M. R. A. Jarrow & W. T. Ziemba (Eds.), *Handbooks in operations research and management science* (Vol. 9, pp. 793–837). Elsevier.

Allen, D. E., & Rachim, V. S. (1996). Dividend policy and stock price volatility: Australian evidence. *Applied Financial Economics, 6*(2), 175–188.

Alli, K. L., Khan, A. Q., & Ramirez, G. G. (1993). Determinants of corporate dividend policy: A factorial analysis. *Financial Review, 28*(4), 523–547. https://doi.org/10.1111/j.1540-6288.1993.tb01361.x

Almeida, H., Campello, M., & Weisbach, M. S. (2004). The cash flow sensitivity of cash. *The Journal of Finance, 59*(4), 1777–1804.

Ambarish, R., John, K., & Williams, J. (1987). Efficient signaling with dividends and investments. *The Journal of Finance, 42*(2), 321–343.

Amidu, M., & Abor, J. (2006). Determinants of dividend payout ratios in Ghana. *The Journal of Risk Finance, 7*(2), 136–145. https://doi.org/10.1108/15255940610648580

Amihud, Y., & Lev, B. (1981). Risk reduction as a managerial motive for conglomerate mergers. *The Bell Journal of Economics*, 605–617.

Andres, C., Betzer, A., van den Bongard, I., Haesner, C., & Theissen, E. (2013). The information content of dividend surprises: Evidence from Germany. *Journal of Business Finance & Accounting, 40*(5–6), 620–645. https://doi.org/10.1111/jbfa.12036

Ang, J. S., Cole, R. A., & Lin, J. W. (2000). Agency costs and ownership structure. *The Journal of Finance, 55*(1), 81–106. https://doi.org/10.1111/0022-1082.00201

Anwar, S., Singh, S., & Jain, P. (2017). Impact of cash dividend announcements: Evidence from the Indian manufacturing companies. *Journal of Emerging Market Finance, 16*(1), 29–60.

Arora, R. K., & Srivastava, A. (2019). Ownership concentration and dividend payout in emerging markets: Evidence from India. *Global Business Review, 22*(5), 1276–1288. https://doi.org/10.1177/0972150918824953

Arslan, Ö., Florackis, C., & Ozkan, A. (2006). The role of cash holdings in reducing investment–Cash flow sensitivity: Evidence from a financial crisis period in an emerging market. *Emerging Markets Review, 7*(4), 320–338. https://doi.org/10.1016/j.ememar.2006.09.003

Asem, E. (2009). Dividends and price momentum. *Journal of Banking & Finance, 33*(3), 486–494. https://doi.org/10.1016/j.jbankfin.2008.09.004

Ashraf, B. N., Bibi, B., & Zheng, C. (2016). How to regulate bank dividends? Is capital regulation an answer? *Economic Modelling, 57*, 281–293. https://doi.org/10.1016/j.econmod.2016.05.005

Asimakopoulos, P., Lambrinoudakis, C., Tsangarakis, N., & Tsiritakis, E. D. (2007). Signaling with mandatory dividends: The case of the Greek stock market. SSRN 984445.

Asquith, P., & Mullins, D. W. Jr. (1983). The impact of initiating dividend payments on shareholders' wealth. *Journal of Business, 56*(1), 77–96.

Attig, N., Boubakri, N., El Ghoul, S., & Guedhami, O. (2016). The global financial crisis, family control, and dividend policy. *Financial Management, 45*(2), 291–313. https://doi.org/10.1111/fima.12115

Attig, N., El Ghoul, S., Guedhami, O., & Zheng, X. (2018). Dividends and economic policy uncertainty: International evidence. SSRN 3295228.

Baba, N. (2009). Increased presence of foreign investors and dividend policy of Japanese firms. *Pacific-Basin Finance Journal, 17*(2), 163–174. https://doi.org/10.1016/j.pacfin.2008.04.001

Babar, M., & Habib, A. (2021). Product market competition in accounting, finance, and corporate governance: A review of the literature. *International Review of Financial Analysis, 73*, 101607. https://doi.org/10.1016/j.irfa.2020.101607

Badru, B. O., & Qasem, A. (2021). Corporate social responsibility and dividend payments in the Malaysian capital market: The interacting effect of family-controlled companies. *Journal of Sustainable Finance & Investment*, 1–24. https://doi.org/10.1080/20430795.2021.1979926

Bae, S. C., Chang, K., & Kang, E. (2012). Culture, corporate governance, and dividend policy: International evidence. *Journal of Financial Research, 35*(2), 289–316. https://doi.org/10.1111/j.1475-6803.2012.01318.x

Baker, H. K. (2009). *Dividends and dividend policy*. John Wiley.

Baker, H. K., & Farrelly, G. E. (1988). Dividend achievers: A behavioral look. *Akron Business & Economic Review, 19*(1), 79–92.

Baker, H. K., Farrelly, G. E., & Edelman, R. B. (1985/1972). A survey of management views on dividend policy. *Financial Management, 14*(3), 78–84.

Baker, H. K., Kapoor, S., & Jabbouri, I. (2018). Institutional perspectives of dividend policy in India. *Qualitative Research in Financial Markets, 10*(3), 324–342. https://doi.org/10.1108/QRFM-07-2017-0067

Baker, H. K., Mukherjee, T. K., & Paskelian, O. G. (2006). How Norwegian managers view dividend policy. *Global Finance Journal, 17*(1), 155–176. https://doi.org/10.1016/j.gfj.2006.06.005

Baker, H. K., & Powell, G. E. (1999). How corporate managers view dividend policy. *Quarterly Journal of Business & Economics, 38*(2), 17.

Baker, H. K., & Powell, G. E. (2000). Determinants of corporate dividend policy: A survey of NYSE firms. *Financial Practice & Education, 10*(1), 29–40.

Baker, H. K., Powell, G. E., & Veit, E. T. (2001). Factors influencing dividend policy decisions of Nasdaq firms. *Financial Review, 36*(3), 19.

Baker, H. K., Saadi, S., Dutta, S., & Gandhi, D. (2007). The perception of dividends by Canadian managers: New survey evidence. *International Journal of Managerial Finance, 3*(1), 70–91. https://doi.org/10.1108/17439130710721662

Baker, M., Nagel, S., & Wurgler, J. (2006). The effect of dividends on consumption. National Bureau of Economic Research Cambridge, MA, USA.

Baker, M., & Stein, J. C. (2004). Market liquidity as a sentiment indicator. *Journal of Financial Markets, 7*(3), 271–299. https://doi.org/10.1016/j.finmar.2003.11.005

Baker, M., & Wurgler, J. (2004a). Appearing and disappearing dividends: The link to catering incentives. *Journal of Financial Economics, 73*(2), 271–288. https://doi.org/10.1016/j.jfineco.2003.08.001

Baker, M., & Wurgler, J. (2004b). A catering theory of dividends. *The Journal of Finance, 59*(3), 1125–1165. https://doi.org/10.1111/j.1540-6261.2004.00658.x

Balachandran, B., Khan, A., Mather, P., & Theobald, M. (2019). Insider ownership and dividend policy in an imputation tax environment. *Journal of Corporate Finance, 54*, 153–167. https://doi.org/10.1016/j.jcorpfin.2017.01.014

Balachandran, B., & Nguyen, J. H. (2018). Does carbon risk matter in firm dividend policy? Evidence from a quasi-natural experiment in an imputation environment.

Journal of Banking & Finance, 96, 249–267. https://doi.org/10.1016/j.jban kfin.2018.09.015

Bali, R., & Hite, G. L. (1998). Ex dividend day stock price behavior: Discreteness or tax-induced clienteles? *Journal of Financial Economics, 47*(2), 127–159. https://doi.org/10.1016/S0304-405X(97)00041-X

Bancel, F., Bhattacharyya, N., Mittoo, U. R., & Baker, H. K. (2009). Cross-country determinants of payout policy: European firms. In *Dividends and dividend policy* (pp. 71–93). John Wiley & Sons, Inc.

Banerjee, S., Dasgupta, S., & Kim, Y. (2008). Buyer–supplier relationships and the stakeholder theory of capital structure. *The Journal of Finance, 63*(5), 2507–2552. https://doi.org/10.1111/j.1540-6261.2008.01403.x

Banerjee, S., Gatchev, V. A., & Spindt, P. A. (2007). Stock market liquidity and firm dividend policy. *Journal of Financial and Quantitative Analysis, 42*(2), 369–397. https://doi.org/10.1017/S0022109000003318

Barclay, M. J. (1987). Dividends, taxes, and common stock prices: The ex-dividend day behavior of common stock prices before the income tax. *Journal of Financial Economics, 19*(1), 31–44. https://doi.org/10.1016/0304-405X(87)90027-4

Baskin, J. (1989). Dividend policy and the volatility of common stocks. *Journal of Portfolio Management, 15*(3), 19.

Basse, T., Gruppe, M., Reddemann, S., & Schwope, F. (2011). Dividend policy issues in the financial crisis: The example of the German automotive industry. *International Journal of Applied Decision Sciences, 4*(3), 247–259. https://doi.org/10.1504/IJADS.2011.040881

Basse, T., & Reddemann, S. (2011). Inflation and the dividend policy of US firms. *Managerial Finance, 37*(1), 34–46. https://doi.org/10.1108/03074351111092139

Bataineh, H. (2021). The impact of ownership structure on dividend policy of listed firms in Jordan. *Cogent Business & Management, 8*(1), 1863175. https://doi.org/10.1080/23311975.2020.1863175

Bates, T. W., Kahle, K. M., & Stulz, R. M. (2009). Why do US firms hold so much more cash than they used to? *The Journal of Finance, 64*(5), 1985–2021.

Baxamusa, M., & Jalal, A. (2014). The effects of corruption on capital structure: When does it matter? *The Journal of Developing Areas, 48*(1), 315–335.

Bebczuk, R. N. (2005). Corporate governance and ownership: Measurement and impact on corporate performance and dividend policies in Argentina. https://www.depeco.econo.unlp.edu.ar/doctrab/doc59.pdf

Bekaert, G., Harvey, C. R., Lundblad, C. T., & Siegel, S. (2011). What segments equity markets? *Review of Financial Studies, 24*(12), 3841–3890. https://doi.org/10.1093/rfs/hhr082

Ben-Nasr, H., & Ghouma, H. H. (2022). Dividend policy and religion: International evidence from firms with Islamic Label. *Emerging Markets Review, 50*, 100840. https://doi.org/10.1016/j.ememar.2021.100840

Benartzi, S., Michaely, R., & Thaler, R. (1997). Do changes in dividends signal the future or the past? *The Journal of Finance, 52*(3), 1007–1034.

Benjamin, S. J., & Biswas, P. (2019). Board gender composition, dividend policy and COD: The implications of CEO duality. *Accounting Research Journal, 32*(3), 454–476. https://doi.org/10.1108/ARJ-02-2018-0035

Benlemlih, M. (2019). Corporate social responsibility and dividend policy. *Research in International Business and Finance, 47*, 114–138. https://doi.org/10.1016/j.ribaf.2018.07.005

Berle, A. A., & Means, G. C. (1932). *The modern corporation and private property.* The Macmillan Company.

Bernanke, B. S. (1983). Irreversibility, uncertainty, and cyclical investment. *Quarterly Journal of Economics, 98*(1), 85–106. https://doi.org/10.2307/1885568

Bertrand, M., & Mullainathan, S. (2003). Enjoying the quiet life? Corporate governance and managerial preferences. *Journal of Political Economy, 111*(5), 1043–1075. https://doi.org/10.1086/376950

Bhabra, G. S., Jeong, J., & Powell, J. G. (2002). Dividend smoothing and the cross-sectional determinants of corporate payout policy. In M. Hirschey, K. John, & A. K. Makhija (Eds.), *Innovations in investments and corporate finance* (Vol. 7, pp. 163–183). Emerald Publishing Limited.

Bhattacharya, S. (1979). Imperfect information, dividend policy, and "the bird in the hand" fallacy. *The Bell Journal of Economics, 10*(1), 259–270. https://doi.org/10.2307/3003330

Black, F. (1976). The dividend puzzle. *Journal of Portfolio Management, 2*(2), 5–8.

Black, F., & Scholes, M. (1974). The effects of dividend yield and dividend policy on common stock prices and returns. *Journal of Financial Economics, 1*(1), 1–22. https://doi.org/10.1016/0304-405X(74)90006-3

Block, J. H. (2012). R&D investments in family and founder firms: An agency perspective. *Journal of Business Venturing, 27*(2), 248–265. https://doi.org/10.1016/j.jbusvent.2010.09.003

Bogolebska, J. (2023). Catering theory of dividend policy in Polish listed companies. *European Research Studies Journal, 26*(2), 197–208.

Bolster, P. J., & Janjigian, V. (1991). Dividend policy and valuation effects of the Tax Reform Act of 1986. *National Tax Journal, 44*(4), 511–518. https://doi.org/10.2307/41788937

Bolton, P., & Scharfstein, D. S. (1990). A theory of predation based on agency problems in financial contracting. *The American Economic Review, 80*(1), 93–106. https://www.jstor.org/stable/2006736

Booth, L. D., & Johnston, D. J. (1984). The ex-dividend day behavior of Canadian stock prices: Tax changes and clientele effects. *The Journal of Finance, 39*(2), 457–476.

Booth, L., & Zhou, J. (2015). Market power and dividend policy. *Managerial Finance, 41*(2), 145–163. https://doi.org/10.1108/MF-12-2013-0346

Borokhovich, K. A., Brunarski, K. R., Harman, Y., & Kehr, J. B. (2005). Dividends, corporate monitors and agency costs. *Financial Review, 40*(1), 37–65. https://doi.org/10.1111/j.0732-8516.2005.00092.x

Boshnak, H. A. (2021). The impact of board composition and ownership structure on dividend payout policy: Evidence from Saudi Arabia. *International Journal of Emerging Markets. ahead-of-print*(ahead-of-print). https://doi.org/10.1108/IJOEM-05-2021-0791

Boyd, J. H., & Jagannathan, R. (1994). Ex-dividend price behavior of common stocks. *Review of Financial Studies, 7*(4).

Brav, A., Graham, J. R., Harvey, C. R., & Michaely, R. (2005). Payout policy in the 21st century. *Journal of Financial Economics, 77*(3), 483–527. https://doi.org/10.1016/j.jfineco.2004.07.004

Bremberger, F., Cambini, C., Gugler, K., & Rondi, L. (2016). Dividend policy in regulated network industries: Evidence from the EU. *Economic Inquiry, 54*(1), 408–432. https://doi.org/10.1111/ecin.12238

Brennan, M. (1970). Tax reform and the stock market: An asset price approach. *The American Economic Review, 23*(4), 417–427.

Brennan, M. J., & Thakor, A. V. (1990). Shareholder preferences and dividend policy. *The Journal of Finance, 45*(4), 993–1018. https://doi.org/10.1111/j.1540-6261.1990.tb02424.x

Brockman, P., Hanousek, J., Tresl, J., & Unlu, E. (2022). Dividend smoothing and firm valuation. *Journal of Financial and Quantitative Analysis, 57*(4), 1621–1647. https://doi.org/10.1017/S0022109021000673

Brockman, P., Tresl, J., & Unlu, E. (2014). The impact of insider trading laws on dividend payout policy. *Journal of Corporate Finance, 29*(0), 263–287. https://doi.org/10.1016/j.jcorpfin.2014.09.002

Brockman, P., & Unlu, E. (2009). Dividend policy, creditor rights, and the agency costs of debt. *Journal of Financial Economics, 92*(2), 276–299. https://doi.org/10.1016/j.jfineco.2008.03.007

Bronars, S. G., & Deere, D. R. (1991). The threat of unionization, the use of debt, and the preservation of shareholder wealth. *Quarterly Journal of Economics, 106*(1), 231–254. https://doi.org/10.2307/2937914

Brown, W. O., Helland, E., & Smith, J. K. (2006). Corporate philanthropic practices. *Journal of Corporate Finance, 12*(5), 855–877. https://doi.org/10.1016/j.jcorpfin.2006.02.001

Buchanan, B. G., Cao, C. X., Liljeblom, E., & Weihrich, S. (2017). Uncertainty and firm dividend policy – A natural experiment. *Journal of Corporate Finance, 42*, 179–197. https://doi.org/10.1016/j.jcorpfin.2016.11.008

Bulan, L., & Hull, T. (2013). The impact of technical defaults on dividend policy. *Journal of Banking & Finance, 37*(3), 814–823. https://doi.org/10.1016/j.jbankfin.2012.10.014

Byrne, J., & O'Connor, T. (2017). Creditor rights, culture and dividend payout policy. *Journal of Multinational Financial Management, 39*, 60–77. https://doi.org/10.1016/j.mulfin.2016.12.002

Caliskan, D., & Doukas, J. A. (2015). CEO risk preferences and dividend policy decisions. *Journal of Corporate Finance, 35*, 18–42. https://doi.org/10.1016/j.jcorpfin.2015.08.007

Campello, M., Graham, J. R., & Harvey, C. R. (2010). The real effects of financial constraints: Evidence from a financial crisis. *Journal of Financial Economics, 97*(3), 470–487. https://doi.org/10.1016/j.jfineco.2010.02.009

Cao, C., Jia, F., Zhang, X., & Chan, K. C. (2016). Does religion matter to dividend policy? Evidence from Buddhism and Taoism in China. *Nankai Business Review International, 7*(4), 510–541. https://doi.org/10.1108/NBRI-12-2015-0033

Cao, L., Du, Y., & Hansen, J. Ø. (2017). Foreign institutional investors and dividend policy: Evidence from China. *International Business Review, 26*(5), 816–827.

Cao, Z., Chen, S. X., Harakeh, M., & Lee, E. (2022). Do non-financial factors influence corporate dividend policies? Evidence from business strategy.

International Review of Financial Analysis, *82*, 102211. https://doi.org/10.1016/j.irfa.2022.102211

Capaul, M. (2003). *Corporate governance in Latin America*. Whither Latin American Capital Markets.

Casey, K. M., & Dickens, R. N. (2000). The effects of tax and regulatory changes on commercial bank dividend policy. *The Quarterly Review of Economics and Finance*, *40*(2), 279–293. https://doi.org/10.1016/S1062-9769(99)00051-4

Castillo, A., & Jakob, K. (2006). The Chilean ex-dividend day. *Global Finance Journal*, *17*(1), 105–118. https://doi.org/10.1016/j.gfj.2006.06.002

Cejnek, G., Randl, O., & Zechner, J. (2021). The COVID-19 pandemic and corporate dividend policy. *Journal of Financial and Quantitative Analysis*, *56*(7), 2389–2410. https://doi.org/10.1017/S0022109021000533

Chang, M., Chang, B., & Dutta, S. (2020). National culture, firm characteristics, and dividend policy. *Emerging Markets Finance and Trade*, *56*(1), 149–163. https://doi.org/10.1080/1540496X.2019.1627518

Chang, K., Kang, E., & Li, Y. (2016). Effect of institutional ownership on dividends: An agency-theory-based analysis. *Journal of Business Research*, *69*(7), 2551–2559. https://doi.org/10.1016/j.jbusres.2015.10.088

Chang, R. P., & Rhee, S. G. (1990). The impact of personal taxes on corporate dividend policy and capital structure decisions. *FM: The Journal of the Financial Management Association*, *19*(2), 21–31.

Chapple, L., Clarkson, P. M., & Gold, D. L. (2013). The cost of carbon: Capital market effects of the proposed emission trading scheme (ETS). *Abacus*, *49*(1), 1–33. https://doi.org/10.1111/abac.12006

Charest, G. (1978). Dividend information, stock returns and market efficiency-II. *Journal of Financial Economics*, *6*(2), 297–330. https://doi.org/10.1016/0304-405X(78)90033-8

Chasiotis, I., Georgakopoulos, G., Konstantios, D., & Toudas, K. (2022). Climate risk and corporate dividend smoothing: Some international evidence. SSRN 4280214. https://ssrn.com/abstract=4280214

Chateau, J.-P. D. (1979). Dividend policy revisted: Within - and out -of-sample tests. *Journal of Business Finance & Accounting*, *6*(3), 355–370. https://doi.org/10.1111/j.1468-5957.1979.tb01097.x

Chatterjee, C., Dutta, P., & Basu, S. (2021). Evidence-based stock price behaviour around cash dividend announcements on an emerging market set-up. *Global Business Review*. https://doi.org/10.1177/09721509211052126

Cheibub, J. A., & Przeworski, A. (1999). Democracy, elections, and accountability for economic outcomes. *Democracy, Accountability, and Representation*, *2*, 222–250.

Chemmanur, T. J., He, J., Hu, G., & Liu, H. (2010). Is dividend smoothing universal?: New insights from a comparative study of dividend policies in Hong Kong and the U.S. *Journal of Corporate Finance*, *16*(4), 413–430. https://doi.org/10.1016/j.jcorpfin.2010.03.001

Chen, Z., Cheung, Y.-L., Stouraitis, A., & Wong, A. W. S. (2005). Ownership concentration, firm performance, and dividend policy in Hong Kong. *Pacific-Basin Finance Journal*, *13*(4), 431–449. https://doi.org/10.1016/j.pacfin.2004.12.001

Chen, X., Chih-Chieh Chris, H., Tsang, A., & Xiang, Y. (2022). Cross-border enforcement of securities laws and dividend payouts. *The British Accounting Review*, *54*(6), 101117. https://doi.org/10.1016/j.bar.2022.101117

Chen, H.-L., Chow, E. H., & Shiu, C.-Y. (2013). Ex-dividend prices and investor trades: Evidence from Taiwan. *Pacific-Basin Finance Journal*, *24*(0), 39–65. https://doi.org/10.1016/j.pacfin.2013.02.004

Chen, J., & Dhiensiri, N. (2009). Determinants of dividend policy: The evidence from New Zealand. *International Research Journal of Finance and Economics*, *34*, 18–28.

Chen, J., Leung, W. S., & Goergen, M. (2017). The impact of board gender composition on dividend payouts. *Journal of Corporate Finance*, *43*, 86–105. https://doi.org/10.1016/j.jcorpfin.2017.01.001

Chen, L. H., & Silva Gao, L. (2012). The pricing of climate risk. *Journal of Financial and Economic Practice*, *12*, 115–131.

Chen, C., & Wu, C. (1999). The dynamics of dividends, earnings and prices: Evidence and implications for dividend smoothing and signaling. *Journal of Empirical Finance*, *6*(1), 29–58. https://doi.org/10.1016/S0927-5398(98)00008-5

Chen, M., Xie, J., & Li, Y. (2022). Heterogeneity of dividend smoothing: A strategic response to peer competition in China. *Pacific-Basin Finance Journal*, *76*, 101874. https://doi.org/10.1016/j.pacfin.2022.101874

Chen, N., & Yang, T.-C. (2017). Democracy, rule of law, and corporate governance – A liquidity perspective. *Economics of Governance*, *18*(1), 35–70. https://doi.org/10.1007/s10101-016-0182-4

Cheung, A., Hu, M., & Schwiebert, J. (2018). Corporate social responsibility and dividend policy. *Accounting and Finance*, *58*(3), 787–816. https://doi.org/10.1111/acfi.12238

Chintrakarn, P., Chatjuthamard, P., Jiraporn, P., & Kim, Y. S. (2019). Exploring the causal effect of religious piety on dividend policy: Evidence from historical religious identification. *Applied Economics Letters*, *26*(4), 306–310. https://doi.org/10.1080/13504851.2018.1467550

Choi, W., Chung, C. Y., & Wang, K. (2022). Firm-level political risk and corporate investment. *Finance Research Letters*, *46*, 102307. https://doi.org/10.1016/j.frl.2021.102307

Choi, J.-H., & Wong, T. J. (2007). Auditors' governance functions and legal environments: An international investigation. *Contemporary Accounting Research*, *24*(1), 13–46. https://doi.org/10.1506/X478-1075-4PW5-1501

Chonko, L. B., & Hunt, S. D. (1985). Ethics and marketing management: An empirical examination. *Journal of Business Research*, *13*(4), 339–359.

Chowdhury, J., & Sonaer, G. (2016). Ex-dividend day abnormal returns for special dividends. *Journal of Economics and Finance*, *40*(4), 631–652. https://doi.org/10.1007/s12197-015-9317-7

Cohen, D. V., & Nelson, K. A. (1992). *Multinational ethics programs: Cases in corporate practice.*

Coleman, J. S. (1988). Social capital in the creation of human capital. *American Journal of Sociology*, *94*, S95–S120. https://doi.org/10.1086/228943

Cong, L. W., Gao, H., Ponticelli, J., & Yang, X. (2018). *Credit allocation under economic stimulus: Evidence from China.* Buffett Institute Global Poverty Research Lab Working Paper (17-108).

Correia da Silva, L., Goergen, M., & Renneboog, L. (2004). *Dividend policy and corporate governance* (p. 325). Connect to electronic book (University of Melbourne only). https://doi.org.ezp.lib.unimelb.edu.au/10.1093/01992593 05.001.0001

Crane, A. D., Michenaud, S., & Weston, J. P. (2016). The effect of institutional ownership on payout policy: Evidence from index thresholds. *Review of Financial Studies, 29*(6), 1377–1408. https://doi.org/10.1093/rfs/hhw012

Cremers, K. J. M., Nair, V. B., & Peyer, U. (2008). Takeover defenses and competition: The role of stakeholders. *Journal of Empirical Legal Studies, 5*(4), 791–818. https://doi.org/10.1111/j.1740-1461.2008.00141.x

Cullinan, C. P., & Bline, D. M. (2003). The effects of labour on accounting choice in Canada. *Canadian Accounting Perspectives, 2*(2), 135–151. https://doi.org/10.1506/J0YC-861K-YV60-M5VA

D'Souza, J., Jacob, J., & Ramesh, K. (2000). The use of accounting flexibility to reduce labor renegotiation costs and manage earnings. *Journal of Accounting and Economics, 30*(2), 187–208. https://doi.org/10.1016/S0165-4101(01)00004-0

Dahl, O. (2000). The grammar of future time reference in European languages. *Empirical Approaches to Language Typology, 6*, 309–328.

Dang, H. N., Vu, V. T. T., Ngo, X. T., & Hoang, H. T. V. (2021). Impact of dividend policy on corporate value: Experiment in Vietnam. *International Journal of Finance & Economics, 26*(4), 5815–5825. https://doi.org/10.1002/ijfe.2095

Das, S. (2017). Firm characteristics and dividend policy in India. *Transnational Corporations Review, 9*(3), 190–200. https://doi.org/10.1080/19186444.20 17.1362862

Dasgupta, S., & Sengupta, K. (1993). Sunk investment, bargaining and choice of capital structure. *International Economic Review, 34*(1), 203–220. https://doi.org/10.2307/2526957

Dasilas, A. (2009). The ex-dividend day stock price anomaly: Evidence from the Greek stock market. *Financial Markets and Portfolio Management, 23*(1), 59–91. https://doi.org/10.1007/s11408-008-0094-6

Dasilas, A., & Leventis, S. (2011). Stock market reaction to dividend announcements: Evidence from the Greek stock market. *International Review of Economics & Finance, 20*(2), 302–311. https://doi.org/10.1016/j.iref.2010.06.003

Daunfeldt, S.-O., Selander, C., & Wikström, M. (2009). Taxation, dividend payments and ex-day price-changes. *Multinational Finance Journal, 13*(1/2), 141–160.

Davaadorj, Z. (2019). Does social capital affect dividend policy? *Journal of Behavioral and Experimental Finance, 22*, 116–128. https://doi.org/10.1016/j.jbef.2019.02.010

De Tocqueville, A. (1988/1840). *Democracy in America* (Trans. George Lawrence). Harper Perennial.

DeAngelo, H., & DeAngelo, L. (1990). Dividend policy and financial distress: An empirical investigation of troubled NYSE firms. *The Journal of Finance, 45*(5), 1415–1431.

DeAngelo, H., & DeAngelo, L. (1991). Union negotiations and corporate policy: A study of labor concessions in the domestic steel industry during the 1980s. *Journal of Financial Economics, 30*(1), 3–43. https://doi.org/10.1016/0304-405X(91)90021-B

DeAngelo, H., & DeAngelo, L. (2006). The irrelevance of the MM dividend irrelevance theorem. *Journal of Financial Economics, 79*(2), 293–315. https://doi.org/10.1016/j.jfineco.2005.03.003

DeAngelo, H., DeAngelo, L., & Skinner, D. J. (1996). Reversal of fortune dividend signaling and the disappearance of sustained earnings growth. *Journal of Financial Economics, 40*(3), 341–371. https://doi.org/10.1016/0304-405X(95)00850-E

DeAngelo, H., DeAngelo, L., & Stulz, R. M. (2006). Dividend policy and the earned/ contributed capital mix: A test of the life-cycle theory. *Journal of Financial Economics, 81*(2), 227–254. https://doi.org/10.1016/j.jfineco.2005.07.005

Delis, M. D., Hasan, I., & Ongena, S. (2020). Democracy and credit. *Journal of Financial Economics, 136*(2), 571–596. https://doi.org/10.1016/j.jfineco.2019.09.013

DeMarzo, P., & Sannikov, Y. (2008). *Learning in dynamic incentive contracts* (pp. 867–876). Mimeo, Stanford University.

Denis, D. J., & Osobov, I. (2008). Why do firms pay dividends? International evidence on the determinants of dividend policy. *Journal of Financial Economics, 89*(1), 62–82. https://doi.org/10.1016/j.jfineco.2007.06.006

Deshmukh, S., Goel, A. M., & Howe, K. M. (2013). CEO overconfidence and dividend policy. *Journal of Financial Intermediation, 22*(3), 440–463. https://doi.org/10.1016/j.jfi.2013.02.003

Dewasiri, N. J., & Abeysekera, N. (2022). Corporate social responsibility and dividend policy in Sri Lankan firms: A data triangulation approach. *Journal of Public Affairs, 22*(1), e2283. https://doi.org/10.1002/pa.2283

Dewasiri, N., & Banda, Y. W. (2015). Dividend policy and stock price volatility: An error corrected approach. *Asia-Pacific Journal of Management Research and Innovation, 11*(3), 165–171.

Dewenter, K. L., & Warther, V. A. (1998). Dividends, asymmetric information, and agency conflicts: Evidence from a comparison of the dividend policies of Japanese and U.S. firms. *The Journal of Finance, 53*(3), 879–904. https://www.scopus.com/inward/record.url?eid=2-s2.0-0038371974&partnerID=40&md5=62419df15133ce d2ef061346577f40dd

Ding, C., Ho, C. Y., & Chang, M. (2021). CEO and CFO equity compensation and dividend payout over the firm lifecycle. *Global Finance Journal, 49*, 100562. https://doi.org/10.1016/j.gfj.2020.100562

Dinh Nguyen, D., To, T. H., Nguyen, D. V., & Phuong Do, H. (2021). Managerial overconfidence and dividend policy in Vietnamese enterprises. *Cogent Economics & Finance, 9*(1), 1885195. https://doi.org/10.1080/23322039.2021.1885195

Dong, B., Chen, Y., & Fan, C. (2022). Local corruption and dividend policy: Evidence from China. *Finance Research Letters, 47*, 102698. https://doi.org/10.1016/j.frl.2022.102698

Driver, C., Grosman, A., & Scaramozzino, P. (2020). Dividend policy and investor pressure. *Economic Modelling, 89*, 559–576. https://doi.org/10.1016/j.econ mod.2019.11.016

Dubofsky, D. A. (1992). A market microstructure explanation of ex-day abnormal returns. *The Journal of the Financial Management Association, 21*(4), 32.

Dubofsky, D. A. (1997). Limit orders and ex-dividend day return distributions. *Journal of Empirical Finance, 4*(1), 47–65. https://doi.org/10.1016/S0927-5398(96) 00012-6

Du, Q., Hasan, I., Wang, Y., & Wei, K. (2020, May 1). Local corruption, whistleblowing, and debt financing. *Whistleblowing, and Debt Financing*.

Dupuis, D. (2019). Ex-dividend day price behavior and liquidity in a tax-free emerging market. *Emerging Markets Review, 38*, 239–250. https://doi.org/10.1016/j.ememar.2019.02.001

Dyer, J. H., Godfrey, P. C., Jensen, R. J., & Bryce, D. J. (2021). *Strategic management: Concepts and cases*. John Wiley & Sons.

Eades, K. M., Hess, P. J., & Kim, E. H. (1984). On interpreting security returns during the ex-dividend period. *Journal of Financial Economics, 13*(1), 3–34. https://doi.org/10.1016/0304-405X(84)90030-8

Easterbrook, F. H. (1984). Two agency cost explanations of dividends. *The American Economic Review, 74*(4), 650.

Efthymiou, V. A., Episcopos, A., Leledakis, G. N., & Pyrgiotakis, E. G. (2021). Intraday analysis of the limit order bias on the ex-dividend day of U.S. common stocks. *International Review of Economics & Finance, 72*, 405–421. https://doi.org/10.1016/j.iref.2020.11.017

El Ghoul, S., Guedhami, O., Kwok, C. C. Y., & Mishra, D. R. (2011). Does corporate social responsibility affect the cost of capital? *Journal of Banking & Finance, 35*(9), 2388–2406. https://doi.org/10.1016/j.jbankfin.2011.02.007

ElBannan, M. A. (2020). Does catering behavior persist? Evidence on dividend sentiment in emerging financial markets. *International Review of Economics & Finance, 69*, 350–373. https://doi.org/10.1016/j.iref.2020.06.016

Elton, E. J., & Gruber, M. J. (1970). Marginal stockholder tax rates and the clientele effect. *The Review of Economics and Statistics, 52*(1), 68–74.

Esqueda, O. A. (2016). Signaling, corporate governance, and the equilibrium dividend policy. *The Quarterly Review of Economics and Finance, 59*, 186–199. https://doi.org/10.1016/j.qref.2015.06.005

Faccio, M., Marchica, M.-T., & Mura, R. (2016). CEO gender, corporate risk-taking, and the efficiency of capital allocation. *Journal of Corporate Finance, 39*, 193–209. https://doi.org/10.1016/j.jcorpfin.2016.02.008

Faleye, O., & Trahan, E. A. (2011). Labor-Friendly corporate practices: Is what is good for employees good for shareholders? *Journal of Business Ethics, 101*(1), 1–27. https://doi.org/10.1007/s10551-010-0705-9

Fama, E. F. (1974). The empirical relationships between the dividend and investment decisions of firms. *The American Economic Review, 64*(3), 304.

Fama, E. F., & Babiak, H. (1968). Dividend policy: An empirical analysis. *Journal of the American Statistical Association, 63*(324), 1132.

Fama, E. F., & French, K. R. (1988). Dividend yields and expected stock returns. *Journal of Financial Economics, 22*(1), 3–25. https://doi.org/10.1016/0304-405X(88)90020-7

Fama, E. F., & French, K. R. (2001). Disappearing dividends: Changing firm characteristics or lower propensity to pay? *Journal of Financial Economics, 60*(1), 3–43. https://doi.org/10.1016/S0304-405X(01)00038-1

Fama, E. F., & French, K. R. (2015). A five-factor asset pricing model. *Journal of Financial Economics, 116*(1), 1–22.

Fan, J. P. H., & Wong, T. J. (2005). Do external auditors perform a corporate governance role in emerging markets? Evidence from east Asia. *Journal of Accounting Research, 43*(1), 35–72. https://doi.org/10.1111/j.1475-679x.2004.00162.x

Farooq, O., & Ahmed, N. (2019). Dividend policy and political uncertainty: Evidence from the US presidential elections. *Research in International Business and Finance, 48*, 201–209. https://doi.org/10.1016/j.ribaf.2019.01.003

Farooque, O. A., Hamid, A., & Sun, L. (2021). Does corporate governance have a say on dividends in Australian listed companies? *Australasian Accounting, Business and Finance Journal, 15*(4), 47–75.

Fee, C. E., & Hadlock, C. J. (2000). Management turnover and product market competition: Empirical evidence from the U.S. newspaper industry. *Journal of Business, 73*(2), 205–243. https://doi.org/10.1086/209640

Felimban, R., Badreddine, S., & Floros, C. (2022). Share price informativeness and dividend smoothing behavior in GCC markets. *Journal of Economic Studies, 49*(6), 978–1001. https://doi.org/10.1108/JES-08-2020-0379

Felimban, R., Floros, C., & Nguyen, A.-N. (2018). The impact of dividend announcements on share price and trading volume. *Journal of Economic Studies, 45*(2), 210–230. https://doi.org/10.1108/JES-03-2017-0069

Ferris, S. P., Jayaraman, N., & Sabherwal, S. (2009). Catering effects in corporate dividend policy: The international evidence. *Journal of Banking & Finance, 33*(9), 1730–1738. https://doi.org/10.1016/j.jbankfin.2009.04.005

Ferris, S. P., Sen, N., & Pei, HoY. (2006). God save the queen and her dividends: Corporate payouts in the United Kingdom. *Journal of Business, 79*(3), 1149–1173. https://doi.org/10.1086/500672

Fisher, G. R. (1961). Some factors influencing share prices. *The Economic Journal, 71*(281), 121–141. https://doi.org/10.2307/2228227

Fliers, P. T. (2019). What is the relation between financial flexibility and dividend smoothing? *Journal of International Money and Finance, 92*, 98–111. https://doi.org/10.1016/j.jimonfin.2018.12.009

Florentsen, B., & Rydqvist, K. (2002). Ex-day behavior when investors and professional traders assume reverse roles: The case of Danish lottery bonds. *Journal of Financial Intermediation, 11*(2), 152–175. https://doi.org/10.1006/jfin.2001.0332

Fonseka, M., & Richardson, G. (2023). The effect of mandatory corporate social responsibility disclosure and performance on firms' dividend decisions: Evidence from China. *Economic Modelling, 120*, 106152. https://doi.org/10.1016/j.econmod.2022.106152

Frankfurter, G. M., & Wood, B. G., Jr. (1997). The evolution of corporate dividend policy. *Journal of Financial Education*, 16–33.

Frankfurter, G., Wood, B. G., & Wansley, J. (2003). *Dividend policy: Theory and practice*. Elsevier.

Frank, M., & Jagannathan, R. (1998). Why do stock prices drop by less than the value of the dividend? Evidence from a country without taxes. *Journal of Financial Economics, 47*(2), 161–188. https://doi.org/10.1016/S0304-405X(97)80053-0

Freedman, R. S. (2006). *Introduction to financial technology*. Elsevier.

Fritz Foley, C., Hartzell, J. C., Titman, S., & Twite, G. (2007). Why do firms hold so much cash? A tax-based explanation. *Journal of Financial Economics, 86*(3), 579–607. https://doi.org/10.1016/j.jfineco.2006.11.006

Fudenberg, D., & Tirole, J. (1995). A theory of income and dividend smoothing based on incumbency rents. *Journal of Political Economy, 103*(1), 75–93. https://doi.org/10.1086/261976

Fukuda, A. (2000). Dividend changes and earnings performance in Japan. *Pacific-Basin Finance Journal, 8*(1), 53–66. https://doi.org/10.1016/S0927-538X(99)00024-4

Fuller, K. P. (2001). The influence of managerial reputation on dividend smoothing. In *Advances in financial economics* (Vol. 6, pp. 83–115). Emerald Publishing Limited.

García-Feijóo, L., Hossain, M. M., & Javakhadze, D. (2021). Managerial social capital and dividend smoothing. *Journal of Corporate Finance, 66*, 101811. https://doi.org/10.1016/j.jcorpfin.2020.101811

Garel, A., & Petit-Romec, A. (2021). Engaging employees for the long run: Long-term investors and employee-related CSR. *Journal of Business Ethics, 174*(1), 35–63. https://doi.org/10.1007/s10551-020-04572-8

Gârleanu, N., & Zwiebel, J. (2009). Design and renegotiation of debt covenants. *Review of Financial Studies, 22*(2), 749–781. https://doi.org/10.1093/rfs/hhn017

Gervais, S., & Odean, T. (2001). Learning to be overconfident. *Review of Financial Studies, 14*(1), 1–27. https://doi.org/10.1093/rfs/14.1.1

Glen, J. D. (1995). *Dividend policy and behavior in emerging markets: To pay or not to pay.* World Bank.

Godfrey, P. C., Merrill, C. B., & Hansen, J. M. (2009). The relationship between corporate social responsibility and shareholder value: An empirical test of the risk management hypothesis. *Strategic Management Journal, 30*(4), 425–445. https://doi.org/10.1002/smj.750

Gomez, P.-Y., & Korine, H. (2005). Democracy and the evolution of corporate governance. *Corporate Governance: An International Review, 13*(6), 739–752. https://doi.org/10.1111/j.1467-8683.2005.00467.x

Gonedes, N. J. (1978). Corporate signaling, external accounting, and capital market equilibrium: Evidence on dividends, income, and extraordinary items. *Journal of Accounting Research, 16*(1), 26–79.

Gonzalez, M., Molina, C. A., Pablo, E., & Rosso, J. W. (2017). The effect of ownership concentration and composition on dividends: Evidence from Latin America. *Emerging Markets Review, 30*, 1–18. https://doi.org/10.1016/j.ememar.2016.08.018

Gordon, M. (1959). Osmotic and ionic regulation in Scottish brown trout and sea trout (*Sulmo truttu* L.), *Journal of Experimental Biology, 36*(2), 253–260.

Gordon, M. J. (1959). Dividends, earnings, and stock prices. *The Review of Economics and Statistics, 41*(2), 99–105.

Gordon, M. J. (1962). The savings investment and valuation of a corporation. *The Review of Economics and Statistics*, 37–51.

Gordon, M., & Lintner, J. (1956). Distribution of income of corporations among dividend, retained earning and taxes. *The American Economic Review, 46*(2), 97–113.

Gounopoulos, D., Huang, W., & Yang, M. (2021). *Innovation and dividend smoothing.* https://www.efmaefm.org/0EFMAMEETINGS/EFMA%20ANNUAL%20MEET INGS/2022-Rome/papers/EFMA%202022_stage-3032_question-Full%20Paper_id-152.pdf

Goyal, A., Jategaonkar, S. P., & Muckley, C. B. (2020). Why do privatized firms pay higher dividends? *Journal of Corporate Finance, 60*, 101493. https://doi.org/10.1016/j.jcorpfin.2019.101493

Graham, J. R., & Harvey, C. R. (2001). The theory and practice of corporate finance: Evidence from the field. *Journal of Financial Economics, 60*(2–3), 187–243. https://doi.org/10.1016/S0304-405X(01)00044-7

Graham, J. R., Michaely, R., & Roberts, M. R. (2003). Do price discreteness and transactions costs affect stock returns? Comparing ex-dividend pricing before and after decimalization. *The Journal of Finance, 58*(6), 2611–2636. https://doi.org/10.1046/j.1540-6261.2003.00617.x

Grant, R. (1991). *Contemporary strategy analysis.* Oxford.

Grennan, J. (2019). Dividend payments as a response to peer influence. *Journal of Financial Economics, 131*(3), 549–570. https://doi.org/10.1016/j.jfineco.2018.01.012

Grullon, G., & Michaely, R. (2007). *Corporate payout policy and product market competition.* Paper presented at the AFA 2008 New Orleans meetings paper.

Grullon, G., Michaely, R., & Swaminathan, B. (2002). Are dividend changes a sign of firm maturity? *Journal of Business, 75*(3), 387–424.

Guedhami, O., Kwok, C. C. Y., & Shao, L. (2017). Political freedom and corporate payouts. *Journal of Corporate Finance, 43*, 514–529. https://doi.org/10.1016/j.jcorpfin.2017.02.002

Gugler, K. (2003). Corporate governance, dividend payout policy, and the interrelation between dividends, R&D, and capital investment. *Journal of Banking & Finance, 27*(7), 1297–1321. https://doi.org/10.1016/S0378-4266(02)00258-3

Guttman, I., Kadan, O., & Kandel, E. (2010). Dividend stickiness and strategic pooling. *Review of Financial Studies, 23*(12), 4455–4495. https://doi.org/10.1093/rfs/hhq096

Gyapong, E., Ahmed, A., Ntim, C. G., & Nadeem, M. (2021). Board gender diversity and dividend policy in Australian listed firms: The effect of ownership concentration. *Asia Pacific Journal of Management, 38*(2), 603–643. https://doi.org/10.1007/s10490-019-09672-2

Habib, A. (2004). Accounting-based equity valuation techniques and the value relevance of dividend information: Empirical evidence from Japan. *Pacific Accounting Review, 16*(2), 23–44. https://doi.org/10.1108/01140580410818478

Haesner, C., & Schanz, D. (2013). Payout policy tax clienteles, ex-dividend day stock prices and trading behavior in Germany: The case of the 2001 tax reform. *Journal of Business Finance & Accounting, 40*(3–4), 527–563. https://doi.org/10.1111/jbfa.12018

Ham, C. G., Kaplan, Z. R., & Leary, M. T. (2020). Do dividends convey information about future earnings? *Journal of Financial Economics, 136*(2), 547–570. https://doi.org/10.1016/j.jfineco.2019.10.006

Handjinicolaou, G., & Kalay, A. (1984). Wealth redistributions or changes in firm value: An analysis of returns to bondholders and stockholders around dividend announcements. *Journal of Financial Economics, 13*(1), 35–63. https://doi.org/10.1016/0304-405X(84)90031-X

Harada, K., & Nguyen, P. (2011). Ownership concentration and dividend policy in Japan. *Managerial Finance, 37*(4), 362–379. https://doi.org/10.1108/03074351111115313

Hart, O. D. (1983). The market mechanism as an incentive scheme. *The Bell Journal of Economics, 14*(2), 366–382. https://doi.org/10.2307/3003639

Hauser, R. (2013). Did dividend policy change during the financial crisis? *Managerial Finance, 39*(6), 584–606. https://doi.org/10.1108/03074351311322861

Haushalter, D., Klasa, S., & Maxwell, W. F. (2007). The influence of product market dynamics on a firm's cash holdings and hedging behavior. *Journal of Financial Economics, 84*(3), 797–825.

He, W. (2012). Agency problems, product market competition and dividend policies in Japan. *Accounting and Finance, 52*(3), 873–901. https://doi.org/10.1111/j.1467-629X.2011.00414.x

Healy, P. M., & Palepu, K. G. (1988). Earnings information conveyed by dividend initiations and omissions. *Journal of Financial Economics, 21*(2), 149–175. https://doi.org/10.1016/0304-405X(88)90059-1

Heinkel, R. (1978). *Dividend policy as a signal of firm value in Essays on financial markets with imperfect information.* Ph.D. Thesis, University of California.

He, T. T., Li, W. X. B., & Tang, G. Y. N. (2012). Dividends behavior in state- versus family-controlled firms: Evidence from Hong Kong. *Journal of Business Ethics, 110*(1), 97–112. https://doi.org/10.1007/s10551-011-1150-0

Hendijani Zadeh, M. (2021). The effect of corporate social responsibility transparency on corporate payout policies. *International Journal of Managerial Finance, 17*(5), 708–732. https://doi.org/10.1108/IJMF-07-2020-0386

He, W., & Zhang, F. (2022). Languages and dividends. *The British Accounting Review, 54*(6), 101132. https://doi.org/10.1016/j.bar.2022.101132

Hietala, P. T. (1990). Equity markets and personal taxation: The ex-dividend day behaviour of Finnish stock prices. *Journal of Banking & Finance, 14*(2–3), 327–350. https://doi.org/10.1016/0378-4266(90)90053-5

Higgins, R. C. (1972). The corporate dividend-saving decision. *Journal of Financial and Quantitative Analysis, 7*(2), 1527–1541.

Hilliard, J., Jahera, J. S., & Zhang, H. (2019). The US financial crisis and corporate dividend reactions: For better or for worse? *Review of Quantitative Finance and Accounting, 53*(4), 1165–1193. https://doi.org/10.1007/s11156-018-0778-6

Hoang, E. C., & Hoxha, I. (2021). A tale of two emerging market economies: Evidence from payout smoothing in China and Taiwan. *International Journal of Managerial Finance, 17*(3), 361–376. https://doi.org/10.1108/IJMF-03-2019-0114

Hoberg, G., Phillips, G., & Prabhala, N. (2014). Product market threats, payouts, and financial flexibility. *The Journal of Finance, 69*(1), 293–324.

Hofstede, G. (1984). *Culture's consequences: International differences in work-related values* (Vol. 5). Sage.

Hofstede, G. (1990). *Cultures and organizations: Software of the mind.* McGraw-Hill.

Hofstede, G., Hofstede, G. J., & Minkov, M. (2010). *Cultures and organizations: Software of the mind* (3rd ed.). Citeseer.

Holder, M. E., Langrehr, F. W., & Hexter, J. L. (1998). Dividend policy determinants: An investigation of the influences of stakeholder theory. *FM: The Journal of the Financial Management Association, 27*(3), 73.

Hossain, A. T., Hossain, T., & Kryzanowski, L. (2021). Political corruption and corporate payouts. *Journal of Banking & Finance, 123*, 106016. https://doi.org/10.1016/j.jbankfin.2020.106016

Hossain, M. N., Rabarison, M. K., Ater, B., & Sobngwi, C. K. (2023). CEO marital status and dividend policy. *Journal of Corporate Finance, 78*, 102342. https://doi.org/10.1016/j.jcorpfin.2022.102342

Ho, S.-J. K., & Wu, C. (2001). The earnings information content of dividend initiations and omissions. *Journal of Business Finance & Accounting*, *28*(7–8), 963–977. https://doi.org/10.1111/1468-5957.00400

Huang, H. H., Kerstein, J., & Wang, C. (2018). The impact of climate risk on firm performance and financing choices: An international comparison. *Journal of International Business Studies*, *49*(5), 633–656. https://doi.org/10.1057/s41267-017-0125-5

Huang, T., Wu, F., Yu, J., & Zhang, B. (2015). Political risk and dividend policy: Evidence from international political crises. *Journal of International Business Studies*, *46*(5), 574–595. https://doi.org/10.1057/jibs.2015.2

Hu, Z., & Chang, J.-C. (2022). Does air pollution affect dividend policy. *Finance Research Letters*, *49*, 103183. https://doi.org/10.1016/j.frl.2022.103183

Imamah, N., Lin, T.-J., SuhadakHandayani, S. R., & Hung, J.-H. (2019). Islamic law, corporate governance, growth opportunities and dividend policy in Indonesia stock market. *Pacific-Basin Finance Journal*, *55*, 110–126. https://doi.org/10.1016/j.pacfin.2019.03.008

Jabbouri, I. (2016). Determinants of corporate dividend policy in emerging markets: Evidence from MENA stock markets. *Research in International Business and Finance*, *37*, 283–298. https://doi.org/10.1016/j.ribaf.2016.01.018

Jacob, C., & Jijo Lukose, P. J. (2018). Institutional ownership and dividend payout in emerging markets: Evidence from India. *Journal of Emerging Market Finance*, *17*(Suppl. 1), S54–S82. https://doi.org/10.1177/0972652717751538

Jain, A. K. (2001). Corruption: A review. *Journal of Economic Surveys*, *15*(1), 71–121.

Jain, P. K., Kuvvet, E., & Pagano, M. S. (2017). Corruption's impact on foreign portfolio investment. *International Business Review*, *26*(1), 23–35. https://doi.org/10.1016/j.ibusrev.2016.05.004

Jakob, K., & Ma, T. (2004). Tick size, NYSE rule 118, and ex-dividend day stock price behavior. *Journal of Financial Economics*, *72*(3), 605–625. https://doi.org/10.1016/S0304-405X(03)00189-2

James, H., Benson, B. W., & Wu, C. (2017). Does CEO ownership affect payout policy? Evidence from using CEO scaled wealth-performance sensitivity. *The Quarterly Review of Economics and Finance*, *65*, 328–345. https://doi.org/10.1016/j.qref.2016.10.003

Javakhadze, D., Ferris, S. P., & Sen, N. (2014). An international analysis of dividend smoothing. *Journal of Corporate Finance*, *29*(0), 200–220. https://doi.org/10.1016/j.jcorpfin.2014.09.007

Jensen, M. C. (1986). Agency costs of free cash flow, corporate finance, and takeovers. *The American Economic Review*, *76*(2), 323.

Jensen, M. C., & Meckling, W. H. (1976). Theory of the firm: Managerial behavior, agency costs and ownership structure. *Journal of Financial Economics*, *3*(4), 305–360. https://doi.org/10.1016/0304-405X(76)90026-X

Jensen, G. R., Solberg, D. P., & Zorn, T. S. (1992). Simultaneous determination of insider ownership, debt, and dividend policies. *Journal of Financial and Quantitative Analysis*, *27*(2), 247–263. https://search.ebscohost.com/login.aspx?direct=true&db=bth&AN=5722920&lang=fr&site=ehost-live

Jeong, J. (2013). Determinants of dividend smoothing in emerging market: The case of Korea. *Emerging Markets Review*, *17*(0), 76–88. https://doi.org/10.1016/j.ememar.2013.08.007

Jeon, J. Q., Lee, C., & Moffett, C. M. (2011). Effects of foreign ownership on payout policy: Evidence from the Korean market. *Journal of Financial Markets*, *14*(2), 344–375. https://doi.org/10.1016/j.finmar.2010.08.001

Jerry, R. G. (1980). *Taxation and the ex-dividend day behavior of common stock prices.*

Jiraporn, P. (2006). Share repurchases, shareholder rights, and corporate governance provisions. *The North American Journal of Economics and Finance*, *17*(1), 35–47. https://doi.org/10.1016/j.najef.2005.03.003

Jiraporn, P., Kim, J. C., & Kim, Y. S. (2011). Dividend payouts and corporate governance quality: An empirical investigation. *Financial Review*, *46*(2), 251–279. https://doi.org/10.1111/j.1540-6288.2011.00299.x

Johnson, S., Boone, P., Breach, A., & Friedman, E. (2000). Corporate governance in the Asian financial crisis. *Journal of Financial Economics*, *58*(1–2), 141–186. https://doi.org/10.1016/S0304-405X(00)00069-6

Johnson, W. C., Kang, J.-K., & Yi, S. (2010). The certification role of large customers in the new issues market. *Financial Management*, *39*(4), 1425–1474. https://doi.org/10.1111/j.1755-053X.2010.01118.x

John, K., & Williams, J. (1985). Dividends, dilution, and taxes: A signalling equilibrium. *The Journal of Finance*, *40*(4), 1053–1070.

Jose, M. L., & Stevens, J. L. (1989). Capital market valuation of dividend policy. *Journal of Business Finance & Accounting*, *16*(5), 651–661. https://doi.org/10.1111/j.1468-5957.1989.tb00044.x

Kalay, A. (1980). Signaling, information content, and the reluctance to cut dividends. *Journal of Financial and Quantitative Analysis*, *15*(4), 855–869. https://doi.org/10.2307/2330564

Kalay, A. (1982). The ex-dividend day behavior of stock prices: A re-examination of the clientele effect. *The Journal of Finance*, *37*(4), 1059–1070. https://doi.org/10.1111/j.1540-6261.1982.tb03598.x

Kale, J. R., & Noe, T. H. (1990). Dividends, uncertainty and underwriting costs under asymetric information. *Journal of Financial Research*, *13*(4), 265. https://doi.org/10.1111/j.1475-6803.1990.tb00631.x

Kale, J. R., & Shahrur, H. (2007). Corporate capital structure and the characteristics of suppliers and customers. *Journal of Financial Economics*, *83*(2), 321–365. https://doi.org/10.1016/j.jfineco.2005.12.007

Kang, E., & Kim, R. (2021). Product market competition, reputation, and dividend policy. *Applied Economics*, *53*(29), 3334–3346. https://doi.org/10.1080/00036846.2021.1877255

Kao, L., & Chen, A. (2013). How product market competition affects dividend payments in a weak investor protection economy: Evidence from Taiwan. *Pacific-Basin Finance Journal*, *25*, 21–39. https://doi.org/10.1016/j.pacfin.2013.08.004

Kaplan, S. N., & Reishus, D. (1990). Outside directorships and corporate performance. *Journal of Financial Economics*, *27*(2), 389–410. https://doi.org/10.1016/0304-405X(90)90061-4

Karpavičius, S. (2014). Dividends: Relevance, rigidity, and signaling. *Journal of Corporate Finance*, *25*, 289–312. https://doi.org/10.1016/j.jcorpfin.2013.12.014

Karpavičius, S., & Yu, F. (2018). Dividend premium: Are dividend-paying stocks worth more? *International Review of Financial Analysis*, *56*, 112–126. https://doi.org/10.1016/j.irfa.2018.01.004

Karpoff, J. M., & Walkling, R. A. (1988). Short-term trading around ex-dividend days: Additional evidence. *Journal of Financial Economics, 21*(2), 291–298. https://doi.org/10.1016/0304-405X(88)90063-3

Karpoff, J. M., & Walkling, R. A. (1990). Dividend capture in NASDAQ stocks. *Journal of Financial Economics, 28*(1–2), 39–65. https://doi.org/10.1016/0304-405X(90)90047-4

Karuna, C. (2007). Industry product market competition and managerial incentives. *Journal of Accounting and Economics, 43*(2), 275–297. https://doi.org/10.1016/j.jacceco.2007.02.004

Kato, K., Kato, K., Loewenstein, U., & Loewenstein, U. (1995). The ex-dividend-day behavior of stock prices: The case of Japan. *Review of Financial Studies, 8*(3).

Kent Baker, H., & De Ridder, A. (2018). Payout policy in industrial and financial firms. *Global Finance Journal, 37*, 138–151. https://doi.org/10.1016/j.gfj.2018.05.005

Khambata, D., & Liu, W. (2005). Cultural dimensions, risk aversion and corporate dividend policy. *Journal of Asia-Pacific Business, 6*(4), 31–43. https://doi.org/10.1300/J098v06n04_03

Kilincarslan, E. (2021). Smoothed or not smoothed: The impact of the 2008 global financial crisis on dividend stability in the UK. *Finance Research Letters, 38*, 101423. https://doi.org/10.1016/j.frl.2019.101423

Kim, W. S., Kiymaz, H., & Oh, S. (2020). Do country-level legal, corporate governance, and cultural characteristics influence the relationship between insider ownership and dividend policy? *Pacific-Basin Finance Journal, 64*, 101457. https://doi.org/10.1016/j.pacfin.2020.101457

Kindleberger, C. P. (2000). Manias, panics, and crashes: A history of financial crises. *The Scriblerian and the Kit-Cats, 32*(2), 379.

Klasa, S., Maxwell, W. F., & Ortiz-Molina, H. (2009). The strategic use of corporate cash holdings in collective bargaining with labor unions. *Journal of Financial Economics, 92*(3), 421–442. https://doi.org/10.1016/j.jfineco.2008.07.003

Kobrin, S. (2022). *Managing political risk assessment: Strategic response to environmental change.* University of California Press.

Koo, D. S., Ramalingegowda, S., & Yu, Y. (2017). The effect of financial reporting quality on corporate dividend policy. *Review of Accounting Studies, 22*(2), 753–790. https://doi.org/10.1007/s11142-017-9393-3

Koussis, N., & Makrominas, M. (2019). What factors determine dividend smoothing by US and EU banks? *Journal of Business Finance & Accounting, 46*(7–8), 1030–1059. https://doi.org/10.1111/jbfa.12399

Kowalewski, O., Stetsyuk, I., & Talavera, O. (2007). *Corporate governance and dividend policy in Poland.* Working papers Article. Financial Institutions Center at The Wharton School.

Krieger, K., Mauck, N., & Pruitt, S. W. (2021). The impact of the COVID-19 pandemic on dividends. *Finance Research Letters, 42*, 101910. https://doi.org/10.1016/j.frl.2020.101910

Kumar, P. (1988). Shareholder-manager conflict and the information content of dividends. *Review of Financial Studies, 1*(2), 111–136.

Kumar, S. (2017). New evidence on stock market reaction to dividend announcements in India. *Research in International Business and Finance, 39*, 327–337. https://doi.org/10.1016/j.ribaf.2016.09.009

Kumar, P., & Lee, B. S. (2001). Discrete dividend policy with permanent earnings. *Financial Management, 30*(3), 55–76.

La Porta, R., Lopez-de-Silanes, F., Shleifer, A., & Vishny, R. (1998). Law and finance. *Journal of Political Economy, 106*, 42.

La Porta, R., Lopez-De-Silanes, F., Shleifer, A., & Vishny, R. W. (2000). Agency problems and dividend policies around the world. *The Journal of Finance, 55*(1), 1–33. https://doi.org/10.1111/0022-1082.00199

Labhane, N. B. (2018a). Dividend policy decisions in India: Standalone versus business group-affiliated firms. *Global Business Review, 20*(1), 133–150. https://doi.org/10.1177/0972150918803990

Labhane, N. B. (2018b). Why do firms smooth dividends? Empirical evidence from an emerging economy India. *Afro-Asian Journal of Finance and Accounting, 8*(3), 237–256. https://doi.org/10.1504/AAJFA.2018.093463

Labhane, N. B., & Mahakud, J. (2016). Determinants of dividend policy of Indian companies: A panel data analysis. *Paradigm, 20*(1), 36–55. https://doi.org/10.1177/0971890716637698

Labhane, N. B., & Mahakud, J. (2018). Dividend smoothing and business groups: Evidence from Indian companies. *Global Business Review, 19*(3), 690–706.

Lakonishok, J., & Vermaelen, T. (1986). Tax-induced trading around ex-dividend days. *Journal of Financial Economics, 16*(3), 287–319. https://doi.org/10.1016/0304-405X(86)90032-2

Lambrecht, B. M., & Myers, S. C. (2010). *A Lintner model of dividends and managerial rents.* National Bureau of Economic Research.

Lamdin, D. J. (1993). Shareholder taxation and aggregate dividend payout: Evidence from the Tax Reform Act of 1986. *Review of Quantitative Finance and Accounting, 3*(4), 459–468. https://doi.org/10.1007/BF02409623

Lam, K. C. K., Sami, H., & Zhou, H. (2012). The role of cross-listing, foreign ownership and state ownership in dividend policy in an emerging market. *China Journal of Accounting Research, 5*(3), 199–216. https://doi.org/10.1016/j.cjar.2012.06.001

Larkin, Y., Leary, M. T., & Michaely, R. (2016). Do investors value dividend-smoothing stocks differently? *Management Science, 63*(12), 4114–4136. https://doi.org/10.1287/mnsc.2016.2551

Lasfer, M. A. (1996). Taxes and dividends: The UK evidence. *Journal of Banking & Finance, 20*(3), 455–472. https://doi.org/10.1016/0378-4266(95)00012-7

Lawson, B., & Wang, D. (2011). Auditor monitoring and dividend payout policy. SSRN.

Leary, M. T., & Michaely, R. (2011). Determinants of dividend smoothing: Empirical evidence. *Review of Financial Studies, 24*(10), 3197–3249. https://doi.org/10.1093/rfs/hhr072

Lease, R. C., John, K., Kalay, A., Loewenstein, U., & Sarig, O. H. (1999). *Dividend policy: Its impact on firm value.* OUP Catalogue.

Lee, K. F. (2020). Peer effects on firm dividend policies in Taiwan. 財務金融學刊, *28*(3), 113–144.

Lei, G., Wang, W., & Liu, M. (2015). Political uncertainty, dividend policy adjustments and market effects. *China Journal of Accounting Studies, 3*(1), 49–83. https://doi.org/10.1080/21697213.2015.1015370

Lewellen, W. G., Stanley, K. L., Lease, R. C., & Schlarbaum, G. G. (1978). Some direct evidence on the dividend clientele phenomenon. *The Journal of Finance*, *33*(5), 1385–1399. https://doi.org/10.1111/j.1540-6261.1978.tb03427.x

Lian, Y., Sepehri, M., & Foley, M. (2011). Corporate cash holdings and financial crisis: An empirical study of Chinese companies. *Eurasian Business Review*, *1*(2), 112–124.

Lieberman, M. B., & Asaba, S. (2006). Why do firms imitate each other? *Academy of Management Review*, *31*(2), 366–385. https://doi.org/10.5465/amr.2006.20208686

Li, Y., Liao, M., & Liu, Y. (2023). How does green credit policy affect polluting firms' dividend policy? The China experience. *International Review of Financial Analysis*, *88*, 102631. https://doi.org/10.1016/j.irfa.2023.102631

Li, W., & Lie, E. (2006). Dividend changes and catering incentives. *Journal of Financial Economics*, *80*(2), 293–308. https://doi.org/10.1016/j.jfineco.2005.03.005

Lintner, J. (1956). Distribution of incomes of corporations among dividends, retained earnings, and taxes. *The American Economic Review*, *46*(2), 97–113. https://www.jstor.org/stable/1910664

Lin, J.-C., & Yu, M.-T. (2023). Managerial overconfidence and dividend stickiness. *Journal of Accounting, Auditing & Finance*. https://doi.org/10.1177/0148558X221150102

Litzenberger, R. H., & Ramaswamy, K. (1979). The effect of personal taxes and dividends on capital asset prices: Theory and empirical evidence. *Journal of Financial Economics*, *7*(2), 163–195. https://doi.org/10.1016/0304-405X(79)90012-6

Loderer, C. F., & Mauer, D. C. (1992). Corporate dividends and seasoned equity issues: An empirical investigation. *The Journal of Finance*, *47*(1), 201–225. https://doi.org/10.1111/j.1540-6261.1992.tb03983.x

Machlup, F. (1967). Theories of the firm: Marginalist, behavioral, managerial. *The American Economic Review*, *57*(1), 1–33. https://www.jstor.org/stable/1815603

Mahenthiran, S., Cademartori, D., & Gjerde, T. (2020). Mandatory dividend policy, growth, liquidity and corporate governance: Evidence from Chile. *Review of Pacific Basin Financial Markets and Policies*, *23*(03), 2050025. https://doi.org/10.1142/S0219091520500253

Manos, R. (2001). *Capital structure and dividend policy: Evidence from emerging markets*. PhD Thesis, University of Birmingham.

Martins, T. C., & Novaes, W. (2012). Mandatory dividend rules: Do they make it harder for firms to invest? *Journal of Corporate Finance*, *18*(4), 953–967. https://doi.org/10.1016/j.jcorpfin.2012.05.002

Masselman, G. (1963). *The cradle of colonialism*. Yale University Press.

McCaffrey, K., & Hamill, P. (2000). Dividend initiation announcements effects in initial public offerings. *Applied Financial Economics*, *10*(5), 533–542. https://doi.org/10.1080/096031000416415

McCluskey, T., Burton, B. M., Power, D. M., & Sinclair, C. D. (2006). Evidence on the Irish stock market's reaction to dividend announcements. *Applied Financial Economics*, *16*(8), 617–628. https://doi.org/10.1080/09603100600639058

McDonald, R. L. (2001). Cross-border investing with tax arbitrage: The case of German dividend tax credits. *Review of Financial Studies*, *14*(3), 617–657. https://doi.org/10.1093/rfs/14.3.617

McGuinness, P. B., Lam, K. C. K., & Vieito, J. P. (2015). Gender and other major board characteristics in China: Explaining corporate dividend policy and

governance. *Asia Pacific Journal of Management, 32*(4), 989–1038. https://doi.org/
10.1007/s10490-015-9443-y

McManus, I., Ap Gwilym, O., & Thomas, S. (2004). The role of payout ratio in the
relationship between stock returns and dividend yield. *Journal of Business Finance
& Accounting, 31*(9/10), 1355–1387. https://doi.org/10.1111/j.0306-686X.
2004.00577.x

Means, D. B., Charoenwong, C., & Kang, Y. K. (1992). Changing dividend policies
caused by the Tax Reform Act of 1986: An empirical analysis. *Journal of
Economics and Finance, 16*(3), 153–160. https://doi.org/10.1007/BF02920317

Megginson, W. L., Ullah, B., & Wei, Z. (2014). State ownership, soft-budget
constraints, and cash holdings: Evidence from China's privatized firms. *Journal
of Banking & Finance, 48*(0), 276–291. https://doi.org/10.1016/j.jbankfin.
2014.06.011

Mehdi, M., Sahut, J.-M., & Teulon, F. (2017). Do corporate governance and
ownership structure impact dividend policy in emerging market during financial
crisis? *Journal of Applied Accounting Research, 18*(3), 274–297. https://doi.org/
10.1108/JAAR-07-2014-0079

Michaely, R., Michaely, R., Murgia, M., & Murgia, M. (1995). The effect of tax
heterogeneity on prices and volume around the ex-dividend day: Evidence from the
Milan stock exchange. *Review of Financial Studies, 8*(2), 369–399.

Michaely, R., & Roberts, M. R. (2012). Corporate dividend policies: Lessons from
private firms. *Review of Financial Studies, 25*(3), 711–746. https://doi.org/10.1093/
rfs/hhr108

Michaely, R., & Vila, J.-L. (1995). Investors' heterogeneity, prices, and volume
around the ex-dividend day. *Journal of Financial and Quantitative Analysis,
30*(2), 171–198.

Miles, R., Charles, S., & Alan, D. (1978). Organizational strategy, structure and
process. *Academy of Management Review, 3*(3), 546–562.

Miller, M. H., & Modigliani, F. (1961). Dividend policy, growth, and the valuation of
shares. In H. R. Vane & C. Mulhearn (Eds.), *Harry M. Markowitz, Merton H.
Miller, William F. Sharpe, Robert C. Merton and Myrin S. Scholes* (Vol. 2, pp.
113–135). Elgar. Elgar Reference Collection. Pioneering Papers of the Nobel
Memorial Laureates in Economics.

Miller, M. H., & Scholes, M. S. (1978). Dividends and taxes. *Journal of Financial
Economics, 6*(4), 333–364. https://doi.org/10.1016/0304-405X(78)90009-0

Miller, M. H., & Scholes, M. S. (1982). Dividend and taxes: Some empirical evidence.
Journal of Political Economy, 90(6), 23.

Milonas, N. T., Travlos, N. G., Xiao, J. Z., & Tan, C. (2006). The ex-dividend day
stock price behavior in the Chinese stock market. *Pacific-Basin Finance Journal,
14*(2), 155–174. https://doi.org/10.1016/j.pacfin.2005.06.004

Minnick, K., & Rosenthal, L. (2014). Stealth compensation: Do CEOs increase their
pay by influencing dividend policy? *Journal of Corporate Finance, 25*(0), 435–454.
https://doi.org/10.1016/j.jcorpfin.2014.01.005

Mishkin, F. S. (1992). Anatomy of a financial crisis. *Journal of Evolutionary
Economics, 2*(2), 115–130. https://doi.org/10.1007/BF01193536

Mishkin, F. S. (1995). Symposium on the monetary transmission mechanism. *The
Journal of Economic Perspectives, 9*(4), 3–10. https://doi.org/10.1257/jep.9.4.3

Mitton, T. (2004). Corporate governance and dividend policy in emerging markets. *Emerging Markets Review*, *5*(4), 409–426. https://doi.org/10.1016/j.ememar.20 04.05.003

Mollah, A. S. (2001). *Dividend policy and behaviour, and security price reaction to the announcement of dividends in an emergency market: A study of companies listed on the Dhaka stock exchange*. PhD Thesis, University of Leeds (Business School). https://etheses.whiterose.ac.uk/700/

Mortal, S., Paudel, S., & Silveri, S. (2017). The impact of market structure on ex-dividend day stock price behavior. *Financial Management*, *46*(4), 1053–1082. https://doi.org/10.1111/fima.12176

Mulchandani, K., Mulchandani, K., & Wasan, P. (2020). Dividends and earnings quality: Evidence from India. *IIMB Management Review*, *32*(2), 166–176. https://doi.org/10.1016/j.iimb.2019.10.001

Muñoz, E., & Rodriguez, A. (2017). Ex-dividend date stock behavior and the clientele effect: Evidence around a tax reduction. *Global Finance Journal*, *32*, 55–61. https://doi.org/10.1016/j.gfj.2016.06.003

Myers, S. C. (1977). Determinants of corporate borrowing. *Journal of Financial Economics*, *5*(2), 147–175. https://doi.org/10.1016/0304-405X(77)90015-0

Myers, S. C., & Majluf, N. S. (1984). Corporate financing and investment decisions when firms have information that investors do not have. *Journal of Financial Economics*, *13*(2), 187–221. https://doi.org/10.1016/0304-405X(84)90023-0

Naranjo, A., Nimalendran, M., & Ryngaert, M. (2000). Time variation of ex-dividend day stock returns and corporate dividend capture: A reexamination. *The Journal of Finance*, *55*(5), 2357–2372.

Nash, R. C., Netter, J. M., & Poulsen, A. B. (2003). Determinants of contractual relations between shareholders and bondholders: Investment opportunities and restrictive covenants. *Journal of Corporate Finance*, *9*(2), 201–232. https://doi.org/10.1016/S0929-1199(02)00007-X

Nguyen, K. H. (2014). Impact of a dividend initiation wave on shareholder wealth. *Applied Financial Economics*, *24*(8), 573–586. https://doi.org/10.1080/09603107.20 14.892197

Nguyen, T.-G. (2020). Stock liquidity and dividend policy: Evidence from an imputation tax environment. *International Review of Financial Analysis*, *72*, 101559. https://doi.org/10.1016/j.irfa.2020.101559

Nguyen, T. T. M., & Tran, Q. T. (2022). Democracy and dividend policy around the world. *The North American Journal of Economics and Finance*, *62*, 101713. https://doi.org/10.1016/j.najef.2022.101713

Nie, J., & Yin, L. (2022). Do dividends signal safety? Evidence from China. *International Review of Financial Analysis*, *82*, 102123. https://doi.org/10.1016/j.irfa.2022.102123

Nishikawa, Y., Hashemi Joo, M., & Parhizgari, A. M. (2021). Languages and dividend policy. *The Journal of Behavioral Finance*, 1–19. https://doi.org/10.1080/15427560.2021.1913158

Nissim, D., & Ziv, A. (2001). Dividend changes and future profitability. *The Journal of Finance*, *56*(6), 2111–2133. https://doi.org/10.1111/0022-1082.00400

Nowak, S., Mrzygłód, U., Mosionek-Schweda, M., & Kwiatkowski, J. M. (2021). What do we know about dividend smoothing in this millennium? Evidence from

Asian markets. *Emerging Markets Finance and Trade, 57*(13), 3677–3706. https://doi.org/10.1080/1540496X.2019.1711367

O'Sullivan, M. A. (2006). Living with the U.S. financial system: The experiences of general electric and Westinghouse electric in the last century. *Business History Review, 80*(4), 621–655.

Ofori-Sasu, D., Clarissa Dzeha, G., Boachie, C., & Yindenaba Abor, J. (2022). The role of board dynamics in explaining payout policy and shareholders' wealth: Evidence from the banking sector in Africa. *Research in Globalization, 5,* 100086. https://doi.org/10.1016/j.resglo.2022.100086

Ohlson, J. A. (1995). Earnings, book values, and dividends in equity valuation. *Contemporary Accounting Research, 11*(2), 661–687. https://doi.org/10.1111/j.1911-3846.1995.tb00461.x

Ozo, F. K., & Arun, T. G. (2019). Stock market reaction to cash dividends: Evidence from the Nigerian stock market. *Managerial Finance, 45*(3), 366–380. https://doi.org/10.1108/MF-09-2017-0351

Paczkowski, J. (2012, March 19). Apple's dividend: Why now? https://allthingsd.com/20120319/apples-dividend-why-now/

Pahi, D., & Yadav, I. S. (2022). Product market competition, agency cost and dividend payouts: New evidence from emerging market. *Journal of Management & Governance, 26*(3), 925–956. https://doi.org/10.1007/s10997-021-09570-0

Pandey, I., & Bhat, R. (2007). Dividend behaviour of Indian companies under monetary policy restrictions. *Managerial Finance, 33*(1), 14–25.

Panousi, V., & Papanikolaou, D. (2012). Investment, idiosyncratic risk, and ownership. *The Journal of Finance, 67*(3), 1113–1148. https://doi.org/10.1111/j.1540-6261.2012.01743.x

Papaioannou, G. J., & Savarese, C. M. (1994). Corporate dividend policy response to the Tax Reform Act of 1986. *Financial Management, 23*(1), 56–63. https://doi.org/10.2307/3666056

Park, H. (2003). Determinants of corruption: A cross-national analysis. *Multinational Business Review, 11*(2), 29–48. https://doi.org/10.1108/1525383X200300010

Partington, G. H. (1989). Variables influencing dividend policy in Australia: Survey results. *Journal of Business Finance & Accounting, 16*(2), 165–182.

Pástor, L. u., & Veronesi, P. (2012). Uncertainty about government policy and stock prices. *The Journal of Finance, 67*(4), 1219–1264. https://doi.org/10.1111/j.1540-6261.2012.01746.x

Patatoukas, P. N. (2012). Customer-base concentration: Implications for firm performance and capital markets. *The Accounting Review, 87*(2), 363–392. https://www.jstor.org/stable/23245608

Pattenden, K., & Twite, G. (2008). Taxes and dividend policy under alternative tax regimes. *Journal of Corporate Finance, 14*(1), 1–16. https://doi.org/10.1016/j.jcorpfin.2007.09.002

Pearce, J. A., & Robinson, R. B. (1985). *Formulation, implementation and control of competitive strategy.*

Pettenuzzo, D., Sabbatucci, R., & Timmermann, A. (2023). Dividend suspensions and cash flows during the Covid-19 pandemic: A dynamic econometric model. *Journal of Econometrics.* https://doi.org/10.1016/j.jeconom.2022.11.008

Pettit, R. R. (1972). Dividend announcements, security performance, and capital market efficiency. *The Journal of Finance, 27*(5), 993–1007. https://doi.org/ 10.1111/j.1540-6261.1972.tb03018.x

Pettit, R. R. (1977). Taxes, transactions costs and the clientele effect of dividends. *Journal of Financial Economics, 5*(3), 419–436. https://doi.org/10.1016/0304-405X(77)90046-0

Phan, T. K. H., & Tran, N. H. (2019). Dividend policy and stock price volatility in an emerging market: Does ownership structure matter? *Cogent Economics & Finance, 7*(1), 1637051. https://doi.org/10.1080/23322039.2019.1637051

Poretti, C., & Blal, I. (2020). The asset-light strategies and the dividend puzzle: International evidence from the hospitality industry. *International Journal of Hospitality Management, 91*, 102639. https://doi.org/10.1016/j.ijhm.2020.102639

Porter, M. E. (1979). How competitive forces shape strategy. *Harvard Business Review, 57*(2), 137–145.

Porter, M. E. (1980). *Competitive strategy: Techniques for analyzing industries and competitors.* Free Press.

Porter, M. E. (2008). The five competitive forces that shape strategy. *Harvard Business Review, 86*(1), 78.

Poterba, J. M., & Summers, L. H. (1984). New evidence that taxes affect the valuation of dividends. *The Journal of Finance, 39*(5), 1397–1415.

Prakash, N., & Yogesh, L. (2021). Market reaction to dividend announcements during pandemic: An event study. *Vision.* https://doi.org/10.1177/09722629211066288

Pruitt, S. W., & Gitman, L. J. (1991). The interactions between the investment, financing, and dividend decisions of major U.S. firms. *Financial Review, 26*(3), 409–430. https://doi.org/10.1111/j.1540-6288.1991.tb00388.x

Pucheta-Martínez, M. C., & Bel-Oms, I. (2016). The board of directors and dividend policy: The effect of gender diversity. *Industrial and Corporate Change, 25*(3), 523–547. https://doi.org/10.1093/icc/dtv040

Qin, W., Liang, Q., Jiao, Y., Lu, M., & Shan, Y. (2022). Social trust and dividend payouts: Evidence from China. *Pacific-Basin Finance Journal, 72*, 101726. https://doi.org/10.1016/j.pacfin.2022.101726

Raaballe, J., & Hedensted, J. S. (2008). *Dividend determinants in Denmark.* SSRN. https://doi.org/10.2139/ssrn.1123436

Rabbani, N. (2017). The announcement effect of cash dividend changes on share prices: Evidence from Dhaka stock exchange. *Review of Pacific Basin Financial Markets and Policies, 20*(04), 1750025. https://doi.org/10.1142/S0219091517500254

Raith, M. (2003). Competition, risk, and managerial incentives. *The American Economic Review, 93*(4), 1425–1436.

Ramezani, M., & Moosavi, S. A. (2015). Market power and dividend policy: Evidence from firms listed in Tehran stock exchange. *Environment Conservation Journal, 16*(SE), 7–14.

Raymond, E. M., & Charles, C. S. (2003). *Organizational strategy, structure, and process.* Stanford University Press.

Renneboog, L., & Trojanowski, G. (2007). Control structures and payout policy. *Managerial Finance, 33*(1), 43–64. https://doi.org/10.1108/03074350710715809

Rhee, K., & Park, K. S. (2018). Changes in dividend smoothing after the financial crisis. *Economics Letters, 172*, 37–39. https://doi.org/10.1016/j.econlet.2018.08.019

Riley, J. G. (1975). Competitive signaling. *Journal of Economic Theory, 10*(2), 174–186. https://doi.org/10.1016/0022-0531(75)90049-6

Robbins, S. P., Bergman, R., Stagg, I., & Coulter, M. (2014). *Management*. Pearson Australia.

Root, A., & Yung, K. (2022). Resolving agency and product market views of cash holdings. *Research in International Business and Finance, 59*, 101518. https://doi.org/10.1016/j.ribaf.2021.101518

Ross, S. A., Westerfield, R., & Jaffe, J. F. (2010). *Corporate finance* (9th ed.). McGraw-Hill/Irwin.

Roy, A. (2015). Dividend policy, ownership structure and corporate governance: An empirical analysis of Indian firms. *Indian Journal of Corporate Governance, 8*(1), 1–33. https://doi.org/10.1177/0974686215574422

Rozeff, M. S. (1982). Growth, beta and agency costs as determinants of dividend payout ratios. *Journal of Financial Research, 5*(3), 249.

Rozycki, J. J. (1997). A tax motivation for smoothing dividends. *The Quarterly Review of Economics and Finance, 37*(2), 563–578. https://doi.org/10.1016/S1062-9769(97)90043-0

Rupasingha, A., Goetz, S. J., & Freshwater, D. (2006). The production of social capital in US counties. *The Journal of Socio-Economics, 35*(1), 83–101. https://doi.org/10.1016/j.socec.2005.11.001

Saadi, S., & Chkir, I. (2008). Taxation and dividend policy: New empirical evidence. *Journal of Corporate Ownership and Control, 5*(4), 266–273.

Saeed, A. (2021). The impact of employee friendly practices on dividend payments: Evidence from emerging economies. *Journal of Business Research, 135*, 592–605. https://doi.org/10.1016/j.jbusres.2021.07.009

Saeed, A., & Zamir, F. (2021). How does CSR disclosure affect dividend payments in emerging markets? *Emerging Markets Review, 46*, 100747. https://doi.org/10.1016/j.ememar.2020.100747

Saens, R., & Tigero, T. (2021). Mandatory dividend rules and the investment decision: The case of Chile. *The North American Journal of Economics and Finance, 56*, 101373. https://doi.org/10.1016/j.najef.2021.101373

Sahu, C. (2000). An empirical test of association between dividend payout and stock returns. *Paradigm, 4*(2), 109–130.

Sarwar, B., & Hassan, M. (2021). Impact of economic policy uncertainty on dividend decision: A moderating role of board financial expertise. *Journal of Public Affairs, 21*(3), e2613. https://doi.org/10.1002/pa.2613

Sawicki, J. (2009). Corporate governance and dividend policy in Southeast Asia pre- and post-crisis. *The European Journal of Finance, 15*(2), 211–230. https://doi.org/10.1080/13518470802604440

Schmidt, K. M. (1997). Managerial incentives and product market competition. *The Review of Economic Studies, 64*(2), 191–213. https://doi.org/10.2307/2971709

Schrand, C. M., & Zechman, S. L. C. (2012). Executive overconfidence and the slippery slope to financial misreporting. *Journal of Accounting and Economics, 53*(1), 311–329. https://doi.org/10.1016/j.jacceco.2011.09.001

Schwartz, S. H. (1992). Universals in the content and structure of values: Theoretical advances and empirical tests in 20 countries. In M. P. Zanna (Ed.), *Advances in experimental social psychology* (Vol. 25, pp. 1–65). Academic Press.

Schwartz, S. H. (1994). Are there universal aspects in the structure and contents of human values? *Journal of Social Issues, 50*(4), 19–45.

Scott, W. R. (1912). *The constitution and finance of English, Scottish and Irish joint-stock companies to 1720* (Vol. 1). The University Press.

Setia-Atmaja, L. (2010). Dividend and debt policies of family controlled firms: The impact of board independence. *International Journal of Managerial Finance, 6*(2), 128–142. https://doi.org/10.1108/17439131011032059

Setiawan, D., Bandi, B., Kee Phua, L., & Trinugroho, I. (2016). Ownership structure and dividend policy in Indonesia. *Journal of Asia Business Studies, 10*(3), 230–252. https://doi.org/10.1108/JABS-05-2015-0053

Shailer, G., & Wang, K. (2015). Government ownership and the cost of debt for Chinese listed corporations. *Emerging Markets Review, 22*(0), 1–17. https://doi.org/10.1016/j.ememar.2014.11.002

Shao, L., Kwok, C. C. Y., & Guedhami, O. (2010). National culture and dividend policy. *Journal of International Business Studies, 41*(8), 1391–1414. https://doi.org/10.1057/jibs.2009.74

Shao, L., Kwok, C. C. Y., & Guedhami, O. (2013). Dividend policy: Balancing shareholders' and creditors' interests. *Journal of Financial Research, 36*(1), 43–66. https://doi.org/10.1111/j.1475-6803.2013.12002.x

Sharma, V. (2011). Independent directors and the propensity to pay dividends. *Journal of Corporate Finance, 17*(4), 1001–1015. https://doi.org/10.1016/j.jcorpfin.2011.05.003

Shefrin, H. M., & Statman, M. (1984). Explaining investor preference for cash dividends. *Journal of Financial Economics, 13*(2), 253–282. https://doi.org/10.1016/0304-405X(84)90025-4

Sheikh, S. (2022a). CEO power and the likelihood of paying dividends: Effect of profitability and cash flow volatility. *Journal of Corporate Finance, 73*, 102186. https://doi.org/10.1016/j.jcorpfin.2022.102186

Sheikh, S. (2022b). Corporate social responsibility and corporate payout policy: The impact of product market competition. *International Journal of Managerial Finance, 18*(1), 49–74. https://doi.org/10.1108/IJMF-09-2020-0465

Shelley, R. B. T. (2007). *SSE to raise dividend 18 per cent in new payout policy.* www.ft.com

Shin, M., Kim, S., Shin, J., & Lee, J. (2018). Labor union effect on corporate cash holdings and their marginal value. *Emerging Markets Finance and Trade, 54*(6), 1391–1413. https://doi.org/10.1080/1540496X.2017.1289085

Shinozaki, S., & Uchida, K. (2017). Ownership structure, tax regime, and dividend smoothing. In T. Naito, W. Lee, & Y. Ouchida (Eds.), *Applied approaches to societal institutions and economics: Essays in honor of Moriki Hosoe* (pp. 41–55). Springer Singapore.

Shleifer, A. (1985). A theory of yardstick competition. *The RAND Journal of Economics, 16*(3), 319–327. https://doi.org/10.2307/2555560

Shleifer, A., & Vishny, R. W. (1986). Large shareholders and corporate control. *Journal of Political Economy, 94*(3, Part 1), 461–488.

Shleifer, A., & Vishny, R. W. (1997). A survey of corporate governance. *The Journal of Finance, 52*(2), 737–783. https://doi.org/10.1111/j.1540-6261.1997.tb04820.x

Short, H., Zhang, H., & Keasey, K. (2002). The link between dividend policy and institutional ownership. *Journal of Corporate Finance, 8*(2), 105–122. https://doi.org/10.1016/S0929-1199(01)00030-X

Sibanda, M. (2014). Do firms smooth their dividends over time? Evidence from the Johannesburg stock exchange. *Journal of Economics, 5*(3), 333–339. https://doi.org/10.1080/09765239.2014.11885009

Silvers, R. (2021). The effects of cross-border cooperation on disclosure enforcement, earnings attributes, and transparency. *Journal of Accounting and Public Policy, 40*(4), 106875. https://doi.org/10.1016/j.jaccpubpol.2021.106875

Spence, M. (1973). Job market signaling. *Quarterly Journal of Economics, 87*, 355–374.

Stevens, J. L., & Jose, M. L. (1992). The effects of dividend payout, stability, and smoothing on firm value. *Journal of Accounting, Auditing and Finance, 7*(2), 213–216.

Stulz, R. M. (2005). The limits of financial globalization. *The Journal of Finance, 60*(4), 1595–1638.

Subramaniam, V. (1996). Underinvestment, debt financing, and long-term supplier relations. *Journal of Law, Economics, and Organization, 12*(2), 461–479. https://doi.org/10.1093/oxfordjournals.jleo.a023371

Subramaniam, V., & Wasiuzzaman, S. (2019). Corporate diversification and dividend policy: Empirical evidence from Malaysia. *Journal of Management & Governance, 23*(3), 735–758. https://doi.org/10.1007/s10997-018-9440-x

Syed, K. B. S., Zainir, F. B., & Isa, M. (2018). Does reputation matter in the dividend smoothing policy of emerging market firms? Empirical evidence from India. *Borsa Istanbul Review, 18*(3), 191–204. https://doi.org/10.1016/j.bir.2017.12.001

Tahir, M., Ibrahim, H., Zulkafli, A. H., & Mushtaq, M. (2020). Corruption, national culture, law and dividend repatriation policy. *Journal of Multinational Financial Management, 57–58.* https://doi.org/10.1016/j.mulfin.2020.100658

Telser, L. G. (1966). Cutthroat competition and the long purse. *The Journal of Law and Economics, 9*, 259–277. https://doi.org/10.1086/466627

Thakur, B. P. S., & Kannadhasan, M. (2019). Corruption and cash holdings: Evidence from emerging market economies. *Emerging Markets Review, 38*, 1–17. https://doi.org/10.1016/j.ememar.2018.11.008

Thanatawee, Y. (2011). Life-Cycle theory and free cash flow hypothesis: Evidence from dividend policy in Thailand. *International Journal of Financial Research, 2*(2). https://doi.org/10.5430/ijfr.v2n2p52

Thieroff, R. (2000). On the areal distribution of tense-aspect categories in Europe. *Empirical Approaches to Language Typology, 6*, 265–308.

Thompson, E. K., & Adasi Manu, S. (2021). The impact of board composition on the dividend policy of US firms. *Corporate Governance: The International Journal of Business in Society, 21*(5), 737–753. https://doi.org/10.1108/CG-05-2020-0182

Tigero, T., Saens, R., & Castillo, A. (2023). Dividend smoothing and ownership concentration: Evidence from Latin America. *Journal of Corporate Accounting & Finance. n/a*(n/a). https://doi.org/10.1002/jcaf.22639

Titman, S. (1984). The effect of capital structure on a firm's liquidation decision. *Journal of Financial Economics, 13*(1), 137–151. https://doi.org/10.1016/0304-405X(84)90035-7

Titman, S., & Wessels, R. (1988). The determinants of capital structure choice. *The Journal of Finance, 43*(1), 1–19.

Tran, Q. T. (2019a). Corporate cash holdings and financial crisis: New evidence from an emerging market. *Eurasian Business Review, 10*(2), 271–285. https://doi.org/10.1007/s40821-019-00134-9

Tran, Q. T. (2019b). Corruption, agency costs and dividend policy: International evidence. *The Quarterly Review of Economics and Finance, 76,* 325–334. https://doi.org/10.1016/j.qref.2019.09.010

Tran, Q. T. (2019c). Creditors and dividend policy: Reputation building versus debt covenant. *European Research on Management and Business Economics, 25*(3), 114–121. https://doi.org/10.1016/j.iedeen.2019.06.001

Tran, D. V. (2020). Economic policy uncertainty and bank dividend policy. *International Review of Economics, 67*(3), 339–361. https://doi.org/10.1007/s12232-020-00344-y

Tran, Q. T. (2020). Corruption and corporate cash holdings: International evidence. *Journal of Multinational Financial Management, 54,* 100611. https://doi.org/10.1016/j.mulfin.2019.100611

Tran, Q. T. (2021). Local corruption and dividend policy: Evidence from Vietnam. *Economic Analysis and Policy, 70,* 195–205. https://doi.org/10.1016/j.eap.2021.02.011

Tran, Q. T., Alphonse, P., & Nguyen, X. M. (2017). Dividend policy: Shareholder rights and creditor rights under the impact of the global financial crisis. *Economic Modelling, 64,* 502–512. https://doi.org/10.1016/j.econmod.2017.03.010

Tran, Q. T., Nguyen, X. M., & Dao, T. H. (2022). Financial crisis and dividend policy: Evidence from an emerging market. *Journal of International Economics and Management, 22*(2), 25–41. https://doi.org/10.38203/jiem.022.2.0046

Tran, Q. T., Nguyen, X. M., Nguyen, T. H. A., Nguyen, T. M., & Truong, T. T. T. (2019). Monetary loosening and dividend policy: Evidence from Vietnamese stock market. *Asian Academy of Management Journal, 24*(2).

Trantidis, A. (2016). Is government contestability an integral part of the definition of democracy? *Politics, 37*(1), 67–81. https://doi.org/10.1177/0263395715619635

Travlos, N. G., Trigeorgis, L., & Vafeas, N. (2001). Shareholder wealth effects of dividend policy changes in an emerging stock market: The case of Cyprus. *Multinational Finance Journal, 5*(2), 87–112.

Twu, M. (2012). Stock market development and the decline of the portion of dividend payers throughout the world. *Financial Review, 47*(2), 401–421. https://doi.org/10.1111/j.1540-6288.2012.00334.x

Ucar, E. (2016). Local culture and dividends. *Financial Management, 45*(1), 105–140. https://doi.org/10.1111/fima.12118

Ullah, I., Majeed, M. A., Fang, H.-X., & Khan, M. A. (2020). Female CEOs and investment efficiency: Evidence from an emerging economy. *Pacific Accounting Review, 32*(4), 443–474. https://doi.org/10.1108/PAR-08-2019-0099

Utami, S. R., & Inanga, E. L. (2011). Agency costs of free cash flow, dividend policy, and leverage of firms in Indonesia. *European Journal of Economics, Finance and Administrative Sciences, 33,* 7–24.

Van Loon, H. W. (1913). *The fall of the Dutch Republic.* Houghton Mifflin.

Villiers, C. D., & Ma, D. (2017). The association between corporate social responsibility and dividend pay-outs. *International Journal of Critical Accounting*, *9*(5–6), 460–480. https://doi.org/10.1504/IJCA.2017.090584

von Eije, H., & Megginson, W. L. (2008). Dividends and share repurchases in the European Union. *Journal of Financial Economics*, *89*(2), 347–374. https://doi.org/10.1016/j.jfineco.2007.11.002

Wang, J. (2012). Do firms' relationships with principal customers/suppliers affect shareholders' income? *Journal of Corporate Finance*, *18*(4), 860–878. https://doi.org/10.1016/j.jcorpfin.2012.06.007

Wang, C. F., & Guo, Y. (2011). Do dividend tax cuts lead firms to increase dividends: Evidence from China. *China Journal of Accounting Research*, *4*(4), 197–209. https://doi.org/10.1016/j.cjar.2010.06.001

Wang, X., Manry, D., & Wandler, S. (2011). The impact of government ownership on dividend policy in China. *Advances in Accounting*, *27*(2), 366–372. https://doi.org/10.1016/j.adiac.2011.08.003

Watts, R. (1973). The information content of dividends. *Journal of Business*, *46*(2), 191–211.

Wei, S.-J., & Kaufmann, D. (1999). *Does grease money speed up the wheels of commerce?* The World Bank.

Wei, Z., Wu, S., Li, C., & Chen, W. (2011). Family control, institutional environment and cash dividend policy: Evidence from China. *China Journal of Accounting Research*, *4*(1–2), 29–46. https://doi.org/10.1016/j.cjar.2011.04.001

Weston, J. F., & Brigham, E. F. (1979). *Managerial finance* (7th ed.). Dryden Press.

White, L. F. (1996). Executive compensation and dividend policy. *Journal of Corporate Finance*, *2*(4), 335–358. https://doi.org/10.1016/0929-1199(96)00003-X

Whitworth, J., & Rao, R. P. (2010). Do tax law changes influence ex-dividend stock price behavior? Evidence from 1926 to 2005. *Financial Management*, *39*(1), 419–445. https://doi.org/10.1111/j.1755-053X.2010.01078.x

Whorf, B. L. (1956). *Language, thought and reality: Selected writings of Benjamin Lee Whorf.* MIT Press.

Williston, S. (1888). History of the law of business corporations before 1800. *Harvard Law Review*, *2*(3), 105–124.

Xu, X., & Li, Y. (2018). Local corruption and corporate cash holdings: Sheltering assets or agency conflict? *China Journal of Accounting Research*, *11*(4), 307–324. https://doi.org/10.1016/j.cjar.2018.05.001

Xu, X., Lin, C., & Yan, Y. (2023). Covid-19 crisis and corporate cash dividend policies: Evidence from Chinese listed companies. *Applied Economics Letters*, *30*(2), 178–184. https://doi.org/10.1080/13504851.2021.1980485

Xu, G., Zhang, D., & Yano, G. (2017). Can corruption really function as "protection money" and "grease money"? Evidence from Chinese firms. *Economic Systems*, *41*(4), 622–638.

Yang, X., Han, L., Li, W., Yin, X., & Tian, L. (2017). Monetary policy, cash holding and corporate investment: Evidence from China. *China Economic Review*, *46*, 110–122.

Yan, Q., & Zhu, H. (2020). Peer influence on dividend policy: Evidence from the Chinese stock market. *Economics Letters*, *192*, 109229. https://doi.org/10.1016/j.econlet.2020.109229

Yaseen, H. (2019). *Dividend policy explained by country's standards of living: An international evidence.* Paper presented at the Global Versus Local Perspectives on Finance and Accounting.

Yensu, J., & Adusei, C. (2016). Dividend policy decision across African countries. *International Journal of Economics and Finance, 8*(6), 63–77.

Ye, K., & Zhang, R. (2011). Do lenders value corporate social responsibility? Evidence from China. *Journal of Business Ethics, 104*(2), 197–206. https://doi.org/10.1007/s10551-011-0898-6

Zainudin, R., Mahdzan, N. S., & Yet, C. H. (2018). Dividend policy and stock price volatility of industrial products firms in Malaysia. *International Journal of Emerging Markets, 13*(1), 203–217. https://doi.org/10.1108/IJoEM-09-2016-0250

Zeng, S., & Wang, L. (2015). CEO gender and corporate cash holdings. Are female CEOs more conservative? *Asia-Pacific Journal of Accounting & Economics, 22*(4), 449–474. https://doi.org/10.1080/16081625.2014.1003568

Zhou, J., Booth, L., & Chang, B. (2013). Import competition and disappearing dividends. *Journal of International Business Studies, 44*(2), 138–154. https://doi.org/10.1057/jibs.2012.36

Printed and bound by CPI Group (UK) Ltd, Croydon, CR0 4YY

11/03/2024

14468758-0005